T H E
CHOCOLATE
BIBLE

THE
CHOCOLATE
BIBLE

The Definitive Sourcebook, with over 600 Illustrations

Christian Teubner
Leopold Forsthofer
Silvio Rizzi
Sybil Gräfin Schönfeldt
Karl Schumacher
Eckart Witzigmann

CHARTWELL
BOOKS, INC.

This edition published in 2010 by:
CHARTWELL BOOKS, INC.
A division of BOOK SALES, INC.
276 Fifth Avenue, Suite 206
New York, New York 10001
USA

ISBN-13: 978-0-7858-1907-3
ISBN-10: 0-7858-1907-X

Library of Congress Catalog Card Number: 97-66093

Original edition
© 1996 Teubner Edition, Germany

English language translation:
© 1997 Transedition Limited, England
All rights reserved

Printed in Singapore

CONTENTS

XOCOLATL
The History of Chocolate

The story of how chocolate came to such prominence in the diet of millions of people around the world began in that dramatic period of world history when the Spanish first conquered the New World.

For centuries the Old World knew nothing of cacao bushes and trees, whose broad crowns swayed beneath the protective canopy of taller trees. Cacao bushes grew in the primeval forest, producing blossom, leaf, and fruit simultaneously. The eighteenth-century Swedish naturalist Carolus Linnaeus named this evergreen tree of Paradise *Theobroma*, meaning "food of the gods." In legends handed down over thousands of years, the native peoples of Central and South America described how the gods alone were worthy of enjoying its fruits.

A tree of life in Paradise

These truly are trees of life. It is claimed that cacao trees appeared in early Western panel paintings of Paradise by monks living in cold and drafty cloisters. They accurately depict trees with thick foliage —

smooth, oblong, leathery leaves, which are reddish in color when they unfurl, turning to a dark green — and dense clusters of small lemon-yellow blossoms with pink calyxes, whose sweet scent is so very attractive to insects, sprouting directly from the trunk on old wood. Centuries later, this flowering phenomenon would engage the interest of numerous botanists, who termed it "cauliflory," meaning "flowering on the stem," from the Greek word *caulos*, a stem or stalk.

Cacao trees and bushes require a constant climate, which you might think appropriate for Paradise; in this case, it is humid air, damp soil, and a temperature that never falls much lower than 68°F: no storms, no blazing sun. In these ideal conditions, the tree grows, flowers, and bears its fruit, also directly on the trunk, but only a short way up the main branches. As they ripen, the green pods swell. They are between 6 and 14 inches long, oval, rounded or pointed at the end, and weigh about one pound. As many as fifty leathery green bean-shaped seeds are tightly packed within, embedded in a pink juicy pulp, slightly acidic but refreshing to the taste. For the Indians living along the Orinoco long ago, this tree had a practical use as a refreshment stand along the way. They plucked the green pods, squeezed out the sharp-tasting pink ambrosia, and threw away the rest. When the pods are ripe, they burst to reveal their strange looking seeds, flattened on the side where they are packed together. Within the seeds are the kernels — reddish brown, and oily while they are still fresh, with an aromatic but bitter taste. This is the original cacao, as it has grown since time immemorial in the tropical forests and islands of the Americas.

Cacahuatl — a form of currency for the Aztecs

The cocoa beans, collected from the pulp of the pod that bursts open after ripening, were later called "sun cacao" by the Spanish. They are attractive, brightly colored, and veined. A local inhabitant out hunting or on a foraging trip through the forest two or three thousand years ago and coming across these bright pebble-shaped beans might have scraped them out of the flesh of the pod. Maybe he bent down to look at them, wondering whether they could be eaten. Perhaps he even tried to eat them; they would have been very hard and rather bitter. When the beans are crushed, however, they turn into a solid paste as a result of their high fat content. It is not possible to say for sure whether the Mayans chewed the crushed cocoa beans just as they were, or whether they mixed the paste with water. Whatever the case, the woods were full of cacao bushes, and beans were available to everyone. With the passage of time, the bushes were cultivated in a simple fashion into small groves. And at a time when the Christian era was just beginning in Europe, cocoa beans heaped up in baskets were being traded in the markets of the Mayan princes. They had a dual purpose, as currency and food.

We know that the Toltecs, who lived in what is now Mexico, were also familiar with the "sun beans," and probably had been for over a thousand years by the time they were conquered by the Aztecs in 1325. The Aztecs gave the beans the name *cacahuatl*. Under their rule, the beans were used principally as a form of exchange, and were the only universally valid currency in which the conquered provinces could pay their taxes to the Aztec rulers.

When the Spaniards, led by Hernando Cortés (1485–1547), in their turn subjugated the Aztecs in 1519, they discovered a huge reserve of cocoa beans said to be worth a vast fortune in the possession of Montezuma II (1480–1520), Aztec emperor of Mexico from 1502 to 1520. Several hundred years later, the naturalist and globetrotter Alexander von Humboldt (1769–1859) also came across cocoa beans being used as a form of currency in Costa Rica.

Cocoa from the ground

At the beginning of the history of cocoa, perhaps as early as the Toltec era, people must have discovered by chance that the "sun beans" tasted quite different if the

La jicara, a hollowed gourd, sometimes lavishly decorated, was a typical Indian drinking vessel used for chocolate at the time of the Spanish conquest (from *El Chocolate*).

© Nestlé, Mexiko

© Nestlé, Mexiko

Ek-chuah, the patron saint of cocoa, as depicted by the Mayans. In the picture to the left, the bones held in his hand symbolize a food of which only the internal part, the seed, is used. The body posture, squatting on one knee, represents the lengthy amount of time required to process cocoa. In the picture to the right, Ek-chuah is shown holding a wooden grinding block with his feet (from *El Chocolate*)

Cacahuatl A sixteenth-century wood carving of a cacao bush growing in the shade of another tree. Cocoa beans are shown spread out on the ground to dry in the sun. (Giralamo Benzoni, Venice, 1565)

secret of fermentation. During the five to ten days that it takes for this chemical reaction to take place, the cocoa flavor develops and is retained, no matter how the cocoa beans are subsequently treated.

This was the first step in the development of the cocoa bean as a popular food. If something promises to taste good, it attracts attention, and it seems to be human nature to then devote some effort to it. First, there came systematic harvesting. The Indians no longer waited for the ripe pods to burst open on the trunk or branch but hacked them off with machetes. This is still done today. They then accelerated the process of decay by simply tossing the ripe pods into moist earth and leaving them to ferment. After a few days they dug out the pods again, stripped off the remains of the decaying shells and washed the remainder of the pulp off the beans in large tubs of water. Only then did they place the beans in the sun to roast. The beans had to become bone-dry to prevent the formation of mold. Since small pieces of shell and fiber still adhered to the beans, the Indians

pod did not burst open on the trunk and dry out, but fell instead onto moist earth, where it began to ferment and rot in the humid heat of the forest. Certainly the beans would not look quite as tempting in the moist and slimy ground. But once they had been rinsed in stream water, then rubbed and cleaned, they tasted much better: milder and yet still flavorful. That was the

Preparation of *xocolatl* in old Mexico. The roasted cacao beans were finely ground and stirred with water and spices until frothy. (Copperplate engraving by Olfert Dapper, 1673)

tipped them onto the ground and trampled them with their bare feet — it looked as if they were dancing.

The beans treated in this way were called "earth cocoa" and underwent further processing before they were consumed: after roasting and shelling, they were ground in a mortar, and formed into fist-sized balls. Pieces were broken off the ball as required and mixed with cold water. The poorer people, who had nothing else, would add a little corn flour. Those who had the ingredients would sweeten the mixture with honey or spice it with chiles.

Cocoa beans are rich — they consist of about 55 percent fat, and also contain proteins and starches. They are a mild stimulant containing two alkaloids, caffeine and theobromine. Theobromine, which was discovered and named by a Russian chemist in 1841, is closely related to caffeine, and is used in medicine as both a stimulant and a diuretic.

Xocolatl — drinking customs among the Indians

In the pre-Columbian era it was, of course, not possible to remove the fat and oil from the cocoa paste or to refine it. As a result, the ground cocoa and water quickly separated, with the cocoa gradually settling, undissolved, to form a sediment, which ranged from crumbly to sludgy. Even for the

A proud Indian with the equipment for preparing *xocolatl*. The vanilla bean shown in the lower picture beside the cacao was used to enhance flavor. (Copperplate engraving, 1685)

The wooden quirl is still an important utensil in the present-day Mexican kitchen. At the market in Ocotlan de Morelos in the state of Oaxaca the *molinillos* (molinets) are piled up for sale. With their ornamental carving, they are small works of art.

Toltecs and Aztecs this was unpleasant and unacceptable. They therefore made *xocolatl* from the *cacahuatl* by adding cold water and stirring vigorously (*xoco* means bitter and *atl* means water). Slaves sat and stirred the cocoa paste energetically with a wooden whisk until it swirled around and remained suspended in the water and the *xocolatl* could be served.

This was how the Spaniards first encountered it. Columbus, however, faced with all the new experiences that assailed his senses, did not realize that cocoa was a food at all. On a trade ship belonging to the Guanache Indians, he discovered what he described as "almonds, which are called cacao, and serve as coins in New Spain."

A mere twenty years later, travelers accompanying Hernando Cortés were so fascinated by Indian drinking customs that they recorded them immediately and in precise detail. A report by Bernial Diaz del Castillo noted that Montezuma drank *xocolatl* several times a day from beakers made of pure gold, and that warriors and nobles of the court, in common with their prince, kept the ground cocoa in golden containers, which they always carried around with them. Whereas higher

© Cadbury Ltd

The meeting of Cortés and Montezuma in 1519. The Aztecs received the Spaniards so warmly because they thought that Cortés was their god Quetzalcoatl, whose return they were awaiting.

ranking Indians spiced the drink with native vanilla, wild honey, pita juice, and occasionally with chile powder, the Spanish officers enhanced it with aniseed, cinnamon, almonds, and hazelnuts, which they had specially sent from Spain for the purpose. Peasants and ordinary soldiers prepared the cocoa mixture more simply. They crumbled the cocoa paste with whatever spices they chose into a gourd, which they filled with water and shook until the mixture was frothy. At the end of the sixteenth century, Francesco Carletti noted:

> This drink was imbibed in a single draft for the miraculous refreshment and satisfaction of the bodily state, to which it gives strength, nourishment, and energy to such a degree that those who are accustomed to drinking it can no longer remain strong without it, even if they eat other nutritious substances. And they also appear to lose weight if they do not have this drink.

Cortés was interested principally in its properties as a stimulant. He wrote, "One beaker keeps a soldier fresh for the whole day." It appears that he succeeded in conquering his hosts with the assistance of their very own drink.

Chocolaterias in the West Indies and the Spaniards' hot chocolate

The Spaniards, for whom drunkenness was a sin, developed a liking for this new drink. Since the Church recognized it as a beverage rather than a food, it could be consumed even during periods of fasting. It soon became the classic accompaniment for the first meal of the day. Over the years "chocolaterias" were established all over the West Indies, where the cocoa was always freshly prepared.

The Spaniards, however, now poured boiling water instead of cold over the cocoa and whisked it. A classic recipe for a whipped chocolate drink still reminds us of this original frothy cocoa. As with the native Indian drink, it is still made with water, but uses modern refined cocoa powder or chocolate. Stiffly beaten egg whites are whisked into the hot chocolate to imitate the classic froth of the Aztec drink, and it is served immediately.

Spain at that time was one of the wealthiest nations in the Western world, and this new fashionable drink was spiced with everything that the market offered: cinnamon and nutmeg, pepper and ginger, and sometimes even sugar. Still the drink continued to be made with water. The countries in which the cacao bush was indigenous all belonged to the Spanish and Portuguese crown, and so for roughly a century cocoa remained a Spanish drink, and a secret.

Chocolate houses in Europe and colonialism

This is how things would probably have remained had the Italians not voyaged to the West Indies around 1600. There they became acquainted with this very special drink and introduced it to Italy at the beginning of the seventeenth century. From there the exotic bean followed conventional trade routes by sea and land over the Alps to the north. England began to make direct imports from Jamaica after it took the island from Spain in 1655, which marks the start of English trade with the West Indies.

In the second half of the seventeenth century, an aristocratic Frenchwoman, Madame D'Aulnoy, traveled to the Spanish court in Madrid to visit relatives. In letters from "the country without forks," as the French contemptuously referred to Spain (Louis XIV, the Sun King, had recently made this implement fashionable as an individual piece of cutlery), she reported on the new national drink, chocolate. It was the focus when ladies gathered together, while their husbands were engrossed in conversation. In the late afternoon, ladies would meet in large, airy assembly rooms. Waiting women would bring in silver dishes filled with candied fruits, each one wrapped individually in gold paper to protect fingers and handkerchief. The new national drink was handed around as an accompaniment: "Each porcelain cup stood on an agate saucer with a gold border, each with a matching

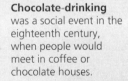

© Info-Zentrum Schokolade

Drinking chocolate as the elixir of life. (Copperplate engraving by Martin Engelbrecht, about 1750)

Chocolate-drinking was a social event in the eighteenth century, when people would meet in coffee or chocolate houses.

sugar bowl. There was iced chocolate, warm chocolate, and some with eggs and milk. There are even women who can drink six cups in succession."

Chocolate became the subject of poems and songs, of learned dissertations in every language, and of secret recipes for doctors and apothecaries. "The first chocolate house" appeared throughout Europe: in Vienna, which ranked as the Eldorado for chocolate drinkers, somewhat later in London, then in Holland, and so on. Chocolate had become socially acceptable in London by the mid-seventeenth century, and the city boasted numerous chocolate houses by 1657. Samuel Pepys noted

Chocolate production
as it looked at the end
of the eighteenth
century is depicted in
this Viennese etching
from 1775, from a
collection entitled
"Scenes from Nature
and the Arts."

© Info-Zentrum Schokolade

laconically in his diary for April 24, 1661, two days
after the ceremonial crowning of Charles II, for
which Pepys had risen at four o'clock in the
morning and celebrated until well in the night,
sustained with appropriate quantities of wine and
other drinks: "Waked in the morning with my head
in a sad taking through the last night's drink, which
I am very sorry for. So rise and went out with Mr.
Creed to drink our morning draught, which he did
give me in chocolate to settle my stomach."

Still preoccupied with their losses from the
Thirty Years' War, the German states were forced
to spend their money on things other than
fashionable drinks. It was not until 1679 that the
Dutch professor Cornelius Bontekoe, personal
physician to the Great Elector, Friedrich Wilhelm
von Brandenburg, prescribed chocolate for his
master. The Great Elector had just gained an
important military success with a victory over the
Swedes at Fehrbellin and was now seeking to add
new glory to his house and state. A few years later,
in 1683, while his emperor in Vienna was fighting
the Turks — who collected coffee as the spoils of
war and kept it in their tents — and waiting to
begin his own advance westwards, Friedrich put a
fleet to sea in order to conquer a piece of this
remarkable New World for himself, as the English,
Spanish, and Dutch had done before him. His
soldiers and sailors, however, went only as far as
the west coast of Africa, where they founded a
colony, which survived only until 1717 and failed
to send any colonial goods to Berlin.

As this mission by an impoverished European
prince indicates, the countries of the New World
had become a cheap market, of which the European
states were taking advantage. Paintings and wall
panels of the seventeenth and early eighteenth
centuries show the ample female figure of Europe
sitting enthroned among gifts laid at her feet by
representatives of the other continents, reflecting

the benefits she gained from the fantastic spread of
colonialism. While the Great Elector craved for
colonies to such an extent that he neglected his
duty to the emperor, the Spanish king, Philip V,
grew so weary of them that in 1728 he sold the
cocoa trade monopoly to an international company,
just as he might sell a plot of land.

The passion of two infantas

Cocoa beans found their way from Spain to the true
heart of European cuisine in France in the wedding
chest of an infanta. In 1615, Anne of Austria, who
was just fifteen and the eldest daughter of Philip of
Spain, married the son of Maria de' Medici, Louis
XIII, who was only four days older. A powerful
queen mother, an even more powerful minister —
Cardinal Richelieu — and a marriage that furthered
their lust for power all played a role in the history of
cocoa. For Anne brought with her to the north not
only a dowry but also recipes for the Spanish drink,
which she feared she would not find at the French
court and which she did not wish to forego. It was
not only the royal bride, neglected by her husband
for almost twenty years, who needed the soothing
effects of *xocolatl*; even Richelieu appears to have

thought highly of cocoa beans. His elder brother noted in his diary that the Cardinal took the drink as a treatment for enlargement of the spleen.

A generation later, in 1660, the next infanta came to Paris to marry, as a guarantee of the everlasting peace between Spain and France. Maria Theresa, daughter of Philip IV, married Louis XIV, son of the unhappy Anne of Austria. Maria Theresa came with a servant whose sole function was to prepare her favorite chocolate drink. She also came

by this time had also been introduced into the Dutch, English, and French colonies. The consequence of increased cultivation was considerable competition on the European market, which brought about a drop in the price of Spanish cocoa, and allowed cocoa products from all the colonies to begin to become generally affordable.

The second reason has to do with taste. Through the addition of bland milk from European cows and sugar from imported sugar cane, which was

John Cadbury's shop in Birmingham, England, can be seen in this street scene from around 1830.

to a man who had chosen the sun as the symbol of his kingdom, "because it is unique, and also for the light it sheds on the other stars."

Louis became the archetypical absolute ruler and, like the sun, had an influence beyond the confines of his own kingdom. He paid subsidies to the German princes on his borders in order to keep the peace, and later attracted their sons to his court at Versailles, where they learned what today are still regarded as the basic rules of etiquette. He loved the extravagance of masked balls and festive occasions, where the nobility, separated from the public by barriers, were handed coffee, tea, and chocolate. These three drinks created a new form of socializing, and started a real revolution in the field of food and drink.

Cocoa — goods from the colonies waiting for the cow

In the seventeenth century chocolate ceased to be a dark, rough drink; it took on the acceptable taste we still appreciate today. This change came about for three reasons. The first was the international trade in cocoa, which began with the cultivation of cacao bushes into trees and systematic planting, and

still expensive, the unique flavor of cocoa could now be fully developed.

The third reason involves industrial production. The fermented and roasted beans were still crushed in mortars, as in Spanish times, or they were ground on a stone, or in carved wooden chocolate mills, such as those still found in Mexico. The resulting product could either be used as it was or shaped into fist-sized cakes, which were then dried and stored until required, when pieces would be broken off. These cakes of cocoa still retained all the cocoa fats, and therefore spoiled easily. The fat became rancid and the taste unpleasant. A French book written in 1708 warns:

Chocolate is a kind of solid paste made up of several constituents. The main constituent is cocoa. The other vegetable constituents are vanilla beans, sugar, cinnamon, Mexican pepper, cloves; some people add orange blossom water, nutmeg or dark ambergris. Good quality xocolate is no more than two or three months old, has no specks of mold, or signs of aging. It should not have any holes made by insects, which can occur in very old stocks. There should be nothing in the taste which is unpalatable or overly spiced. When sampling, there should be no rancid smell or acidic taste.

Beans and nuts are roasted over an open fire in the traditional Mexican way, to develop their flavor before they are made into chocolate bars.

A Mexican tradition
The traditional way of making chocolate has been handed down from generation to generation

It may have been Spanish nuns in Mexico who first had the idea of shaping chocolate into bars and slabs. Convent kitchens were regarded as a kind of laboratory where improved and more exquisite chocolate recipes were created. It was here that the technique of roasting and grinding cocoa beans was perfected.

In pre-Columbian times in Mexico, kitchens of the rural population were equipped in much the same way as the kitchens of many rural people there today. The traditional hearth consists of stones,

usually arranged in a semicircle, and coated with clay. A perforated metal sheet holds the nuts and seeds for roasting. The draft for the fire beneath this roasting surface is produced by a fan made of rushes. An important feature of the kitchen is the *metate*, a three-legged quern, or primitive type of hand-operated mill, which is used as an all-purpose mixer. The stone is about 12 x 16 inches, flat in the middle and rising slightly toward the ends. It is made of gray or black porous basalt — its slight roughness assists grinding — and stands on the

Patience and stamina are the most important requirements for this method of chocolate-making. The cocoa beans have to be ground for a prolonged period until the emerging fat forms a pliable mass.

Almonds, cinnamon, and cocoa, a combination from times past. Before the Spanish arrived, Mexican chocolate was prepared without sugar, a commodity then unknown to the Indians.

floor. Its stone legs are of different lengths, so that it inclines at the angle that requires the least amount of effort to be used. The women kneel at the narrow end of the quern and reduce the cocoa to a fine powder with a continuous movement of a *metlapil*, or oblong stone, back and forth.

In the traditional chocolate recipe, 4½ pounds of sugar and 3½ ounces of cinnamon stick and almonds are added to 2 pounds of cocoa beans. First, the cinnamon is reduced to a fine powder. Next, it is ground into a sticky mixture with the cocoa and roasted almonds. Then the sugar is worked in evenly. When the mixture becomes malleable, it is pressed into cakes or bars, or shaped into balls.

The Chocolate Drinker
by French painter Jean-
François de Troy
(1679–1752).

© Iinfo-Zentrum Schokolade

The recipe it gives for the drink states: "To prepare a drink, take a coffee pot and pour in sufficient water for the purpose. Set it on the flame and when it begins to boil, add for each portion two-thirds of an ounce of grated or finely chopped chocolate with an equal quantity of sugar. Allow the whole to boil for half of a quarter-hour."

By this time, industrialization was starting in France. Under Louis XIV, who, in addition to throwing parties and promoting good manners, tried to stimulate all forms of domestic output, the preparation of cocoa powder became mechanized. The cocoa cake was placed in steam-driven grinders or rollers, where the heat generated by the friction of grinding melted the fat — called cocoa butter — contained in the beans. Part of the cocoa butter was pressed out under high pressure. The remaining mass was pressed into flat, round cakes, and became the raw material for cocoa powder and chocolate. There is some dispute as to who first stumbled upon the idea of making this semi-processed product, these rock-hard blocks, into something as gently melting as eating chocolate. But one thing is certain: chocolate was used at first solely for drinks, and continued to be available to the upper echelons of society throughout Europe until the middle of the nineteenth century.

In the seventeenth century, Voltaire and his friend King Friedrich of Prussia, Augustus III, King of Poland and Elector of Saxony, and his prime minister, Count Brühl, were all also devotees of chocolate. Friedrich sometimes liked to drink his with pepper and mustard. He offered chocolate as a reward to those people who had helped him by word or deed, yet otherwise forbade his subjects to drink this exotic product on economic grounds. The Elector of Saxony, on the other hand, recommended Brühl to procure chocolate in Vienna and Rome by courier, and granted numerous coffee houses the privilege of preparing the drink.

The great German writer Friedrich von Schiller, who preferred to read and write undisturbed in the peace of the night and therefore slept late into the morning, liked to be awoken with a cup of chocolate; he also kept himself awake at night with chocolate. In one of his early historical dramas, *Fiesco*, set in Italy in 1547, the hero says: "Before you prepare the chocolate, Madame, come and talk to me!" At that time, Madame would have been able to do this only in the New World; it would be a long time before anyone could prepare chocolate in Italy. Schiller's contemporary, the German lyric poet August Bürger was also a devotee of drinking chocolate. Most of all he enjoyed drinking it at breakfast at an inn at Göttingen in the presence of the ladies who kept him company.

The first half of the nineteenth century in Europe reflected bourgeois taste and values, which, for political reasons, were forced into a private world. The private reading circle and the garden bower were important for the development and concealment of progressive ideas. A cup of coffee or a bowl of chocolate was used as the excuse to meet and talk about politics undisturbed. At this time, the drink was also used to categorize and differentiate people. It was reported how such-and-such a celebrity had a liking for chocolate, and people thought that imitating such a person in this way would make them more like him.

Hot chocolate — a morning drink with social cachet

Coffee, tea, and chocolate also claimed their own platform, their own time of day. Thus, hot chocolate was drunk in the morning, tea in the afternoon; hot chocolate was for receptions and family gatherings, coffee was taken after meals.

Some middle-class citizens had more time than they do today. A mayor, for example, was permitted by the nature of his profession to return home at four or five o'clock in the afternoon to take a cup of hot chocolate or coffee with his family. He had the time to do this because towns were smaller then and could be crossed on foot.

In the course of time manual labor was increasingly replaced by machines. This picture shows the individual stages of production at Maison Masson in France.

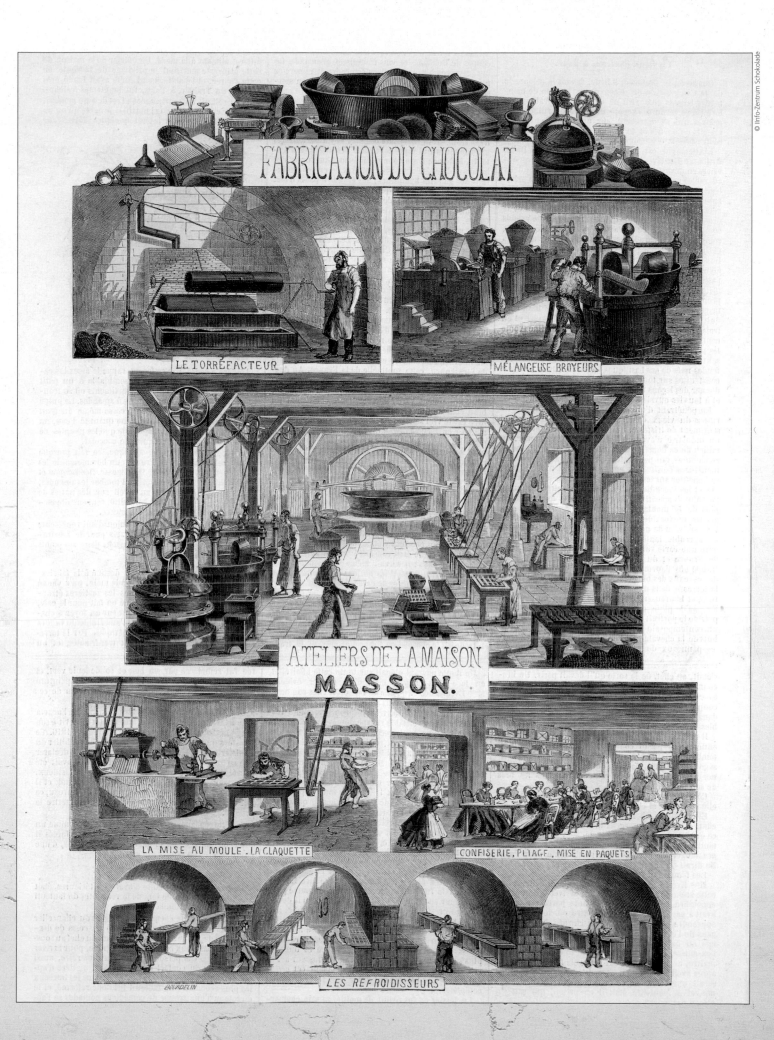

FABRICATION DU CHOCOLAT

LE TORRÉFACTEUR

MÉLANGEUSE BROYEURS

ATELIERS DE LA MAISON MASSON.

LA MISE AU MOULE. LA CLAQUETTE

CONFISERIE, PLIAGE, MISE EN PAQUETS

BOURDELIN

LES REFROIDISSEURS

Tin boxes were for decades the best form of packaging for cocoa powder. They preserved freshness and flavor particularly well. This container originates from about 1900.

From chocolate factories and cioccolatieri to the Swiss chocolate-maker's art

Chocolate candy is the highest quality end product to come from the Aztec bean, but it was able to emerge only in the machine age. A glimpse inside an encyclopedia from the nineteenth century showing circuit diagrams would amaze the reader with the multiplicity of machines for processing chocolate.

The English followed their Spanish competitors in this field. The first chocolate factory in Britain was established in 1728. The first in German territory was built in 1756 by the Prince of Lippe, who had become acquainted with the brown delicacy while serving as an officer with the Portuguese and did not want to forego it when he returned home. By 1781 there were eight factories in Munich alone. In 1776, while the colonists in America had more important issues on their mind, and quite a few years before the French Revolution, Louis XVI granted the royal privilege of manufacturing chocolate.

The first manufactured products were not at all like those we are familiar with today. Fundamentally, they were prepared in the same way as they had been for centuries in Mexico and other cacao-growing countries, where stone rollers ground the cocoa cake. Only now there were no slaves kneeling in front of stone slabs crushing the cocoa with rollers that looked like rolling pins. In the early factories this manual labor was replaced by steam power. Human hands were still used to press the brown liquor into molds, but machines took over again to shake them into shape and then turn them out.

Chocolate became popular, and was adapted to national tastes. Soon, newer and milder aromas wafted out of the confectioners' pans. At first, the Italians called themselves *cioccolatieri*, chocolate-makers, and went from fair to fair boiling up the brown liquid in large pans. This was a few years after the fall of Napoleon, when the ordinary citizen could again look forward to enjoying life.

At the same time, food chemistry, already a scientific discipline, discovered the value of the individual basic nutrients. So upon the advice of an English doctor and botanist, some bland milk was kneaded into the crumbly brown cocoa mass, and the dark cake gained a hint of the color that passed

Automatic vending machines for selling chocolate candy were very popular around 1890. This vending machine, known as the "Mercury," is decorated in a neo-Gothic style.

into usage as "chocolate brown." The milk made it easier for the workers to press the brown mass into molds with their fists and pestles.

Decades of experimentation began everywhere: for example, the powdered cocoa was mixed with sugar water and even with wine. In 1828 C. J. van Houten of the Netherlands patented a process for separating the cocoa butter from the basic brown block. In the previous century the English had begun adding milk to their chocolate drink, but the high import duties on cocoa beans kept the prices of the chocolate high. In 1831 the Englishman John Cadbury developed a dozen or so cocoa drinks that became the foundation of his chocolate business when the import duties were lowered not many years later.

It was the Swiss, however, who made the first true chocolate candy from the crumbly mass. As so often happens, this success was based on the work of others who had gone before. The itinerant cioccolatieri from Italy had been the models for the first small craft businesses in Switzerland, and many of these manufacturers had learned the confectionery trade in Italy, mainly in Turin, which had become the nation's center for chocolate-making skills. This was precisely the case with François-Louis Cailler. At his factory in Vevey, he improved the stone rollers, driving them with water power. By 1830 he was already offering a whole range of expensive and reasonably priced varieties, so that there was something for everybody. The confectioner Philippe Suchard achieved top international recognition. In 1826, he established a chocolate factory in a small room in Serrières, where, with one other worker, he could produce no more than 55 pounds of candy a day; nonetheless, the scarce product won him a gold medal at the World Exhibition in Paris in 1855.

The secret of factory-made chocolate is "conching." This is the process by which after day-long grinding and stirring a product as smooth and soft as silk is produced from the crumbly, coarse material. In 1847 the English chocolate-maker Joseph Fry combined additional cocoa butter with the chocolate liquor and sugar to improve the texture and quality of chocolate.

In 1863, Daniel Peter, who had learned from his neighbor Heinrich Nestlé how to dry milk, tried an experiment to make a finished product by mixing one delicate raw material with the other. He called this milk chocolate product "Gala-Peter" and won a certificate at the 1878 World Exhibition.

America joins the club

To most Americans, the name Hershey is probably synonymous with chocolate, and some people might assume that the candy takes its name from the town of Hershey, Pennsylvania, rather than the other way around.

Milton Snavely Hershey was born near Hockerville, Pennsylvania, on September 9, 1857, when confectioners in Europe were building factories and experimenting with recipes for chocolate that could be eaten like candy. From a poor rural family, Hershey left school at the age of fifteen to be apprenticed to a confectioner in Lancaster, Pennsylvania. Apparently, he learned his craft well, and when he completed his apprenticeship in 1876 felt sufficiently confident to set up his own candy shop in Philadelphia. The business survived for six years, after which Hershey went to New York. His efforts to establish a thriving candy factory there also ended in failure.

Fortunately, he persevered. Back in Lancaster, he experimented with adding milk to caramels, and found he had created an extremely popular new candy. His initial success led him to establish the Lancaster Caramel Company, which continued to manufacture caramels to his new recipe in the 1890s while Hershey himself turned his attentions to the study of chocolate. After he sold the Lancaster Caramel company for an astonishing $1 million, he concentrated on perfecting a formula for chocolate candy bars. By 1903 he had succeeded, and began building a factory at what became known as Hershey, Pennsylvania. The factory became the world's largest chocolate manufacturing plant, producing the familiar bars, kisses, syrup, and other products that we associate with the name.

Chocolate — the star of advertising

Advertising has always been used as a means of introducing new products to consumers, and as a way of continuing to promote established ones. Before the advent of mass circulation newspapers and magazines, artisans and manufacturers of all kinds relied on handbills and posters displayed within their locale, signs on their delivery vehicles, and the use of their name or identifying mark on the products they made, all means of advertising that continue to this day.

With the growth of towns and large cities, and the increase in manufactured products generally, the way things were bought and sold changed too. Large retail businesses and department stores took the place of small traders and market stall operators. These establishments were designed to sell a large volume of goods to a wide audience, and had to find ways to attract consumers. They needed to make people aware of what was available, and convince them to buy those products. This was the beginning of what has become one of the biggest businesses in the world: mass-market advertising.

Cocoa and chocolate products were ideal subjects for this nascent industry. Although they had been manufactured since the late nineteenth century, it was in the early twentieth century that an increasing number of factories were being built, particularly in Switzerland, Austria, and Germany.

The color signs and posters of those early decades can still grab our attention today. Some are a reflection of the popular art of the period, others were themselves the popular art of the period.

Mass-market advertising. Advertisements for chocolate products were of a very high artistic standard. While enameled advertising signs withstood the passage of time, posters were more transient.

When you open a package of cocoa, even if your eyes are closed, you recognize the incomparable and unmistakable aroma of the brown powder. The Old World, already familiar with spices from the East, seemed to have awaited this gift from the New World. It would complement the aromas and taste of cinnamon and vanilla; it would counterbalance the sweetness of sugar in a way that differed from any food grown in its own latitudes. Almost immediately, it became the symbol of exquisite sweetness. Nothing was or is as mild or smooth as cocoa or chocolate, and yet its slight hint of bitterness is a fine finishing touch.

Cocoa beans are not unlike pebbles in appearance. If they fell out of a sack at your feet you probably would not give them a second glance. It was centuries after their discovery that people worked out the secret of capturing their flavor. Patience is needed to cultivate the tree, patience and experience to handle its fruits, and patience and scientific know-how to produce the treasured result.

COCOA

"Brown gold" is the name that has been given to the product processed from the beans. Just as it requires painstaking effort to mine gold from the depths of the Earth so that we can enjoy its beauty, it takes great effort and industriousness to extract the brown essence from the bean. The reward is chocolate of the highest quality.

have not yet formed their own canopy need the shade of other "mother" trees, which may be provided by banana, monkey bread or citrus trees.

The small pink blossoms of the cacao tree sprout in bunches from old wood on the trunk (cauliflory) and on strong side branches (ramiflory) where leaves dropped from the axils in previous years. At first glance the rather foul-smelling flowers look like orchids, but closer observation shows that they differ quite distinctly in their five-part structure: five sepals, five white or bright red petals, five sterile and five fertile stamens, together with a superior node crowned by a five-columned stigma, with five cells. The cacao

Cultivation of the cacao plant begins in the nursery, as here at a research station in Sabah, Malaysia. Seedlings are grown from fresh cacao beans in growing bags, plastic bags pierced with holes. For research purposes, the plants are also reproduced from cuttings. This allows characteristics of different plants to be combined.

After about fourteen days, the two cotyledons (seed leaves) have pushed up to the light from the bean and the first true leaves have formed. The split bean can be clearly seen on the stem of the tap root, which has made its way down into the soil.

The cocoa plant
A gift from the gods

The wild form of the cacao tree comes from the Rio Negro region, the largest western tributary of the Amazon and the headwaters of the Orinoco, and belongs to the family Sterculiaceae. One characteristic of this family is a tap root pushing deep into the ground, and another is flowers and pods sprouting directly from the trunk. This unusual method of fruit production on the trunk is occasionally seen in other plant families. The cacao, or cocoa, tree is a species of the genus *Theobroma*, which means "food of the gods." Its full botanical name is *Theobroma cacao*. Other cultivated species, such as *Theobroma angustifolia*, *Theobroma bicolor* and *Theobroma pentagona* are of no significance for commercial cocoa production.

In the wild, *Theobroma cacao* grows to about 50 feet, but under cultivation it is restricted to a maximum height of 26 feet. Usually, the tree trunk splits into five main branches, from which the subsidiary branches grow upward at an angle and spread out in stages like a fan. The shiny evergreen leaves are oval and measure up to 1 foot long. The mature trees form a shady canopy, and in effect shade themselves, which is an essential condition for their survival. Young trees that

tree generally starts to flower from its fifth year, and is fully productive from its tenth year. Pollination has to occur within a few hours of the blossoms opening. In the wild, less than 5 percent of the blossoms that open are pollinated naturally by flies, midges, or ants. In cultivation the flowers are pollinated manually by plantation workers.

After fertilization, the node swells rapidly; it takes about five months for the pod to ripen. As is the case with many tropical trees, the flowering period and formation of the fruit are not distinctly separated. It is possible to see blossoms and ripe and unripe pods on the tree simultaneously. The ovoid fruits are up to 14 inches

In the nursery the small trees are grown for twelve months before they are transferred to the plantation. In the research station at Sabah, two main varieties of cacao bean are cultivated, those with fruits that turn from green to yellow when they are ripe, and those that turn from dark red to orange. After three to four months, the plants are grafted or crossed with each other. They are planted out when they are about 3 feet tall. The lower picture shows a new planting on the site of an old plantation that has been cleared. Other trees have been planted specifically to provide shade.

long, hard and leathery, yellow to reddish brown, and weigh between 10½ and 18 ounces. Inside the pod, the compartment walls become slimy, and form a bittersweet gelatinous white or pinkish pulp. Twenty-five to fifty bean-shaped seeds nestle there, in five rows ranged around a central spindle. They are ¾ to 1½ inches long and ⅓ to ¾ inch wide. Each tree yields a maximum of 4½ pounds of beans a year.

Theobroma cacao has two main varieties: Criollo and Forastero. Criollo, meaning "Creole cocoa," is native to Ecuador and Venezuela. Nowadays it is cultivated in several Central American countries, and is also used for propagating new varieties in Southeast Asia. Its fruit pods are long and pointed, and the seeds produce white or cream-colored cotyledons (seed leaves). The tree itself grows only at high altitudes where there is a high rainfall. It does not have a high yield but produces the finest, and most expensive, grade of cocoa. It is used principally to make dark chocolate. Forastero, meaning "stranger," produces the ordinary or common grade of cocoa. The pods are round and the cotyledons are violet. The tree grows at lower altitudes and is more productive than the Criollo. More than 90 percent of cocoa currently comes from plantations of Forastero and its hybrids (Cundeamor, Angoleta, Amelonado, Consum, and Calabacillo). It is the main variety in West Africa and Brazil. This ordinary grade of cocoa is used almost exclusively for cocoa powder and milk chocolate. The two basic varieties are also crossed with each other.

Continuous monitoring of plant development during the growing season is necessary to produce perfect beans. Here, the plants are being inspected by a representative of the Nestlé company on a plantation owned by a farmer on the Ivory Coast.

The delicate blossoms of the cacao tree smother the branches in their hundreds. Their beauty lasts for only a few hours, during which time they have to be pollinated. To ensure success, plantation workers perform the laborious task by hand, using fine brushes to transfer the pollen to the stigma.

The different colors of the fruits are no indication of type. The high quality Criollo bean is still cultivated in Latin America. Africa is the main producer of the ordinary grade Forastero cocoa, with Southeast Asia in close competition. Overall raw cocoa production has shifted greatly in recent decades: whereas in the 1920s Central and South America were the leading producers, in the 1970s Africa took over this position, and new plantations in Southeast Asia have been catching up. Asian research institutes have experimented with the relative importance of shading trees. They have pruned whole branches to produce bigger and better fruit, and found that the increased amount of sun does not seem to have done the trees any harm.

© Kartographie Huber

Areas of cultivation

The biggest producers of cocoa beans are near the Equator

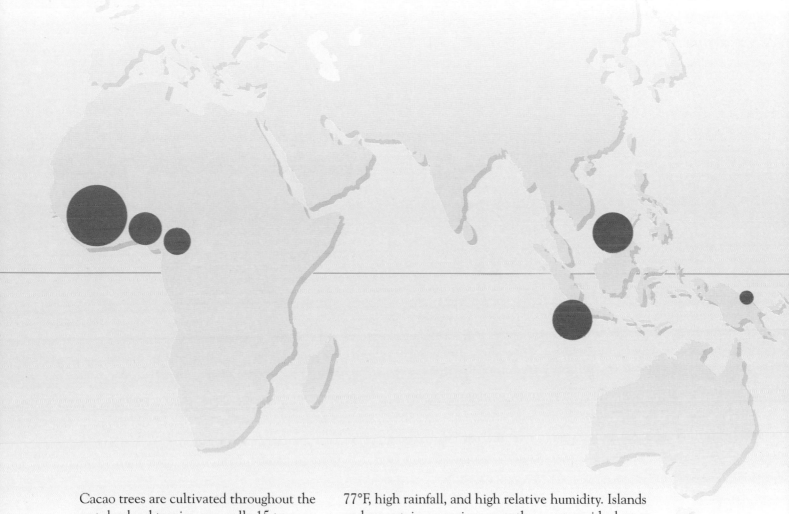

Cacao trees are cultivated throughout the wet, lowland tropics, generally 15 to a maximum of 20 degrees north and south of the Equator. For growth and development the trees require an average temperature of 77°F, high rainfall, and high relative humidity. Islands and mountainous regions near the coast are ideal areas for cultivation.

World harvest 1993 (2,662,250 tons) by country of origin	
Country	**%**
Ivory Coast	32.1
Ghana	8.9
Nigeria	5.8
Indonesia	9.1
Malaysia	9.4
Papua New Guinea	1.5
Dominican Republic	1.9
Mexico	1.8
Brazil	14.3
Columbia	2.3
Ecuador	3.1
Venezuela	0.6
Other	9.2

The cocoa harvest

A delicate crop requires careful handling

Although the cacao tree may flower and ripen intermittently through the year, the main period is from October to March, when 80 percent of the world cocoa crop is harvested. In Africa, the main harvest usually begins at the end of the rainy season and lasts until the early part of the dry season. A second, smaller, harvest may also take place at the start of the following rainy season, but drying the beans becomes a problem if it rains.

The real harvest, when the pods are removed from the trunk, calls for the utmost care. They are cut down by hand, just as they were at the time of the Aztecs. Long sharp blades, often fixed to long poles to reach the higher-growing pods, are used to remove them from the tree trunk. Care is taken to ensure that neither the remaining blossom nor any unripe pods are damaged. The cuts on the tree are then sealed so that new flowers will grow. The timing of the harvest varies with each pod. It takes five to six months from fertilization to the point of ripening, which can usually be determined by the color. Green pods generally become yellow, red pods become orange. Only the dark violet pods scarcely change color and are therefore difficult to judge. The state of ripeness can also be tested by ear. In ripe pods, the beans have become detached from the pulp and rattle when shaken. The timing has to be just right. If the pods are unripe, the beans are hard to remove and the subsequent fermentation is spoiled. Overripe pods, which do not fall from the trunk, offer ideal conditions for the beans to start germinating again.

Yields vary enormously according to the region and the intensity of cultivation. Whereas the small farmer might produce anything from 185 to 640 pounds an acre, the large plantations in Malaysia, for example, can produce up to 2,750 pounds an acre.

As with all natural products, yields may vary qualitatively as well as quantitatively. The manufacturers of proprietary products — chocolate bars, chocolate coatings, and powdered cocoa — therefore buy their raw materials from different regions and make up for the variation in quality by blending.

Harvesting the world over does not vary: Whether in Africa, Latin America, or Southeast Asia, skilled plantation workers use long poles with specially shaped blades to pull down the ripe fruit without damaging the branches, blossoms and unripe fruits.

Cocoa in art

Naïve painting from Haiti: everyday scenes from the plantation

A small art collection, started at the instigation of chocolate connoisseur Rolf Italiaander, proves that cocoa is not simply a food, but also a luxury of a special kind. Mr. Italiaander, who gleaned

Joyful at a Good Harvest by Gontran Durocher (b. 1945, Port-au-Prince), oil on canvas, 25 x 25 inches.

Donkey Waiting to Finish Work by Franklin Joseph-Jean (b. 1960, Port-au-Prince), oil on hardboard, 19½ x 21¾ inches

his knowledge of chocolate and its cultural history from the cacao-growing areas of the world, set Haitian folk painters the task of portraying the theme of cocoa production in pictures. The brilliantly colored paintings in the collection reflect life revolving around the cultivation of cacao and tell of the sorrows and joys of daily work on the plantation. All the pictures reproduced here belong to the Gustav Hamester Collection.

Farmer's Family on Harvest Day by Ulysses K. Joseph (b. 1960, Limbé), oil on canvas, 14 x 19½ inches.

The cacao seeds can be clearly seen in this section that has been cut open. They are violet in color and become brown only after fermentation.

The seeds are carefully removed by hand. While still at the collection points, the pods are split open by plantation workers, who remove the seeds and pulp from the pods. They have to be skillful not to damage the seeds.

Fermentation
The crucial step on the route from cocoa bean to raw cocoa

In a tropical climate, fermentation is a naturally occurring process, in which microorganisms naturally present on the pods cause the flesh inside, which contains sugar, to decompose and release the cocoa beans.

The freshly harvested pods have to be handled with great care, as they are very prone to spoilage and pressure. The beans have to be removed from the pods as quickly as possible after harvesting, since otherwise, with optimum conditions of moisture and warmth within the pods, they would start to germinate, which would render them useless for fermentation. The beans are removed from the pod while they are still at the collection points on the plantation. The workers take each pod and split it in half with a well-aimed blow from a machete or wooden stick. They remove the damp beans, covered with the moist pulp, manually, put them into baskets or other containers, and take them to that part of the plantation where the fermentation process is carried out.

Fermentation methods vary according to the size of the plantation. On the smaller plantations the beans are left to ferment between banana leaves. The beans begin to sweat in the hot sun, and are turned regularly until all the moisture is sweated out. On large plantations the beans are fermented in wooden crates. The piles of crates are sometimes arranged in steps. Fresh beans are added at the top, and then begin to ferment in the heat. Each day the hot beans that have started to ferment are scooped into a lower box, which also has the effect of stirring them. Depending on the variety, they ferment in two (Criollo) to eight (Forastero) days.

During this period, the sugary pulp in the pod is converted into alcohol by the effects of anaerobic microorganisms (yeasts) and the build-up of heat — up to 122°F. With the addition of oxygen, which is provided by mixing and turning the beans, the alcohol turns into acetic acid. Fermentation kills the germ in the seed, so that it is no longer able to germinate. The cells' walls become transparent, and the cell sap spreads into the bean, and the whitish-yellow bean turns to a beautiful chocolate brown. The bitter substances break down and the typical chocolate flavor starts to develop. The beans now begin to become plump, the temperature drops slightly, and fermentation continues for a few days longer. The aromatic substances that develop during fermentation are a precursor of the true cocoa flavor, which develops further when the beans are roasted. Poor fermentation impairs aroma and flavor, and ultimately the quality of the finished product. Only the fermented seeds are referred to as cocoa beans.

Banana leaves are widely used for fermentation. The broad-leaved banana trees are already cultivated on plantations to provide shade for the cacao trees.

During fermentation the biochemical structure of the seed changes. The initially white pulp of the fruit becomes the typically brown cocoa color, flavors develop, and the bitter taste becomes milder.

Wooden crates are used to ferment large quantities of seeds. Each day the seeds are turned by scooping them from one crate to another. After five to seven days, the process is complete and the seeds are dried.

Drying

The final stage of processing on the plantation reduces the high water content of the cocoa beans

In order to make the beans fit for handling or storage for later processing, the high water content has to be reduced from 50 percent to between 5 and 7 percent. As a rule, drying is the last step to be carried out on the plantation. The fermented cocoa beans are either spread out loosely on mats or wire racks, or placed in huge, flat wooden boxes in a layer 2 to 4 inches deep, and exposed to the hot, tropical sun. They are continuously turned by hand to assist the flow of air and to prevent the formation of mold. They can also be dried artificially using special drying equipment. The drying process lasts for five to seven days. During this time, the flavor of the cocoa bean develops further, and the character of each particular variety becomes apparent. The beans dry more quickly and do not stick together if they are washed after fermentation. There is always the risk, however, that the shells will break during washing. When the beans are dried and ready for transport to market, they are referred to as raw cocoa.

The dried cocoa beans, each weighing around 1 to 2 grams, contain a tiny cacao rootlet, which is equal to approximately 1 percent of the weight. This is useless for further processing, as it has an unpleasant taste. In a later processing step, the shells of the beans, which are 10 to 17 percent of the total weight, are removed. They may be ground and used for ersatz tea or coffee, or pulverized and used for the extraction of theobromine.

Even at the road side beans can be seen drying, as here, where a small farmer sits in front of an imposing termite hill.

The sun is a perfect energy source for drying. The beans acquire a very pure taste. This cannot always be said of those dried under cover, where fire is used to hasten the process.

Manual labor is a necessary part of the drying process. The beans are picked over and turned continuously to distribute the heat uniformly.

Nutritional value of the cocoa bean

In common with tea and coffee, cocoa has a high alkaloid content, making it a stimulant. However, in contrast to those two substances, cocoa ranks not only as a stimulant but also as a food. The cocoa bean, with its high fat content (up to 55 percent), combined with 14 percent protein, 9 percent starch, 2.6 percent minerals as well as 5 percent water and 14 percent salt-free essences, concentrates a high nutritional value into the smallest volume. The alkaloid theobromine is present (1.5 percent), as is caffeine (0.2 percent). Despite this nutritional composition and the fact that chocolate is a very enjoyable food, we are often advised to enjoy it in moderation.

Selection of the best qualities of cocoa bean ensures the quality of the end product.

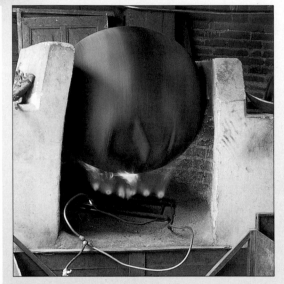

Cocoa beans are roasted in a rotating steel drum over an open fire. After twenty minutes, the drum is opened to check the progress. Depending upon the condition of the beans, the process may last for up to forty minutes. The drum is then opened again. The hot beans fall into a wooden tray and are carefully turned as they cool.

Traditional production

Using the simplest equipment

In the Mexican state of Oaxaca, time appears to have stood still. There are businesses here that make chocolate in the way they have always done. The dry cocoa mass, sweetened with sugar, is pressed into molds and, in time, turns as hard as stone. The pressed chocolate cakes are used to prepare drinking chocolate. Our palates would miss the smooth melting sensation that we have come to associate with chocolate.

This raw chocolate, or chocolate liquor, which later becomes rock hard, is used in Mexico almost exclusively for the preparation of drinking chocolate or for *mole*, the world-famous piquant chocolate sauce served chiefly with turkey.

Raw cocoa

Cocoa varieties and their market

The division of cocoa into two categories — ordinary or common cocoa, and fine cocoa, in itself gives some indication of the volumes being traded on the world market. Firstly, there is the fine grade cocoa (Criollo), high in quality but limited in quantity. With a fine aroma and essential oils, this cocoa is grown principally in Central and South America and in Southeast Asia. It commands a relatively high price.

Secondly, there is ordinary cocoa (Forastero), which makes up almost 90 percent of the world cocoa market, and forms the basis of most chocolate blends. Nowadays, the largest quantities of ordinary cocoa are produced in Africa (Ghana, Ivory Coast, Nigeria, and Cameroon), supplying mainly the European market. Next comes Brazil, which chiefly supplies North America, and then Asia, which is rapidly increasing its production figures.

The trade in raw cocoa is conducted on commodity futures markets in New York, London, and Paris before the actual harvest starts. Contracts for the purchase of specified quantities and qualities of raw cocoa are agreed in advance between the cocoa producers worldwide and the brokers and buyers, who are primarily the food corporations and chocolate manufacturers of the industrialized countries. Cocoa futures trading is intended to keep the market stable. Deeply impenetrable to the lay person, the world market in cocoa is supposed to operate according to the market forces of supply and demand. Although there have been several pronounced jumps in price since the 1960s, caused by political or climatic events, the cocoa market has remained largely stable in the 1980s and 1990s. Unfortunately, this has been at the cost of the producer countries around the Equator.

To make high quality chocolate products, the beans must be of high quality. Here in storage in a Swiss factory that makes couverture, the piled-up jute sacks contain beans of the best provenance. Each blender has its own recipe for mixing beans of individual varieties.

Dark brown beans, such as these top-quality beans from Venezuela, with their pleasant aroma, are neither bitter nor acidic, and are best suited for making dark bitter chocolate and for enriching standard mixtures.

Very light brown beans, with their mild flavor, mild aroma and low acidity, are the basis of very light milk chocolates. Here is an example of a high quality bean from Java.

From Africa come most of the ordinary grade beans, such as these from Saô Tomé, an island off the coast of Gabon.

These dark brown to blackish-brown beans of a high-quality cocoa from Ecuador are distinguished by a strong bitter taste, which is barely acidic. They are used for making bitter chocolate.

These dark brown beans from Grenada are used to make dark bitter chocolate and to enrich standard grades. They have a strong, sharp, slightly bitter but barely acidic taste.

Ordinary grade cocoa beans are often medium brown, fairly strong in aroma, and astringent. They are used as the basis of practically all chocolate liquor. These beans come from the Ivory Coast.

Storage

In reserve and as a hedge against unforeseen price rises on the world market

When the raw cocoa reaches the chocolate factories, each delivery is inspected for quality. Only the best raw materials will ensure a high-quality end product. Experts take samples from the sacks and check whether the cocoa beans supplied meet the specifications. The raw beans must be sound and,

Random samplings are taken to check the quality of the beans. A stainless steel tube with a sharp point is pushed into the sack and then withdrawn, full of beans.

Well-tempered Climatically controlled storage conditions are essential for the large quantities of beans held by chocolate manufacturers. Large stocks protect the manufacturers against unforeseen fluctuations in world market prices and guarantee the consistent quality of their products.

© Info-Zentrum Schokolade

Roasting, one of the most important steps on the long and complicated route from bean to chocolate, develops the flavor and the color.

without exception, must have been fermented, dried, and transported without damage. When the samples have passed the inspection, the sacks of beans are cut open and the beans stored loose in large silos to await processing. The entire process is conducted under controlled conditions in which temperature, humidity, and ventilation are regularly monitored to maintain the sensitive product in peak condition.

Cleaning

An essential process to ensure quality

The raw cocoa beans are kept in the silo until they are required for processing. When they are needed, the beans must first be thoroughly cleaned, as the cleanliness of the cocoa is a determining factor for quality in subsequent production. Special cleaning equipment, incorporating strong suction devices, riddles (special strainers), and brushes as well as magnets, separates and removes small stones, nails, bits of wood and fibers from the sacks. Then, measurable values of the beans, such as fat and water content, are carefully determined.

The cleaning plant removes the last of the impurities. Sieves and brushes as well as pneumatic and magnetic devices are used to clean the beans as carefully as possible, to ready them for the next stage of processing.

Roasting

The most important step in developing flavor and color

The secret of any chocolate product lies in the roasting, which is the next stage in the manufacturing process. The cocoa beans are rigorously sorted and then roasted in large electrically powered machines for 10 to 35 minutes to achieve the desired degree of browning. After the initial drying phase, in which water content of the beans is reduced to 3 percent and the shells become loosened from the kernel for later removal, the actual phase of flavor development begins. The reaction temperature has to be set according to the variety. For ordinary cocoa (usually the African varieties), the range is between 248 and 266 °F. For fine cocoa, the temperature is below 248°F. The color change that is initiated here determines the ultimate shade of brown of the chocolate. The beans may be roasted whole, in which case the hard shell becomes loosened, or the raw beans are shelled, broken up, and then roasted. The techniques used vary considerably — the classic roasting drum is now used only in small enterprises; a modern roasting plant is computer-controlled and no longer requires a master roaster to follow the tricky process visually.

The beans are split open in the cracking plant. The shells, which have already become detached from the nibs in the roasting process, are separated by blasts of air.

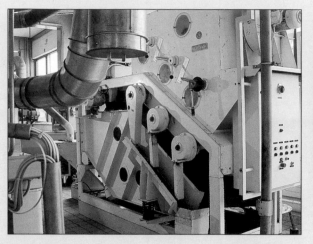

Cracking and grinding

Getting to the essence of the bean

As soon as the roasted beans have cooled, they are cracked open in a continuous crushing plant. Large rollers break the hard shells, which have become detached from the kernels during the roasting process. A powerful current of air uses the differing specific gravity of the components to blow the broken pieces of shell away from the broken cocoa particles. The shell fragments are collected and dispatched to the chemical industry, which extracts the theobromine. The broken cocoa particles that remain, known as "nibs," trickle out from the machine in coarse pieces. Another quality test is performed at this point to ensure that even the tiniest impurities have been removed. Nibs must contain more than 50 percent fat, but no more than 3 percent water and 2 percent foreign bodies (such as shells and seed membrane).

The cocoa nibs have to undergo a further grinding process to separate them into their constituent parts, cocoa butter and powder. They are crushed in special pin mills and are then ground to a fine cocoa paste. This ruptures the cellular tissue of the nibs and causes the fat located in the cells, the cocoa butter, to be released. The heat of friction melts the cocoa butter, which then envelops the cell particles, along with the protein and starch particles. The shiny brown chocolate liquor is pumped off from the mills and held in heated tanks to await further processing. When the liquor cools, it sets hard.

The broken kernels leave the cracking plant. Corrugated rollers reduce the beans into small pieces, which are separated from pieces of shell by powerful currents of air. They are then checked once more for impurities.

The nibs, the broken particles that emerge as coarse pieces when the shells have been removed, are the basic product for chocolate production. They are finely ground in pin mills to produce cocoa liquor.

The hard cocoa bean shells are a waste product as far as the production of chocolate is concerned. For the chemical industry, however, they are a valuable raw material containing a high percentage of theobromine, an alkaloid that contains caffeine.

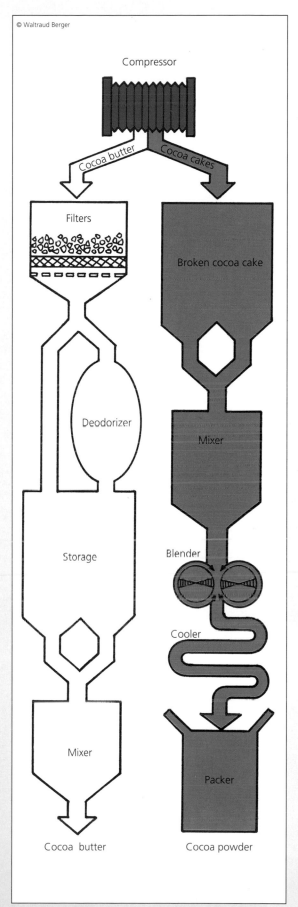

© Waltraud Berger

Compressor

Cocoa butter | Cocoa cakes

Filters

Broken cocoa cake

Deodorizer

Mixer

Storage

Blender

Cooler

Mixer

Packer

Cocoa butter | Cocoa powder

A dark brown glossy mass flows out of the grinding mill. It is the basic material for cocoa powder, cocoa butter, and for chocolate of all sorts. The quality of this intermediate product determines the quality of the finished product.

The route from cocoa liquor to cocoa butter. Powerful hydraulic presses remove as much of the cocoa butter as desired. The residual liquor is ground to cocoa powder.

© Cadbury Ltd.

The pale yellow cocoa butter leaves the presses after being filtered. Depending on how it will be used next, it is formed either into large blocks (see below) or into slabs weighing between 4 and 11 pounds for the confectionery industry. It is solid at room temperature.

The round cocoa cakes drop from the press directly onto the conveyor belt, which transports them to the crushers. There they are broken into pieces the size of hazelnuts and later ground into powder.

Butter and powder
Transforming the chocolate liquor

After the chocolate liquor is produced, the processes for making cocoa butter and cocoa powder diverge. The warm liquor is heated and compressed to remove most of the fat. Hydraulic rams press the chocolate liquor, heated to between 176 and 194°F, into chambers against stainless steel sieves with minute perforations. As the pressure increases, the pale yellow cocoa butter flows out. The duration depends upon the desired fat content of the compressed cocoa cakes. When the compressing chambers are opened, the cakes drop onto a conveyor belt, which moves them immediately to the next stage of production.

The liquid cocoa butter still contains individual particles of cocoa and other impurities, which are removed in various filtering stages. The pale yellow fat is trapped in containers and formed into blocks. If it is stored in a cool, dry place, cocoa butter will keep almost indefinitely. Its pleasant taste hints at the flavor

Non-alkalized: 10–12 percent fat

Alkalized: 10–12 percent fat

of cocoa. At room temperature, cocoa butter is hard and brittle. It has a melting point between 89 and 95°F. The chocolate industry uses it in the manufacture of eating chocolate, icings, and confectionery coatings. This high-quality and very valuable fat, which is responsible for the good melting properties and the crisp snap of chocolate, naturally commands a price. This has led to the search for substitutes.

The residual compressed cocoa cakes, which do not contain much fat, are used to make cocoa powder. But first the crushed cake has to be treated with an alkali salt (potassium carbonate), in order to increase the pH value and neutralize the acidity. Without this treatment, the cocoa powder would not be soluble and would float on the surface of liquids. As well as improving suspension, alkalization makes it possible to determine the color. Lecithin, an emulsifier made from soya bean, is also usually added to powder to be dissolved in cold drinks. The picture below shows a selection of cocoa powders. The alkalizing process can also be carried out on the crushed cocoa kernels (nibs).

After they have been alkalized, the compressed cocoa cakes are crushed and ground into fine powder by large machines. Cocoa powder is categorized according to its fat content, which depends, of course, on the residual amount of fat in the cake; highly defatted cocoa powder contains about 10 percent fat, while lightly defatted powder contains around 20 percent.

Cocoa "press," or "cakes" (2 inches thick, 17½ inches in diameter) really do look like cakes. But the chocolate liquor, which has been compressed until it is almost devoid of fat, is as hard as rock.

Different types of cocoa powder, in various colors and with varying fat content, are produced for various uses.

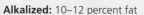

Alkalized: 10–12 percent fat   **Non-alkalized:** 20–22 percent fat   **Alkalized:** 20–22 percent fat

CHOC

The quality of the ingredients we use in cooking is all-important in determining the quality of the end product. What, then, affects the quality of chocolate? First and foremost it is the proportion of high-quality cocoa beans in the blend. Chocolate that is referred to as "fine" is made from a blend containing at least 40 percent high-quality beans. The technical name for the type of chocolate used to make chocolate bars and candies, icings, and cream fillings is "couverture," and is the term used throughout this book to distinguish the ingredients from the finished product. Couverture contains cocoa solids, cocoa butter, sugar, vanilla, and lecithin, and is delicious to eat without further processing.

The proportion of cocoa liquor to sugar is important. The higher the ratio, the darker and more bitter the chocolate. Semisweet and bittersweet chocolate must contain at least 50 percent total dry chocolate liquor. Milk chocolate has at least 25 percent total dry cocoa solids combined with 14 percent dry milk solids, 3.5 percent milk fats, and a maximum of 55 percent sugar.

White chocolate is not really chocolate at all. It is made from cocoa butter, which lacks the components that give cocoa its color and taste. It contains no other elements of the cocoa bean, and for this reason legally must be called "white confectionery coating."

Dark and milk couverture are available in fine stores: Be sure to read the label carefully. White couverture may be available only from specialty stores and by mail order (see page 235).

OLATE

Stone rollers grind the chocolate to a fine powder. Technology has produced the means to do what the Aztecs could achieve only by using muscle power and a grinding stone.

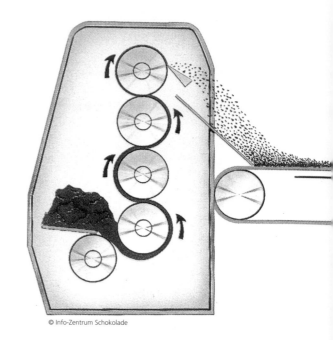

A five-roller mill, drawn schematically, with arrows indicating the direction of rotation, shows how the cocoa is drawn by the rollers from the bottom up to the top.

Grinding to a fine powder

One of the most important stages in making chocolate

The basic ingredient for making chocolate is, of course, the chocolate liquor, but in order to give it its characteristic taste and good melting properties other ingredients are added according to established recipes: more cocoa butter, sugar, cream or milk powder for milk chocolate, spices or flavorings such as vanilla, coffee, or cinnamon, and sometimes hazelnuts, almonds, or other solid ingredients. Some manufacturers use cocoa solids made from a blend of different varieties of bean. Others blend the liquors of two or more varieties. A certain amount of cocoa butter always remains in the chocolate liquor after initial processing, but the quantity is not always sufficient, and in those cases it has to be supplemented. This applies particularly to milk chocolate, which contains only 25 percent chocolate liquor, and to white chocolate, which contains none at all.

In ordinary chocolate, with or without milk, the maximum proportion of sugar is 55 percent. The same is true for white chocolate. For extra bitter chocolate, which has a cocoa component of up to 70 percent, the proportion is correspondingly reduced. In milk chocolate and in white chocolate,

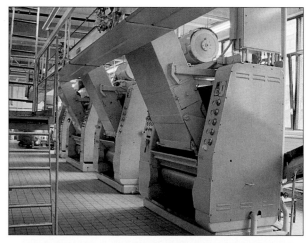

The steel rollers are covered in a thin film as the chocolate liquor moves upwards over the five rollers. At the top, it is scraped off with a knife and drops as a powder onto a conveyor belt.

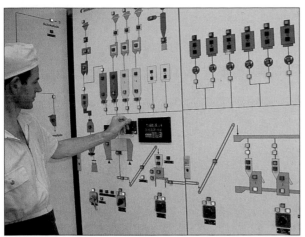

Mixing and measuring are now largely electronically controlled, but the recipes remain the secret of the master mixer and are checked by him or her.

milk powder makes up between 7 and 25 percent of the total volume and affects the taste of the finished chocolate, depending on how it is treated. It can, for example, be lightly caramelized. A few manufacturers even use condensed milk, which is pressed into a solid, dry liquor with sugar.

The ingredients are mixed at a temperature between 104 and 122°F, and then pass to preliminary crushers, where they are reduced to a particle size of 0.2 mm — small, but not small enough. The multi-stage fine grinding equipment reduces this size by a factor of ten. The fluffy chocolate powder, which is scraped from the final roller with a blade, has a granular diameter of 0.02 mm — a particle size that the human tongue can no longer detect. This smooth texture is the aim of a good chocolate manufacturer.

Conching
From chocolate liquor to couverture

In order to bring the taste of the basic chocolate liquor to the peak of perfection and to make it flow readily, another stage in refining is called for: conching. Conches were originally long stone troughs in which the ground chocolate was pounded around and around at a temperature of 86°F, often for several days at a time. In addition, there were round stone troughs in which the liquor was pounded with a stone ball. Modern rotary conches reduce the process to only a few hours, and, with a load of 2¼ to 5½ tons, can handle far larger quantities than the old stone conches.

In the first stage, dry conching, the moisture content of the liquor is reduced to less than 1 percent. At the same time, unwanted volatile flavors evaporate, and a soft film of cocoa butter envelops the particles of the solids. After approximately ten hours the liquor is liquefied by adding cocoa butter, and it is then conched even more vigorously in order to obtain a really homogeneous substance. This stage can last up to four hours to achieve the desired quality. Depending on the recipe used, three hours before conching ends, more cocoa butter is added together with an emulsifier, lecithin, which makes the chocolate flow more readily, improving its pouring quality.

Today there are more efficient and cheaper methods of refining, in which homogenization and taste enhancement are carried out in separate stages. The manufacturers of leading products, however, will not depart from the old methods, because they produce the best results.

Conching is a refining process that converts the chocolate liquor into a creamy liquid by continuous kneading and through the heat generated by friction. After several hours, the crumbly chocolate liquor turns into liquid chocolate.

Intermediate holding vats. The conched chocolate is stored temporarily in huge containers kept at a temperature between 113 and 131°F. The chocolate is kept in motion by mechanical or pneumatic means to prevent the cocoa butter from settling.

Gloss and delicate creaminess, the characteristics of a good-quality chocolate, are already obvious in the liquid phase, when the chocolate is "tempered," the final important step before it is poured into molds.

Tempering and forming

Small bars of chocolate and large blocks of couverture

The chocolate liquor is now at a temperature between 113 and 131°F. In order to give it that familiar silky finish, it has to be tempered. The liquor is cooled down in several stages to about 82°F and then reheated to 89°F. This process stabilizes the fat crystals, so that in addition to

The spotlessly clean molds pass automatically beneath the filling dispensers, through a shaking device to remove air bubbles, and then move on to the cooling section.

having luster and texture, the chocolate breaks with a sharp snap. It is now ready for consumption, and needs only to be poured into bars or blocks, then cooled and packaged.

The term "couverture" comes from the French word *couvrir*, meaning "to cover" or "to coat." This reflects the fact that this special quality chocolate was originally used mainly for chocolate coatings. Today, it continues to be used for this purpose in the candy industry and in baking and patisserie, but it is also eaten in this plain form by people who really appreciate fine chocolate.

The fully hardened blocks of couverture are inverted while still in the cooling chamber, automatically turned out, and placed on the conveyor belt. Defective blocks are picked out and returned to be melted down again.

The small bars pass automatically along the conveyor. "Depositing" is the term used to describe the process when the prewarmed molds are filled, shaken, and cooled. "Demolding" is when the molds are inverted, the blocks are tapped out, and drop onto the conveyor belt to be packaged.

A uniform gloss on perfect blocks of couverture. Depending on the manufacturer, couverture for industrial use may weigh between 4 and 11 pounds. Much smaller packages are available for home use.

Couverture
The professional view

Please note:
In the recipes in this book, "couverture" is always dark couverture. Milk chocolate couverture and white couverture are always explicitly designated.

Couverture is also sold grated and in the form of chocolate buttons. It melts more rapidly like this and can be used for tempering warm couverture (see pages 52–3).

Storing couverture. Couverture, including broken pieces, should always be stored carefully, wrapped in acetate if possible. Since it is very susceptible to other flavors, the place where it is kept, as well as the packaging, should be free of odors. Stored in a cool, dry place, dark couverture will keep for up to 15 months. The more sensitive milk chocolate and white couverture will keep well for up to 10 months.

The main difference between couverture and the type of chocolate used for chocolate bars and other commercial chocolate products is the high cocoa butter content. This allows it to flow more easily, a property that is very important to the confectionery industry, which uses it for molding and coating the most varied products, from chocolates to cakes. The quality of chocolate and couverture depends on the quality of the cocoa beans and the processing, and this is often reflected in the price. The ease with which couverture can be worked depends ultimately on its consistency, and here the industry has a vast palette of products to offer. When technical experts look at the range of couvertures available, they do not use terms such as "semisweet," "bittersweet," and so on, which we see on bars of chocolate. They deal in hard facts, and look at the percentages of the ingredients:

> *1. cocoa solids*
>
> *2. sugar*
>
> *3. total fat content*

The formula on industrial couverture packaging may look something like this: 60/40/38. This means that there is 60 percent cocoa solids, 40 percent sugar, and 38 percent total fat content. This describes a bitter couverture, which is the most frequently used. If it contains less than 60 percent cocoa components, the couverture is "semisweet;" if it contains more than 60 percent, it is "extra bitter." A 70/30/38 indicates 70 percent cocoa solids and only 30 percent sugar. In milk chocolate couverture the average ratio of cocoa solids is about 36 percent. Its formula is: 36/42/38. The third figure, the total fat content, indicates the viscosity of the couverture. The higher the total fat content, the greater the viscosity.

From top to bottom:
Extra bitter couverture, for icing
Pure cocoa butter for thinning couverture
Milk chocolate couverture of varying shades
White couverture, with no cocoa solids, only cocoa butter, which therefore cannot be called "chocolate"
Bitter couverture, the couverture used for confectionery and patisserie

COOKING
WITH
CHOC(

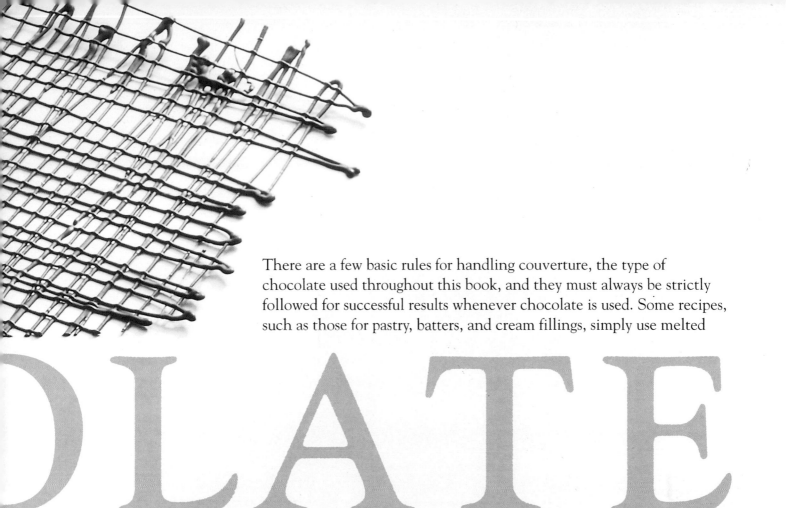

There are a few basic rules for handling couverture, the type of chocolate used throughout this book, and they must always be strictly followed for successful results whenever chocolate is used. Some recipes, such as those for pastry, batters, and cream fillings, simply use melted

chocolate. However, some recipes call for melted couverture to be turned back into its original solid state, which means that it must be tempered, a process described on pages 52–3.

Liquid, tempered couverture is an ideal material for people with creative flair. It can be molded or piped, and offers tremendous scope for decoration. It can also be combined with other ingredients to develop new flavors for confectionery and patisserie. There is no limit to what the creative mind can devise, but it is important to remember that this is a high-quality commodity and should be treated accordingly.

There are also a few important points to remember about some of the other ingredients. For all the recipes in this book, use only fresh, unsalted butter, whole milk, heavy cream, large eggs, and all-purpose flour, unless otherwise specified. Sift flour before measuring, and again afterward if the recipe requires it. Always prepare gelatin appropriately (see Glossary) before using it. Read each recipe all the way through before beginning to use it.

Tempering couverture

Temperature is crucial when working with chocolate for patisserie and confectionery

Couverture is the special type of chocolate used in patisserie and confectionery, which flows more readily than the type of chocolate found in candy bars. The consistency you need will depend on what you are using it for, such as covering cakes or coating candies. For many uses, couverture must be melted first, then tempered. When it is heated (the temperature must never exceed 104°F), couverture loses its binding properties. The sugar, cocoa solids, and cocoa butter separate. Tempering binds them together again, and the couverture returns to its original state: hard chocolate with a lovely sheen.

TEMPERING LARGE QUANTITIES

There are three methods for tempering couverture. The first method is extremely precise and is not suitable for working with small quantities. The couverture is cut into small pieces and heated to exactly 91.4°F, which is the melting point of cocoa butter. It is then simply stirred, ready for instant use. This process can be carried out only with highly accurate tempering equipment, since the melting point and maximum working temperature are identical.

THE TABLE METHOD

The second method of tempering is the one most frequently used. It is both quick and highly suited to small quantities. Again, the couverture is cut into small pieces and melted, but the maximum temperature is 104°F. About half of the melted couverture is poured

The table method:

Melt the chopped couverture over hot water at a maximum temperature of 104°F, stirring gently until all the pieces have melted.

Pour at least half of the couverture onto a marble or stainless steel slab, and spread with a spatula and palette knife.

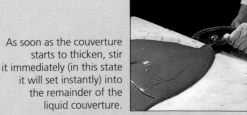

Using a palette knife, work the couverture. Use the spatula to remove any couverture that sets on the palette knife.

As soon as the couverture starts to thicken, stir it immediately (in this state it will set instantly) into the remainder of the liquid couverture.

The injection method:

Stir grated or finely chopped couverture into the warm couverture in batches.

The couverture begins to thicken when sufficient grated couverture has been added. Now reheat gently.

onto a marble or stainless steel slab and worked with a palette knife or spatula until it begins to set. It is then returned as quickly as possible to the rest of the warm couverture. Speed is of the essence, as only a short time elapses between thickening and solidifying. If the couverture as a whole is not cool enough — below 86°F, the point at which couverture begins to thicken — the

Couverture can be held ready for use in thermostatically controlled tempering equipment. Dark couverture is held at between 86 and 91°F, milk chocolate couverture (because of the milk fat content) between 86 and 89°F.

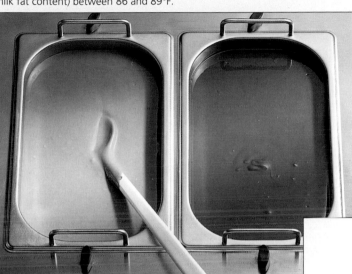

procedure has to be repeated. The cooled couverture must then be carefully reheated until it reaches 89°F. This is the mean temperature at which the couverture is sufficiently viscous to be worked easily. The temperature range for working lies between 86 and 91°F. Below these temperatures, the couverture thickens and dries with a matt surface; above these temperatures, the cocoa butter separates from the cocoa solids, and the couverture has to be tempered again.

THE INJECTION METHOD

The third method of tempering is very simple indeed. Grated or very finely chopped couverture is stirred ("injected") in small quantities at a time into melted couverture of the same type. This is repeated until the couverture starts to become visibly more viscous and the small particles dissolve only slowly. It is then carefully heated until it reaches the ideal temperature of 89°F.

Accurate temperature measurement is no problem with today's technology. There is a wide range of high-precision thermometers available.

Dipping a palette knife into the tempered couverture is the simplest way to check if it is ready. If the couverture has been properly tempered and the temperature of the palette knife is between 68 and 77°F, the couverture will start to harden at the thinnest point (see small inset picture below) after a few minutes. To ensure a correct sheen, however, in addition to the couverture temperature, the room temperature should ideally be 68°F and, most importantly, the temperature of the item to be iced must be between 68 and 80°F.

Correctly and incorrectly tempered. A silky gloss is the ideal couverture surface. If the couverture is too warm, it takes a long time to reach the setting point, and will then show stripes on a matt background.

-30°/+120°C

32.0

ON OFF

D 2020

Rolls, flakes, and fans

Attractive decorations for patisserie, confectionery and desserts

CHOCOLATE ROLLS

Making chocolate rolls is easy, but it calls for a little practice, as you have to work quickly. The couverture remains at the right consistency for making rolls only for a short time, so it is important to spread only small areas of chocolate at a time.

Chocolate rolls:

Using a palette knife, spread the melted couverture thinly over a marble slab until it becomes pliable and the surface is matt.

Form rolls by holding a spatula at an acute angle and shaving the couverture from the slab.

Small rolls:

Using a knife, score the spread couverture into strips to make rolls of the desired size.

Holding the spatula at an acute angle and moving it across the strips, shave off the couverture. When they are cold, the rolls can be snapped apart.

The marble slab and the room in which you are working also need to be at the right temperature, between 72 and 75°F.

CHOCOLATE FANS

There are two techniques for creating this decoration. In the first method, the couverture is converted into a sticky mass by adding oil or nougat. The quantities used depend upon the quality of the couverture, the ambient temperature, and the temperature of the marble slab. The lower the temperature, the more fat is required. Heat the couverture mixture to between 86 and 89°F, spread it onto a marble slab, and work it until it sets, as shown in the picture sequence below.

For the more fascinating, high-speed "professional method," heat a large (20 x 25 inches), smooth, clean baking sheet to 122°F. Temper 5 ounces of couverture at 104°F, and then use a small paint-roller (made of foam, not lambs' wool!) to spread it onto the baking sheet. Place the baking sheet in the refrigerator to cool for at least 1 hour, or for longer until required. Then let it stand in an ambient temperature of about 72°F until it becomes malleable. Proceed to shape it as shown below.

Decorating a cake: Karl Schuhmacher places the outer ring of fans on the cake. He will place a smaller ring on top, and fill the center with a third piece (see below).

Chocolate flakes:

Holding a sharp knife at an acute angle, shave wafer-thin flakes from a block of couverture. Do not hold the knife at a right angle, or whole pieces will break off.

A grater will produce very small flakes. When decorating a cake, grate flakes directly onto it.

Chocolate fans:

First method: Use a palette knife to spread couverture tempered at between 86 and 89°F onto a marble slab.

Second method: Spread couverture tempered at 104°F in portions onto a large baking sheet using a foam roller.

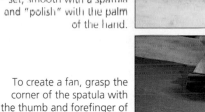

In the first method, when the couverture has begun to set, smooth with a spatula and "polish" with the palm of the hand.

To create a fan, grasp the corner of the spatula with the thumb and forefinger of the left hand and push the spatula forward with the right hand.

The chocolate wrinkles up on the left-hand side, forming the folds of the fan.

The fans can go directly on top of a cake as decoration, or they may be placed on a baking sheet lined with parchment paper and set aside for use later.

Spreading and cutting out shapes

The simplest way to make decorations

This method is very simple. You use a ruler to cut straight edges and a cutter to produce fancy shapes. Of course, it is still important to work carefully and precisely. This starts with spreading the properly tempered couverture as thinly and evenly as possible onto a sheet of parchment paper. In order to get rid of the lines made by the spreader, lift the paper once or twice and allow it to fall back onto the work surface. The surface of the chocolate will become beautifully smooth. If the couverture is spread onto acetate (see pages 64–5) instead of parchment paper, the underside will have a sheen similar to chocolate that has been poured into a mold. Pipe lines or decorations using couverture of a different color onto the surface before it sets. To make a decoration with the comb, you will need two thin layers, one on top of the other.

You can make these decorations and store them for later use. If you wish to store pieces of spread chocolate, keep them small so that they will remain flat. Large areas spread on paper tend to bulge due to the tension, and are difficult to use. The best way is to cut out the decorative elements as soon as the

Spreading and cutting:

Spread the tempered couverture as thinly and evenly as possible onto parchment paper or acetate. Lift the paper and let it fall back onto the counter. This makes the surface even smoother.

Just before the couverture sets, take a warm knife and cut it into 6 x 8-inch pieces to prevent it bowing.

Turn the slab of couverture onto a second piece of parchment paper or acetate, and peel away the first piece. To get different decorative effects, use either the glossy surface or the matt underside.

Cut into pieces of the desired size before the couverture has hardened fully. At this stage it will not splinter. Nevertheless, warm the knife slightly and wipe the blade on a damp towel after each cut.

couverture has been spread and before it is completely cold. This means that you have to work swiftly and, if possible, in a warm room with a warm work surface. In this case, you do not need to use a warmed knife or cutter. However, if the couverture is quite cold, use a warmed knife or cutter and allow it to melt its way gently through the chocolate, which would otherwise break. This entails the irksome task of cleaning the knife or cutter after each cut.

This type of decoration is used a lot in patisserie and confectionery. If the chocolate strips are made somewhat thicker, they can be enjoyed on their own.

To make a grooved pattern, spread a very thin layer, allow it to firm up, then spread a second layer on top. Make straight or wavy lines.

Stamp out shapes with a warm cutter, or cut out geometric shapes using a knife.

Stripes and waves

*Interesting effects created
with two layers*

This is a relatively simple technique. Spread a strip of tempered couverture onto parchment paper, or better still, onto acetate (see pages 64–5). The first layer has to be fairly thick, so that it remains stable when you comb it. When it has set slightly (do not allow it to set hard), fill the gaps with very thin couverture of a contrasting color and then smooth it over. The width of the stripe depends on the spacing of the notches on the comb, and the angle at which the comb is drawn. Various shapes can be made with a knife or cutter. This is best done before the couverture has fully hardened.

Wavy lines are a popular pattern. Turn the comb from side to side as you drag it over the first layer of couverture, varying the spacing.

To make stripes:

Spread a layer of tempered white couverture onto parchment paper. Using a strip of wood as a guide, drag a broad comb over it.

When the first layer has set slightly, pour the contrasting couverture onto it. The contrasting couverture should be as thin as possible.

Use an angled palette knife to smooth over. Lift the parchment briefly and let it fall back onto the table, so that the couverture distributes itself evenly.

The decorating comb is a very simple tool. Draw grooves on a piece of cardboard with the help of a ruler and cut them out with a sharp knife; the spacing depends upon how broad a stripe is required.

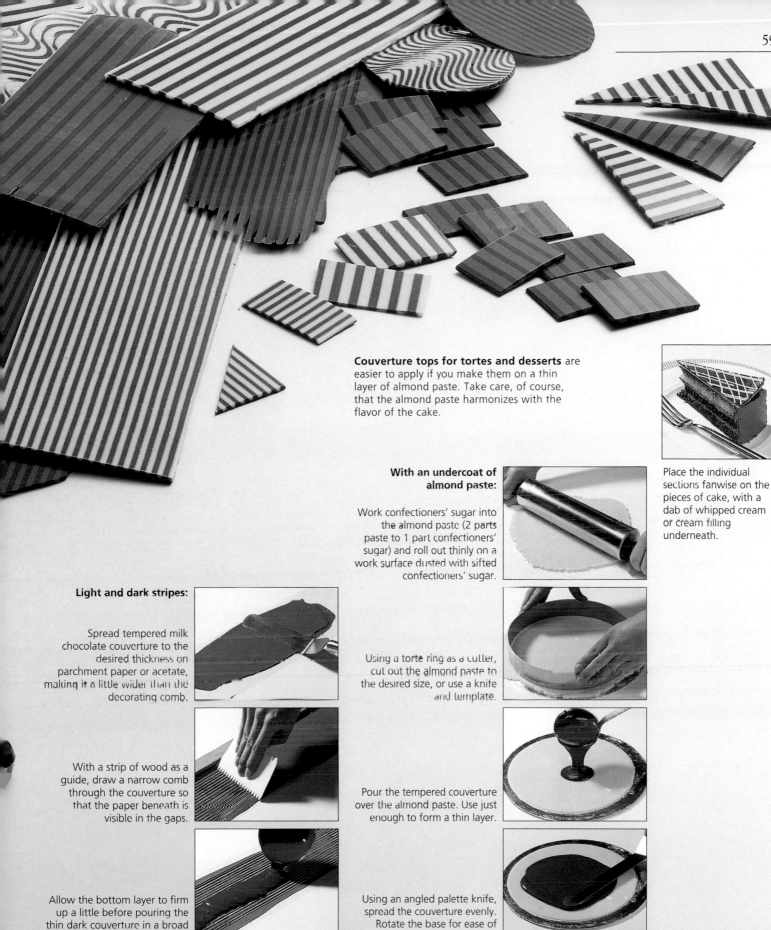

Couverture tops for tortes and desserts are easier to apply if you make them on a thin layer of almond paste. Take care, of course, that the almond paste harmonizes with the flavor of the cake.

Place the individual sections fanwise on the pieces of cake, with a dab of whipped cream or cream filling underneath.

With an undercoat of almond paste:

Work confectioners' sugar into the almond paste (2 parts paste to 1 part confectioners' sugar) and roll out thinly on a work surface dusted with sifted confectioners' sugar.

Light and dark stripes:

Spread tempered milk chocolate couverture to the desired thickness on parchment paper or acetate, making it a little wider than the decorating comb.

Using a torte ring as a cutter, cut out the almond paste to the desired size, or use a knife and template.

With a strip of wood as a guide, draw a narrow comb through the couverture so that the paper beneath is visible in the gaps.

Pour the tempered couverture over the almond paste. Use just enough to form a thin layer.

Allow the bottom layer to firm up a little before pouring the thin dark couverture in a broad band over the top.

Using an angled palette knife, spread the couverture evenly. Rotate the base for ease of spreading.

Using an angled palette knife, spread the darker couverture into the gaps. Lift the paper and let it drop again.

While the couverture is still liquid, pipe a lattice pattern of white couverture on top. Cut into sections while still soft.

Chocolate leaves

What could be more beautiful or more natural than using real leaves to copy nature?

These decorations are among the easiest to make. The only special materials you require are fresh leaves with interesting shapes. They must be sturdy: Soft leaves are no good, as they tend to collapse under the weight of the chocolate, and are difficult to separate from it. Stout leaves, such as bay or vine, citrus or beech, are ideal molds, and are easily separated from the

The upper surface of a leaf is not always the best side to use. The underside often has a prettier structure and gives more interesting results.

An autumnal heart
This is only one example of the wonderful effects that can be created with chocolate leaves. Here, the leaves are used to decorate a chocolate heart-shaped cake made using the recipe for Chocolate and Red Currant Torte (see page 90).

chocolate. Avoid leaves with fine hairs.

Pick leaves when they are fresh and firm, then clean them with a piece of fine cloth or cotton. The pictures show how to dip the leaves in the couverture or paint them with chocolate using a brush. Be careful not to let any couverture run over the edges or get on the back of the leaf, or it will be difficult to remove the molded leaf at these points.

All types of couverture — bitter, milk chocolate, and white — are suitable when they have been properly tempered.

To make chocolate leaves:

Draw the leaf over the surface of the couverture. Only smooth leaves, such as orange or bay, are suitable. This is a quick and easy method.

Use a pastry brush to paint couverture on curved leaves that have an uneven surface. Brush from the center to the edges so that the reverse of the leaf remains clean.

Wait until the couverture has hardened before removing the leaf. Grasp the leaf by the stalk and peel off carefully.

Flowers — thick and thin. The solid flowers with five petals (top) are piped using thick couverture and a large round tip. The large flowers (above) are drawn first on paper or cardboard, then overlaid with parchment paper and the outlines piped with thin filaments of couverture.

Piped decorations

Use a pastry bag to make very simple or highly sophisticated decorations for patisserie and confectionery

To make a paper pastry bag: Cut a triangle of parchment paper. Grasp the middle of the long side with the thumb and forefinger of the left hand. With the right hand, bring the top corner down to the middle, folding under and around to form a cone shape.

Hold the paper with the left hand beneath the point thus created and use the right thumb to push the paper in the direction of the point. Now roll up the paper cone completely.

The point must be completely tight. Fold the projecting end of the paper over to the inside, to hold the pastry bag in shape.

Spoon in the couverture or icing, taking care to keep the edges clean.

Holding the seam firmly, fold the top over. Squeeze the air out of the bag. Fold the ends from the outside in.

Cut off the tip of the bag with a sharp pair of scissors. The size of the opening will determine the thickness of the piping.

Using a pastry bag made of parchment paper or wax paper is a quick and easy way to make decorations, but requires a bit of practice. Small disk shapes are the easiest to make. Line a baking sheet with parchment paper. Fill the pastry bag with tempered couverture and pipe tiny mounds spaced a little way apart, as the chocolate should run slightly. These small disks can be assembled to make flowers.

To make decorations consisting of thin threads, add a few drops of water or sugar syrup to thicken the couverture. The couverture has to be strong enough so that the thread does not break (always hold the pastry bag ½ to ¾ inch above the paper). If you want to make a complicated design, first draw it on paper, then cover it with acetate or parchment paper and pipe the couverture onto the outline of the design. If you want to pipe decorations directly onto cakes or candies, then you will have to keep the design in your head, and practice it several times first.

Stars made by the filling-in method:

Draw the stars on paper and place a sheet of transparent parchment paper or acetate on top. Pipe the outline using white couverture.

Fill in the centers with dark couverture (thinned with a little cocoa butter) at room temperature. Give the paper a sharp tug so that the couverture spreads out evenly.

This type of decoration can be used on tortes, cakes, slices, and roulades, and for dessert dishes.

Chocolate lattice can be used for all sorts of interesting decorative effects. Shapes can be cut from it with a knife or stamped out with a cutter.

Flower petals are an easy shape to start with. They can simply be left as an open filigree design or filled in with thin couverture.

Drops and buttons are the simplest decoration, used mainly in patisserie but also for sealing or decorating candy. They can also be sprinkled with croquant. Piped onto parchment paper, they will keep well.

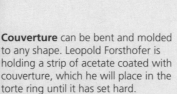

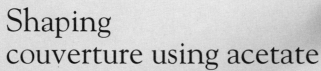

Couverture can be bent and molded to any shape. Leopold Forsthofer is holding a strip of acetate coated with couverture, which he will place in the torte ring until it has set hard.

Shaping
couverture using acetate

Acetate can be used with chocolate in a variety of ways

Acetate is sold in sheets, rolls, and strips in art supply stores. Similar materials, such as Bake-O-Glide, Silpat, and Rodoïde, specially designed for use in baking and candy making may be available from specialty stores or mail order outlets (see page 234), and can be used wherever the text calls for acetate. All these materials are ideal for shaping and bending chocolate. Couverture that has set on acetate retains a high surface sheen, whereas that which has set on parchment paper becomes matt.

Choose the type of acetate according to the shape you want to make. A strong acetate is best for rings and teardrops, because the couverture requires no further shaping after it has solidified. A rubber band is sufficient to hold the ring together. For a more complicated shape, such as a heart, use a thinner acetate because it is more pliable and the couverture clings better to the shape as it sets. Thin acetate is also used to make cones that are to be filled later. To make them, roll the film like a pastry bag (see page 62) and secure it with adhesive tape, fill it with couverture, and leave it to dry on a rack. Before the couverture sets hard, trim off the ends to neaten.

For trouble-free shaping with acetate, make sure that the couverture is properly tempered (see pages 52–3). The kitchen and the work surface must also be warm; 72 to 75°F is ideal, because then the couverture sets slowly, allowing you more time to work.

After shaping, place the couverture in a cool room or refrigerator. When the couverture is completely cold, it will detach itself from the acetate. The advantage of acetate is that it is possible to see where the couverture is detached and where it is still adhering.

Two-tone effects are another possibility: One color of couverture is piped onto acetate in a lattice pattern, or in stripes or spots. A second layer is spread over it to cover the surface. For the general method, see pages 58–9. Here the strips are not allowed to harden, but are formed immediately into bows, teardrops, rings or other shapes.

Chocolate rings:

Place acetate strips ½ inch apart on a work surface or on parchment paper. Mark off the length (that is, the diameter of the ring) with another piece of acetate strip laid crosswise.

Pour the tempered couverture over the acetate strips and spread evenly beyond the edges. The thickness will depend on the use.

Two-tone teardrop shapes:

Place acetate strips spaced apart on parchment paper Pipe a lattice pattern using tempered white couverture.

As soon as the couverture starts to set at the edges, remove the strip of acetate lying crosswise that determines the length of the strips.

As soon as the white couverture starts to set, spread the tempered dark couverture, which should be as thin as possible, over the top.

Grasp the individual acetate strips in turn and lift off, immediately forming them into rings by bringing the ends of the soft couverture around to meet each other.

Before the couverture sets, lift the strips and bend them into teardrop (or other) shapes.

The acetate strip now forms the outside of the ring and is held in position by a rubber band. Refrigerate until set hard.

Press the ends of the strips together. Refrigerate until cold and then remove the strip of acetate.

When the couverture has hardened fully, it detaches itself from the acetate strip, which can now be carefully removed.

Chocolate molds

Easter eggs, Easter rabbits and Santa Claus are the most popular shapes, but there are many others

Using molds is not difficult, provided that the couverture is precisely tempered (see pages 52–3) and that the molds are absolutely clean. Any impurity will cause the couverture to stick or be covered with specks. It could also make it difficult to release the shape from the mold, or cause it to break. To prevent these problems, be sure to wash the mold thoroughly and, after drying, give it a final rub with a fine cotton cloth.

Although Santa Claus, the Easter rabbit, and Easter egg are probably the most popular chocolate figures, there are molds for many others. (Molds for

making chocolate candy shells are described in the chapter "Chocolate Candies.") They may be made of metal, plastic, or stainless steel. The only prerequisites are that the internal surface is smooth and the mold does not narrow at the top, so that the figure can be removed.

How to make figures using a mold is described in detail in the two picture sequences below. The thickness of the chocolate wall depends on the viscosity of the couverture when it is poured out of the mold. You may have to pour in a second coat of couverture if the first one is too thin, or if a more robust shape is required. In this case, the first coat must be allowed to set slightly before the step is repeated. This technique is used for figures that would otherwise be rather fragile. Where a case is to be filled with a delicate pastry cream, the chocolate must be thick enough to withstand further processing.

Transparent molds make it easy to see when the figure is ready to be removed. As the chocolate sets, it shrinks slightly, allowing air to penetrate between it and the wall of the mold.

Filling molds: Fasten the two halves of the mold together with clips and half fill with tempered couverture. Tap the mold once sharply to release any air bubbles, and then fill up to the top.

Pour out the couverture and allow to drain briefly. Ideally, a layer of chocolate about ⅛ inch thick should coat the inside of the mold.

Place on a wire rack over parchment paper to drip. When the couverture has firmed up slightly, lift and trim the edges neatly.

Spread tempered couverture onto parchment paper, stand the figures on it and press them into it. Allow to harden fully.

As soon as air penetrates between the mold and the chocolate, release the clips and open the mold. Trim off any untidy edges.

Chocolate cases:

Fill clean molds with couverture, pour out, and place on a wire rack to drip.

Refrigerate until they firm up. Remove from the molds after a short period at room temperature.

Eggs:

Pour the tempered couverture into the mold until it runs over the top.

In one swift, deft movement, invert the mold over the receptacle and allow the chocolate to run out.

Suspend between wooden strips over parchment paper and allow to drip.

When the couverture has firmed up but is still soft, scrape off the excess around the edges.

When the shapes have hardened fully in the refrigerator (this is apparent when transparent molds are used), turn them out.

To join two halves together, warm the edges briefly on a warm baking sheet.

Press the two halves of the egg together to fit, and trim off any unevenness with a knife.

When it comes to classic recipes for pastries and cakes, chocolate is plainly not held in the same awe as it is in the making of individual chocolate candies, where it is the whole *raison d'être*. For cakes, confectionery, and fillings, it is merely a flavoring. The only exceptions to this are ganache cream, which is based on chocolate, and those fancy cakes

SSERIE

and tortes that occasionally use pure chocolate as a hard topping. Soft icings made with couverture are, however, increasing in popularity.

All three types of couverture are used for patisserie, although the more bitter taste of dark couverture is more popular, because its stronger flavor provides more contrast when combined with pastry or spongecakes, fillings or icings. Milk chocolate couverture and white couverture come into their own when mixed with roasted hazelnuts and almonds or combined with coffee.

The importance of chocolate in patisserie can be judged from some of the famous recipes that owe their very existence to it: Sachertorte from Vienna, Bûche de Noël (Yule Log) from France, Rigo Jansky and Dobostorte from Budapest, Imperial Torte from Munich, and, last but not least, Black Forest Cherry Cake, which is famous worldwide. These classics, made to their original recipes, are still in demand, but modern conveniences such as freezers now make it much easier to produce considerably lighter cream fillings at home, as this chapter will show.

The new art of cake-making

Nature uses our sense of smell to tempt us to try new foods. Although spices from the East were well known in Europe in the Middle Ages, new foods were in short supply until the beginning of the sixteenth century. It was only then that a wealth of previously unknown raw ingredients from other parts of the world, particularly the Americas, enabled cooks and bakers to experiment and create new dishes. Chocolate became one of the most popular of these new ingredients.

Under the Hapsburg emperors in Vienna, the delicate skills of the pastry chef and the confectioner had long flourished. It was the confectioners who first began to experiment with candied and spiced ingredients, and Vienna became the world focus for everything that was sweet. Bakers from Burgundy, who had devised new recipes for the wedding of Maria of Burgundy and the young Maximilian, and were later drawn to Vienna, reported that they encountered many new influences, including Saracen, Sicilian, Turkish, Venetian, and Arabic. When the age of chocolate began, it was the Viennese court confectioners, whose talents were without equal, who established themselves as the leaders in this field too.

For a long time chocolate remained a stranger at the baker's door. Perhaps the fact that cocoa did not yet have the cocoa butter removed and spoiled easily may have been partly responsible. It may also be that traditional bakers were not receptive to new ideas. The cost may have been too high. Even the arbitrary warnings issued from time to time by bishop or doctor thundering against the beans from America, blaming them for all the ills and vices of the time, may have played a part. The true nutritional values of all foods were still unknown, so it was impossible to counter these attacks by producing facts. Claims that chocolate was soothing or stimulating, sinful or good for the stomach were only assumptions.

Pattern for a torte decoration for a Roman almond torte shown in Carl Gruber's book *Confectionery in Words and Pictures*, the "indispensable work for confectioners, patissiers, preserved goods manufacturers and every household," published in Frankfurt am Main in 1896.

Chocolate triumphs at last

In the end, chocolate and cocoa powder found their way into the bakery, too. Bakers and pastry chefs appreciated their unique taste, and discovered that they combine exquisitely with almonds and flour, honey and cream. Nowadays chocolate cookies, cakes, tortes, and pastries are common foods, many based on recipes developed in the nineteenth century. People continue to create exciting new ways to use chocolate, but some of the early recipes became classics that have never been equaled.

The Hotel Sacher was a popular meeting place for the city's epicures at the turn of the century. Its reputation was built largely on the Sachertorte, which needs only a whisper of freshly whipped, lightly sweetened cream to add the finishing touch.

The Sachertorte

The most famous chocolate cake in the world comes from Austria. Franz Sacher (1816–1907), the son of an estate manager for the princes of Schwarzenberg, is said to have first baked it in 1832, when he was only sixteen years old. In 1888 his son Edward, already a *chef de cuisine*, said:

It is my father's creation. He made the cake for the first time while still a trainee in the home of Metternich and it was placed on the old man's table fifty-six years ago, where it was received with general applause. The Prince praised him highly. Since that time, after my father set up as the proprietor of a wine shop and delicatessen, the torte has been in continuous production. No cook or confectioner can copy it. The proof is that my torte appears daily on the table of Their Majesties and the Crown Prince and his wife. You can find it all over Vienna and in the larger towns. In fact, it appears on menus everywhere as a well-known specialty. I have four people working with me day and night all the year round in a specially designed kitchen. Some days we sell and dispatch between 200 and 400 Sachertortes.

By the end of the century, 20,000 Sachertortes a year were going "to the four corners of the earth." The secret of this torte lies in the quality of the chocolate and its moist, firm texture. In the next generation, the recipe was handed down like a national treasure by the renowned Anna Sacher in her cooking school, and thus was saved for posterity. Only the "Sacher" satisfied the tastes of royalty and gourmet alike.

Traditionally, in Vienna, tortes and other sweet dishes made with flour had been regarded as a dessert — that is, they were served only after a meal. But in 1955, when the first tourists started streaming back into Vienna after the end of World War II, cakes and tortes were ordered along with an afternoon cup of coffee. Sachertorte was offered not only by the Hotel Sacher, but also by the Demel confectionery a few hundred yards away. A veritable torte war broke out, which was not settled until 1958, when a judicial decision on the one true Sachertorte was handed down. Perhaps the judge did not have to look further than the *Appetit-Lexikon* (Gastronomic Dictionary) of 1894, which states "Sachertorte is a chocolate torte of a superior kind, distinguished from its imitators by the chemise of apricot jam it wears beneath its glossy chocolate robe... ."

The well-equipped bakery even in those days provided the confectioner with a large number of molds and aids to give him free rein in his creative work.

To bake is to measure

The ingredients for success are the correct techniques, utensils, and equipment

Baking with chocolate and cocoa

The principles for baking with chocolate or cocoa are the same as those that apply to making cakes in general. Chocolate, in the form of couverture or cocoa powder, is only one of a number of ingredients added for flavor in a recipe. It can be added to any mixture, from shortcrust pastry, through different types of cake batter and dough, to meringue. Unlike many other flavorings, however, chocolate and cocoa powder contain a high percentage of fat, which has to be taken into account when you combine them with other ingredients. In doughs and batters such as shortcrust pastry or pound cakes, which already contain a high proportion of fat, this is not a problem. But it is trickier with spongecake batters and particularly with meringue, which consists solely of egg whites and sugar. These mixtures react sensitively to the addition of fat, so you must be especially careful to follow the instructions when blending the various ingredients. Success depends on following the method carefully and on using the correct amount of each ingredient.

The right tools

Successful baking requires a certain amount of equipment, and the recipes in this book use a number of different size and shape cake pans and molds. You do not need to have a perfectly laid out kitchen like a professional, but the basic equipment should be of a high quality. Nobody today would willingly give up modern electric appliances, but it has to be said that a true feel for preparing baked goods can be gained only by performing the processes by hand first. Only then is it possible to judge which steps can be carried out by machine without any loss of quality.

The ideal collection of basic equipment comprises a set of measuring cups and spoons, a wooden rolling pin for pastry, bowls and basins varying in size from 8 to 14 inches (plastic will do but stainless steel is better), whisks in various sizes, and spatulas and spoons made of plastic or wood for stirring and blending. An electric hand mixer and a tabletop mixer are also useful. A hand blender, which has a small flat blade like a blender or liquidizer, is essential in some recipes, as it allows you to

Whisks are an indispensable tool in the bakery. They come in a variety of sizes for manual use. For electric mixers, different styles are available for mixing and beating.

Using a torte ring:

Place a torte ring on a piece of parchment paper cut to size. Turn up tightly around the edges. Do not grease the ring. Pour in the batter.

Invert the baked cake and leave to cool; this evens out any bumps. Peel off the parchment paper.

Slip a sharp knife around the edge of the ring and remove the cake.

Electrical appliances make it easy. When dough is kneaded by hand or a batter is beaten with a whisk, the professional baker automatically uses the most varied range of movements to obtain the optimum consistency. The process is explained here, using a Viennese spongecake batter as an example. With a hand whisk, vertical beating movements are alternated with horizontal movements to reincorporate into the beating process those parts of the mixture that adhere to the sides of the bowl. When an electric hand mixer is used, the limitations soon become apparent. The hand mixer can beat the mixture only in a horizontal plane; only the speed is variable. The vertical movements therefore still have to be performed by hand. In addition, the beaters are very small, so the hand mixer has to be moved around within the bowl to incorporate the whole of the mixture. This is not a very satisfactory method, because it does not give optimum results. The large tabletop mixer is rather more successful. It works like a commercial mixing machine, in which the mixing head, in addition to having large, rotating beaters, also rotates around the bowl. The shape of the bowl allows the batter around the sides to run back into the beating process.

amalgamate the mixture thoroughly without introducing air bubbles. A sieve or sifter is ideal for mixing flour, cornstarch, cocoa powder, and other powdery ingredients. It is also handy for straining cream mixtures. The standard selection of kitchen knives should include a round-ended 10-inch knife with a smooth cutting edge on one side and a serrated blade on the other. There should also be several palette knives — the universal bakery tool — and an angled palette knife, which is ideal for spreading, as well as pastry brushes, the indispensable plastic dough scraper, and a pastry bag with a range of tips. A thermometer — a chocolate thermometer or even an Insta-Read meat thermometer — is essential for monitoring and controlling the temperature of ingredients and mixtures. See pages 232–3 for illustrations of a range of useful equipment.

Cake pans

The basic requirements are a springform pan, a square pan, a fluted mold, and a loaf pan. Shiny aluminum rings are used commercially to make tortes, because they are both simpler to use than cake pans, and have the advantage of producing a very evenly baked spongecake. The recipes that follow show the kind of results that can be achieved.

Oven temperature and timing

Recipes should be followed as closely as possible to obtain the best results. This applies to the measuring as well as to the method. The weak link

in the chain always lies in the baking stage itself — in the temperature and timing. Familiarity with your own oven and a little effort will yield satisfactory results.

The oven can be a problem. Each has its own characteristics, whether it relies on conventional radiant heat, is fan-assisted, or a combination of the two, making it impossible to lay down hard and fast rules. In order to obtain the best results, follow the manufacturer's instructions for the first time in a trial baking. Note down any adjustments made to temperature or timing to ensure future success.

Some oven-manufacturers' guides and some cookbooks recommend that cakes be placed in a cold oven so that energy is not wasted on preheating. Similarly, they may advise switching off the oven before the end of cooking and using the residual heat to complete the process. These energy-saving methods can work if you really know the oven and are very familiar with the recipe. However, it is best not to attempt them when trying out new recipes. In this book, all recipes call for the oven to be preheated to the required temperature. This ensures that the baking action is consistent, which is particularly important for cakes that need a long baking period. Cakes made with lighter batters require careful monitoring. This means looking at the cake at some point before it is fully baked, and watching it throughout the last phase. Ovens with a glass door are a boon, but in some cases you have to open the oven door to test for doneness. The cake is unlikely to collapse now.

Spongecakes — light and dark

An all-purpose cake that can be made in advance and frozen

VIENNESE SPONGECAKE

This basic spongecake, also known as Genoese spongecake, is so versatile that it is well worth keeping on hand. In this recipe the eggs are not separated but beaten whole with the sugar. Whether you beat the batter in a double boiler and then again when it is cold, which is the traditional way, or beat it only when it is cold does not affect the end result. An electric mixer is recommended, as using a whisk is rather laborious.

Makes one 9-inch cake
For the light-colored spongecake:
5 eggs
2 egg yolks
¾ cup sugar
pinch of salt
½ teaspoon grated lemon zest
1 cup flour
¼ cup cornstarch
3 tablespoons oil
3 tablespoons milk
For the dark spongecake:
5 eggs
2 egg yolks
¾ cup sugar
pinch of salt
scraped contents of ½ vanilla bean
1 cup flour
¼ cup cocoa powder
3 tablespoons oil
3 tablespoons milk
You will also need:
9-inch torte ring 2 inches deep

Both cakes are made in the same way, with the exception of two ingredients: the light-colored spongecake calls for grated lemon zest and cornstarch, while the dark spongecake includes the contents of half a vanilla bean and cocoa powder.

Preheat the oven to 400°F. Prepare the batter as illustrated in the picture sequence, and bake for 30 minutes. If necessary, cover the spongecake with foil halfway through the baking period to prevent it from over-browning. Always check that the cake is done by pricking with a wooden toothpick.

Small quantities — a problem

To make a successful spongecake, you need a specific minimum quantity of the individual

Viennese spongecake batter:

Use a hand mixer to beat the eggs, egg yolks, sugar, salt, and lemon zest or vanilla together until frothy.

Move the hand mixer around in circles, so that the batter becomes uniformly creamy and firm.

Sift the flour and cocoa powder or cornstarch onto paper and trickle slowly into the frothy mixture, stirring constantly with a wooden spatula.

Heat the oil and milk together to 86°F. Pour into the batter in a thin stream and blend in with the spatula.

Pour the mixture directly from the bowl into the torte ring, which has been prepared with parchment paper (see page 72), and smooth the top.

To cut a deep base with a torte knife, keep the knife as level as possible and rotate the cake a little after each cut until completely cut through.

ingredients so that they can be measured accurately. Whisking also requires a minimum volume, which means that the quality of a spongecake using less than 5 eggs cannot be guaranteed.

Minimum quantities are not usually a problem for the professional, who is generally making the batter for several cakes at a time. This gives better results than trying to make a single cake. But if you follow the method correctly, the difference should be barely noticeable.

Deep-freezing — the solution

Properly packaged cakes of all kinds can be stored for lengthy periods without loss of quality. This efficient and economic way of preparing very large quantities in advance is of great use to the professional and, on a smaller scale, to the home cook. Most domestic ovens are limited to one 9–10-inch round cake at a time. Sometimes, however, only a part of a spongecake will be used as a base for a torte, so the remainder can be deep frozen for use later. And while baking in batches will not produce the same number of cakes as a professional can, it allows you to keep a few cakes in the freezer for whenever you need them.

Using a thread is a little easier. Make a little cut with a cake knife and insert the thread. Pull the ends of the thread together around the cake — the result is an evenly sliced base.

The recipes on the following pages show tortes that require only one or two thin bases, or a combination of different bases, such as a dark and a light-colored spongecake. These can be sliced from deep bases (1½–2 inches), with the remainder being deep frozen in one piece, or cut up into thinner layers (⅜–⅝-inch thick — wooden slats are useful here) ready for use later. To freeze spongecakes baked on parchment paper, leave the parchment in place, stack the individual layers on top of each other, and wrap the stack in acetate or plastic wrap. Individual layers can then be removed as required. Spongecakes baked in other shapes (for slices, roulades, or Moors' Heads) can be frozen in the same way.

To freeze sliced torte bases place between layers of parchment paper or acetate (see page 64) and place the whole stack between two pieces of cardboard.

Wrap the stack in plastic wrap or place in a freezer bag. You can remove the bases one at a time as required and put the rest back in the freezer.

Chocolate spongecake

For tortes baked in a ring or springform pan with grated walnuts for flavoring

Adding cocoa powder or couverture to practically any spongecake batter can transform it into a batter for making bases for chocolate tortes. The warm, melted butter is blended in at the end. When the egg yolks and egg whites are beaten separately, stir the butter and chocolate together until foamy before adding them. When other fatty ingredients, such as hazelnuts or almonds, are called for in the recipe, you can add them directly to the butter mixture or mix them in later with the flour.

Makes one 10-inch cake
For the spongecake:
8 eggs, separated
½ cup sugar
6 tablespoons ground walnuts
scraped contents of ½ vanilla bean
3½ oz couverture
6 tablespoons butter
½ cup flour mixed with 1⅛ cups cake crumbs
You will also need:
10-inch springform pan or torte ring 2 inches deep

If using a springform pan, lightly grease the base only and sprinkle with crumbs, or line with parchment paper; never grease the sides. Preheat the oven to 375°F and bake for 35–40 minutes. Loosen the baked spongecake from the sides with a knife. Remove the torte ring as shown on page 72.

Melt the couverture over hot water and stir it into the mixture while lukewarm.

Continue to whisk until the couverture is blended completely into the mixture. Then stir in the lukewarm melted butter.

Whip the egg whites into soft peaks with the rest of the sugar. Stir a third of the whipped egg whites into the couverture mixture, using a circular motion.

Chocolate spongecake:

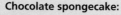

Put the egg yolks, about a quarter of the sugar and the ground nuts into a bowl and mix. Add the scraped contents of the vanilla bean.

Add the remainder of the whipped egg whites, trickle in the flour and bread crumb mixture, and fold in.

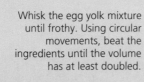

Whisk the egg yolk mixture until frothy. Using circular movements, beat the ingredients until the volume has at least doubled.

Pour the batter into the prepared springform pan or torte ring. Smooth the top with a dough scraper.

BLACK FOREST CHERRY CAKE

Use the recipe on page 76 to make one 10-inch cake base or the recipe on page 78–9 to make three bases the same size on parchment paper.

For the filling:

1 lb jar Morello cherries with juice (15 oz fruit)
scant ½ cup sugar
½ cinnamon stick
2 heaping teaspoons cornstarch
3¼ cups cream

To moisten:

¼ cup kirsch mixed with 3 tablespoons sugar syrup

To decorate:

chocolate curls or rolls and confectioners' sugar

Drain the Morello cherries, reserving the juice. Bring 1 cup of the juice to a boil with about one third of the sugar and the cinnamon. Remove the cinnamon stick. Mix the cornstarch with a little cold water, add to the juice, and cook until thick. Set aside 16 cherries for decoration. Add the remainder to the thickened juice and stir in gently, being careful not to crush the fruit. Bring

Black Forest Cherry Cake has admirers worldwide. It is a prime example of a very simple combination of flavors. The basis is chocolate spongecake and lightly sweetened whipped cream; additional flavor is provided by the sour cherries and, last but not least, the kirsch.

Spread the bottom layer with the whipped cream, then pipe 4 large rings of whipped cream on top. Fill the gaps between the rings with the cherry filling. Place the second layer of spongecake on top, press down, and moisten with the kirsch and sugar syrup.

to a boil again and then remove from the heat. Allow to cool. Whip the cream with the remaining sugar until stiff. Prepare the torte as shown in the pictures. Then spread a layer of cream on top and add the third layer of spongecake. Sprinkle with kirsch and sugar syrup. Spread cream around the sides. Cover the top with chocolate curls. Pipe cream rosettes around the edge and decorate with cherries. Dust the center of the cake with confectioners' sugar.

An open, even texture is the sign of a good chocolate spongecake. It should be evenly baked but not dry. The consistency of the meringue is decisive. It must be airy and light, yet somewhat creamy, so that it binds well with the egg yolk and butter batter and the flour mixture in the final phase. This is achieved by whipping the sugar and egg whites together from the start.

Chocolate spongecake baked on parchment paper

This chocolate spongecake, baked on parchment paper, is perfect for tortes, roulades, and slices

In this spongecake mixture, the very delicate chocolate flavor is provided by the couverture and a small amount of cocoa powder. The batter is spread onto individual pieces of parchment paper to bake. The mixture can also be baked on a baking sheet lined with parchment paper, and then cut into strips to make filled slices as shown on the facing page. It can also be used for making roulades.

Makes four 10-inch or six 9-inch round cakes, or one 15 x 16-inch cake

For the spongecake:
½ cup butter
pinch of salt
2 oz couverture, melted
7 eggs, separated
½ cup + 2 tablespoons sugar
1 cup flour
¼ cup cocoa powder
You will also need:
baking sheets, parchment paper

Assemble the ingredients and ensure that, apart from the couverture, they are all at room temperature. The couverture does not have to be tempered, but it should not be lumpy, and must not be hotter than 89°F or the butter will become too soft.

Line the baking sheets with parchment paper and, using a torte ring as a guide, draw circles of the required size with a pencil.

Preheat the oven to 400°F. Follow the directions in the picture sequence, and bake for 8–10 minutes. Check for doneness after 6–7 minutes and remove from the oven at this time if necessary.

CHOCOLATE AND BLACKBERRY SLICES
This uses the recipe for the chocolate spongecake above minus the cocoa powder.

Makes 12–15 slices

For the filling:
2¼ cups cream, scraped contents of ½ vanilla bean
5 oz finely chopped couverture, 3 tablespoons dark rum
For the spongecake:
6 tablespoons butter, pinch of salt, 2 oz couverture
5 eggs, separated

Chocolate spongecake baked on parchment paper:

Cream the soft butter, add the salt, and slowly dribble in the melted couverture.

Continue to stir until the butter and couverture have bound together to form a frothy mixture.

Add the egg yolks one at a time and stir in.

Whip the egg whites with the sugar to form soft peaks (not stiff and dry). Fold in carefully.

Sift the flour and cocoa powder together on paper. Trickle into the mixture and fold in.

Spoon the mixture onto the circles drawn on parchment paper, and spread evenly to fill the outlines.

scant ½ cup sugar, ¾ cup flour

For the syrup:

½ lb fresh blackberries, ½ cup + 2 tablespoons sugar

2 teaspoons lemon juice, 2 tablespoons water

3 tablespoons blackberry liqueur, 1 teaspoons dark rum

To decorate:

2 oz grated couverture, 1 tablespoon cocoa powder

⅔ cup lightly sweetened whipped cream, 15 blackberries

You will also need:

15 x 12-inch baking sheet

Make the filling a day in advance. Put the cream and vanilla in a saucepan, and bring to a boil. Add the couverture, stirring gently until it melts: Do not let it boil. Pour into a bowl and blend briefly with a hand blender until it is smooth and thoroughly combined. Allow to cool, then cover and refrigerate for 24 hours.

Preheat the oven to 400°F. Prepare the spongecake as shown in the picture sequence opposite. Bake for 12–15 minutes, watching for doneness.

To make the syrup, bring the blackberries, sugar, lemon juice, and water to a boil, stirring constantly. Simmer for 20 minutes, then strain. Reserve the syrup, cool, and mix with the liqueur and rum.

Remove the paper from the cold spongecake, and cut the cake into 3 strips, each 4 inches wide. Whip up the cream filling with a hand mixer, and mix in the rum. Brush the first strip of cake with the blackberry syrup, then spread it with a layer of chocolate cream filling. Place the second strip of cake on top and repeat the procedure. Top with the third strip and brush it with blackberry syrup. Coat the whole torte with the remainder of the chocolate cream, and sprinkle with grated couverture. Dust with sifted cocoa powder and cut into slices. Decorate each slice with whipped cream and a blackberry.

Chocolate slices: The spongecake has been baked on parchment paper, cut into slices, and then layered with chocolate cream flavored with blackberries and alcohol.

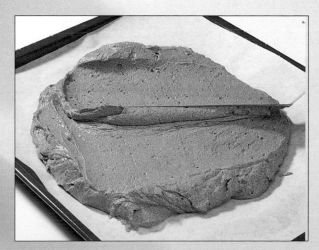

Line a 12 x 15-inch baking sheet with parchment paper. Spoon the batter onto it, spread with a palette knife to an even depth, and smooth the top so that it bakes uniformly.

Using a pastry bag with a round tip, pipe the cream filling in a spiral, working from the center outwards, onto the cooked meringue bases and then assemble.

Chocolate-filled meringue
Sweet fluffy meringue and bitter chocolate — a perfect recipe for fine tortes

GANACHE ICING

This is the counterpart to pure chocolate icing made with couverture. Ganache icing does not harden fully — it remains gently melting — and can be used anywhere a soft texture is required. It is perfect for tortes with a soft filling (mousse) and on small cakes with a delicate texture. It can be made with dark or light couverture (see page 100).

Makes 3 cups
½ cup milk, 3 fl oz cream
¼ cup sugar, ¼ cup water
6½ teaspoons glucose syrup
12 oz couverture

Prepare the icing as shown in the pictures below. The finished icing keeps well in the refrigerator. It can then be reheated as required in a microwave oven or over hot water while stirring gently. Use at a temperature of 86°F.

To make ganache icing:

Mix the milk, cream, sugar, water, and glucose syrup in a saucepan.

Bring the mixture to a boil, stirring constantly, and remove from the heat.

Add the finely chopped or grated couverture and stir until it has completely melted.

To blend thoroughly, place the hand blender in the icing, switch on, and mix with a circular motion. Do not let the blender come to the surface, or air bubbles will be trapped.

CHOCOLATE MERINGUE TORTE

Makes one 8-inch torte
For the bases:
4 egg whites, ½ cup sugar
1 cup confectioners' sugar
2 tablespoons cornstarch, 3 oz couverture, grated
For the filling:
1¾ cups cream, 5 oz couverture
You will also need:
baking sheets, parchment paper
1 recipe ganache icing (see left)

Prepare the bases and cream filling a day in advance. To make the bases, whip the egg whites with the sugar until stiff. Sift the confectioners' sugar with the cornstarch over the mixture and fold in. Blend in the couverture. Cover the baking sheet with parchment paper and draw 3 circles, each 8 inches in diameter. Spoon the mixture into a pastry bag with a round tip. Starting from the center, pipe a continuous spiral to fill each circle. Preheat the oven to 125°F and dry the meringues overnight, leaving the oven door slightly ajar. Remove from the parchment paper with care.

To make the cream filling, bring the cream to a boil. Cut the couverture into small pieces and stir into the cream until it melts. Transfer to a bowl and blend with a hand blender. Allow to cool overnight. The next day, whip the filling with a hand mixer. Cover the bases as shown top left on page 80, then stack the bases on top of each other. Coat the sides of the torte with the remaining filling. Chill. Cover the torte with the ganache icing.

FLAKY MERINGUE TORTE

To convert the cream filling into a fine mocha cream, add 1 tablespoon instant coffee powder.

Makes one 7-inch torte

For the bases:

6 egg whites, ¾ cup sugar

1½ cups confectioners' sugar, 2 tablespoons cornstarch

For the filling:

1 cup cream, 5 oz couverture, 4 teaspoons dark rum

To decorate:

1 cup cream, 4 teaspoons sugar, cocoa powder for dusting

You will also need:

baking sheets, parchment paper

Whip the egg whites with the sugar until stiff. Sift the confectioners' sugar and cornstarch into the meringue mixture and fold in gently. Pipe 5 bases, each 7 inches in diameter, and bake as for the preceding recipe. Crush one base into crumbs. Prepare the cream filling and beat with the rum until frothy. Pipe the filling onto 3 of the bases, as described in the preceding recipe. Assemble the 4 bases into a torte. Whip the cream with the sugar and coat the torte. Sprinkle the meringue crumbs on top and dust with a little sifted cocoa powder.

Chocolate and almond torte

Almonds and chocolate complement each other perfectly in this torte

The torte base, made with almonds and chocolate, is filled with ganache cream and then the whole torte is wrapped in almond paste. The icing can be made from a thin layer of pure couverture, as here, or a ganache icing, which is softer.

Makes one 9-inch round torte
For the bases:
2 oz almond paste, 5 egg yolks, ½ cup butter
½ cup + 2 tablespoons sugar, pinch of salt
scraped contents of ½ vanilla bean
4 egg whites
½ cup ground almonds, unblanched

1 oz grated couverture, ½ cup flour
For the filling:
1⅛ cups cream, 7 oz couverture
¼ cup confectioners' sugar, ½ cup softened butter
For the coating:
7 oz almond paste, ¾ cup confectioners' sugar
For the icing:
5 tablespoons milk, 5 tablespoons cream, 1 tablespoon glucose syrup
2 tablespoons sugar, 7 oz couverture
You will also need:
9-inch springform pan/torte ring 2 inches deep
1 tablespoon croquant (see page 230) to sprinkle on top

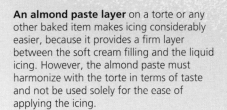

Prepare the cake bases and chocolate cream filling a day in advance. Preheat the oven to 375°F. To make the batter, place the almond paste in a bowl and work in the egg yolks with a spatula until smooth. Add the butter, half the sugar, salt, and vanilla, and cream well. Whip the egg whites with the remaining sugar until stiff. Using a spatula, blend the stiffly beaten egg whites carefully into the creamed mixture with a circular motion. Mix the almonds and couverture with the flour and fold in. Wrap parchment paper around the torte ring as shown on page 72, and spoon in the mixture. Smooth the top. Bake for 45–50 minutes. Leave the oven door open just a crack to allow the excess steam to escape. Rest the cake overnight.

To make the chocolate cream filling, bring the cream to a boil. Cut the couverture into small pieces, add to the cream, and stir. When it melts, place a hand blender in the cream, switch on, then blend thoroughly, using a circular motion. Refrigerate the cream overnight. The next day, let the cream mixture return to room temperature, then whip with a hand mixer. Stir in the confectioners' sugar, then the softened butter, 1 tablespoon at a time.

Cut the torte base into three layers. Cover the bottom and middle layers thickly and evenly with filling. Stack the three layers. Coat the sides and top with the remainder of the filling and allow to cool slightly.

To make the almond paste covering, work the confectioners' sugar into the almond paste on a clean surface. Dust the work surface (marble is ideal) with sifted confectioners' sugar and roll out the almond paste evenly to ⅛ inch. Use to cover the torte as shown in the picture sequence.

To make the icing, bring the milk to a boil with the cream, syrup, and sugar. Cut the couverture into small pieces and add, stirring as it melts. Place a hand blender in the icing, switch on, and blend using a circular motion. Coat the torte as shown and sprinkle with almond or pistachio croquant.

An almond paste layer on a torte or any other baked item makes icing considerably easier, because it provides a firm layer between the soft cream filling and the liquid icing. However, the almond paste must harmonize with the torte in terms of taste and not be used solely for the ease of applying the icing.

Use your hands or a palette knife to press the almond paste carefully against the sides so that it covers the torte without wrinkles.

Trim off the excess almond paste with a palette knife or ordinary knife.

Place the torte on a wire rack and place this on parchment paper or a baking sheet. Pour the icing over the top.

Use a palette knife to smooth the icing over the top, allowing the icing to run down the sides of the torte.

When the sides are covered with icing, smooth over the top a final time to get as smooth a finish as possible.

To cover and ice using almond paste:

Roll out the almond paste thinly and fold in half. Place over one half of the torte and unfold.

Using your hands, smooth out from the center to remove air bubbles between the cream filling and the almond paste.

A pure couverture coating is hard. A softer icing, such as ganache, can be used instead. It has a gently melting consistency, but it lacks the bitter taste of pure chocolate.

Iced with couverture

Imperial torte is a good example of a torte iced with pure chocolate

A torte or cake iced with pure chocolate is a sensuous pleasure. However, because the chocolate is very hard and does not bind with the soft cream filling, it is not easy to cut through cleanly with a fork, and it usually breaks away. When a thin layer of almond paste is placed on top of the filling, the couverture binds with it, making it easier to eat (see page 91).

IMPERIAL TORTE
Makes one 10-inch torte
For the bases:
7 eggs
½ cup sugar
¾ cup + 2 teaspoons flour
½ cup cornstarch
¼ cup warm butter
For the chocolate butter cream:
2¼ cups milk
3 egg yolks
½ cup cornstarch
1 cup sugar
scraped contents of ½ vanilla bean
½ cup cocoa powder, 1¼ cups butter
4 oz couverture, melted
You will also need:
baking sheets, parchment paper
10 oz tempered couverture

Preheat the oven to 410°F. To make the bases, beat the eggs with the sugar until uniformly creamy and firm. Sift the flour and cornstarch together onto parchment paper and add gradually to the egg mixture, stirring constantly. When thoroughly blended, stir in the butter and mix thoroughly again. Line the baking sheets with parchment paper and use a pencil to draw 7 circles, each 10 inches in diameter. Divide the mixture evenly between them and smooth the tops. Bake until light brown.

This chocolate cake is ideal for festive occasions, and at the top of the list of favorite cakes for many people.

CHOCOLATE LAYER CAKE

Makes one 9-inch cake

For the cake:

½ cup butter, heaping ¼ cup confectioners' sugar

pinch of salt, 6 eggs, separated

4½ oz couverture, melted, ¾ cup sugar, 1 cup flour

For the filling:

1 cup butter, 1 cup cocoa powder

pinch of salt, 1¾ cups confectioners' sugar

scraped contents of ½ vanilla bean, 7 fl oz cream

You will also need:

9-inch springform pan, parchment paper

Begin a day in advance. Preheat the oven to 375°F and line the base of the springform pan with parchment paper. Cream the butter with the confectioners' sugar and salt. Add the egg yolks one at a time and blend in the melted couverture. Whip the egg whites with the sugar until stiff. Stir one third of the egg whites into the chocolate mixture. Fold in the remainder with the flour. Spoon the batter into the prepared pan. Smooth the top, and bake for 50 minutes. Remove from the oven and allow to cool. The next day, remove the cake from the pan and cut horizontally into 4 thin layers (see page 75).

To make the cream filling, cream the butter and gradually add the cocoa powder, salt, confectioners' sugar, and vanilla. Whip the cream until stiff and stir it into the butter mixture. Use half of the filling to cover each of the layers, and then place one on top of the other. Use the rest of the filling to coat the sides thickly. Use a palette knife to flick up the chocolate into peaks, the traditional decoration for this cake.

To make the butter cream, blend 2 tablespoons of the milk with the egg yolks and cornstarch. Bring the remaining milk to a boil with the sugar, vanilla, and cocoa powder. Stir in the cornstarch mixture and allow it to return to a boil several times. Cool and then strain. Beat the butter until fluffy and gradually stir in the cooled cream mixture. Finally, stir in the melted couverture.

Spread the cake bases with the chocolate butter cream, reserving some for the sides, and assemble the torte. Allow to cool slightly. Trim the sides of the torte and spread with the remaining butter cream. Allow to cool again. Place on a wire rack and stand it on parchment paper. Coat as thinly as possible with the tempered couverture. Cut into 16 pieces with a warm knife.

Truffle here is not the black fungus, but a ball of gently melting ganache cream filling with a chocolate coating. It tops the truffle torte, named in its honor, which is filled with a ganache cream.

Truffle torte

A classic among chocolate tortes with a gently melting filling

TRUFFLE TORTE

This torte takes its name from the chocolate confection, but the expected truffle filling has been replaced by a light chocolate cream.

Makes one 9½-inch torte

For the chocolate cream:

2¼ cups cream
5 oz couverture

Chocolate cream filling:

Bring the cream to a boil in a saucepan, and stir in the chopped couverture.

Melt the couverture in the hot cream, stirring constantly and evenly.

Use a hand blender to mix the chocolate cream filling thoroughly.

The next day, just before finishing the torte, whip the cream until stiff with a hand mixer.

For the bases:

2 oz couverture

7 tablespoons soft butter

scraped contents of ½ vanilla bean

pinch of salt

5 egg yolks

4 egg whites

½ cup sugar

¾ cup flour, sifted

To decorate:

chocolate curls

cocoa powder for dusting

You will also need:

9½-inch torte ring

baking sheets, butter and flour for the baking sheets

Prepare the chocolate cream a day in advance so that it has time to become really creamy. Bring the cream to a boil, add the couverture, melt and blend as shown in the picture sequence on page 86. When fully blended, allow to cool. Cover and refrigerate for 24 hours.

Preheat the oven to 410°F. To make the chocolate spongecake, melt the couverture over hot water. Add the soft butter, vanilla, and salt, and beat with a hand mixer. Stir in the egg yolks one at a time. In a separate bowl, whip the egg whites with the sugar into soft peaks. Combine both mixtures and carefully fold in the flour. Grease the baking sheets and dust with flour. Use the torte ring to mark out five 9½-inch circles in the flour. Spread out the batter evenly. Bake for about 9 minutes.

Remove from the oven and immediately cut to shape, using the torte ring as a cutter. Use a long-bladed knife to loosen the bases from the baking sheet. Allow to cool. Just before assembling the torte, whip up the cream filling with a hand mixer. Assemble the torte as shown below and dust with sifted cocoa powder.

To assemble a truffle torte:

Spread a base with cream filling. Alternate the remaining bases with layers of cream.

Spread cream filling around the sides and smooth off neatly at the top.

Holding the torte in one hand, sprinkle the top with chocolate flakes.

Use a large palette knife to press the chocolate flakes loosely to the sides of the torte.

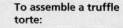

A big copper pan is still used in the Hotel Sacher to melt the couverture. Master confectioner Friedrich Pfliegler can test the temperature of couverture between his finger and thumb as accurately as a thermometer. With his experience, there is no question of a mistake.

Sachertorte

This torte has become the symbol of Viennese confectionery worldwide. Unfortunately, it has had many imitators. Karl Schuhmacher has a simple solution to the problem: He relies on the best ingredients and professional methods, as he explains:

Sachertorte is a timeless composition of the most important and finest ingredients from the confectioner's kitchen with no additives: pure chocolate, butter, eggs, sugar, flour, and apricot jam. What makes them into a Sachertorte is the quality of the individual ingredients and the way they harmonize perfectly with each other. Anything else is just an ordinary chocolate torte with ordinary chocolate icing and often looks nothing like the real thing. It is important to remember that, above all, the Sachertorte must be served correctly. It must be served fresh with freshly beaten, lightly sweetened cream, which the Austrians call "*Schlagobers.*" Without this cool, smooth, elegant finishing touch, the pleasure is incomplete. It would be a sin, a crime even, if the waiter did not recommend it. The sweet velvety coating is a cooked chocolate icing.

Makes one 9-inch torte
For 1 Sachertorte base:
4 oz couverture
½ cup soft butter, ¼ cup + 2 teaspoons confectioners' sugar, 6 eggs, separated
½ cup + 2 tablespoons sugar, 1 cup flour, sifted
For the icing:
2 cups sugar, ¾ cup water
13 oz couverture, chopped
You will also need:
9-inch springform pan, parchment paper
about ¾ cup apricot jam for filling and spreading

Preheat the oven to 350°F. To make the batter, melt the couverture in a double boiler over hot water. Cream the soft butter and confectioners' sugar with the couverture tempered at 89°F. Stir in the egg yolks one at a time. In a clean bowl, whip the egg whites and sugar until stiff. Combine the two mixtures and fold in the sifted flour. Line the base of a springform pan with parchment paper. Spoon in the batter and smooth the top. Bake for 55 minutes. Allow to cool. Invert the pan onto parchment paper dusted lightly with sugar. Use a small knife to ease the torte from the sides,

and remove from the pan. Cut the base in half horizontally. Heat and strain the jam, and use half to sandwich the two layers together. Place the torte on a piece of cardboard cut to the same size. Coat the torte thinly with the remainder of the hot jam. Gently emphasize the rounded edges of the top. The apricot masking is a base for the icing. It also helps to keep the cake moist and the chocolate glossy.

The recipe for the chocolate icing is generous enough for two tortes. To get a really smooth surface, the icing has to be poured over the torte, as shown in the pictures opposite. A certain amount always sticks to the pan, strainer, and table top. It can be scraped up and used again after reheating. Place the iced torte immediately on a firm base and set aside. When the icing has set hard, use a small knife to trim the sides where it has run. Carefully slip a clean damp palette knife under the torte to release it and place on a cake plate.

Couverture icing:

Place the sugar and water in a large saucepan, and bring to a boil.

Stir the couverture, which has been cut into pieces or melted, into the sugar solution.

Boil to the thick thread stage (230°F). Use a damp brush to keep washing down the edges of the pan so that crystals do not form.

Strain the icing into a smaller pan to avoid crystals forming on the sides and building up into lumps.

Pour part of the icing onto a marble slab, while continuing to stir the contents of the pot to prevent a skin forming.

Work the couverture continuously with a palette knife. When it begins to firm up and look somewhat lighter in color, return it to the pot, stir well, pour onto the table, and work again. Return it to the pot once more.

Place the torte on a wire rack over a baking sheet and pour the chocolate directly from the pot onto the top of the torte.

Spread the icing over the top with one or two strokes of the palette knife and then spread evenly around the sides.

Provenance sealed with chocolate.
A seal is a sign of the very best quality. The Sacher seal can appear only on the original product, of course, a torte from the Hotel Sacher.

Chocolate fillings, with the accent on fruit

Fruit flavors blend perfectly with chocolate cream fillings

Flavoring the torte base with a little liqueur produces a really great effect. The torte should not be served too cold. The full flavor can develop only when the fillings are soft and creamy.

CHOCOLATE AND RED CURRANT TORTE

A filling of soft chocolate butter cream sandwiched with a layer of red currant jelly is a wonderful combination in this cake.

Makes one 10-inch torte
For the bases:
5 egg whites, ½ cup + 2 tablespoons sugar
pinch of salt
scraped contents of ½ vanilla bean
1 tablespoon flour
1 cup ground almonds, unblanched
2 oz grated couverture
For the chocolate cream:
3½ oz couverture, 1 cup + 2 tablespoons soft butter
3 eggs, ½ cup + 2 tablespoons sugar
To spread and to moisten:
½ cup red currant jelly
3 tablespoons sugar syrup
3 tablespoons cognac
To decorate:
¼ lb chocolate rolls
confectioners' sugar
You will also need:
baking sheets, parchment paper

Prepare the bases a day in advance. Preheat the oven to 400 °F. Whip the egg whites with the sugar and salt until stiff. Mix in the contents of the vanilla bean just before the end. Mix the flour with the almonds and couverture, and carefully fold into the meringue mixture so that it loses as little volume as possible.

Cover the baking sheets with parchment paper and draw three circles 10 inches in diameter. Spread the meringue mixture on the parchment paper evenly, using an angled palette knife. Bake until light brown. Check after 10 minutes' baking time, and then watch until done. Remove the meringue bases from the baking sheets and allow to cool on the parchment paper. Stack, wrap, and rest overnight.

ORANGE SLICES

Makes 28 slices

1 recipe torte bases (page 90), omitting the grated couverture

For the filling:

7 fl oz cream, 10 oz couverture

3 tablespoons Cointreau

For the almond paste coat:

7 oz almond paste, ¾ cup confectioners' sugar

¼ cup finely chopped candied orange peel

4 teaspoons Cointreau

You will also need.

¼ cup strained orange marmalade

tempered couverture for icing

Spread the torte base dough onto a 15 x 16½-inch baking sheet. Bake and cut into three strips lengthwise.

Bring the cream to a boil, add the couverture and let it melt. Cool, then beat with the liqueur until frothy. Sandwich the cake together with the filling. Spread the top with marmalade. To make the coating, work the almond paste with the other ingredients. Dust the counter with confectioners' sugar and roll out the almond paste to 5 x 16½ inches. Place on the cake. Spread very thinly with couverture. When it starts to thicken, make diagonal lines with a knife. Cut the cake in half lengthwise, and divide each half into 14 pieces.

To make the chocolate cream, melt the couverture over hot water and cool to 86°F. Cream the soft butter and stir in the couverture. Beat the eggs with the sugar until frothy and gradually stir into the butter mixture.

Remove the parchment paper from the torte bases and spread the first base with half of the red currant jelly. Spread a third of the chocolate cream on top of the jelly and place the second base on top. Mix the sugar syrup with the cognac. Using a broad brush, spread half of the cognac mixture as evenly as possible over the second torte base. Then spread with the remainder of the red currant jelly, and half the remaining chocolate cream. Top with the third layer. Dribble the remainder of the cognac mixture on top. Spread the remainder of the cream evenly over the sides and top.

Attach the chocolate rolls while the cream is still soft. Use a palette knife to press the rolls onto the sides first, and then sprinkle rolls on the top. Sift confectioners' sugar on top.

A strip of acetate is a very simple but effective aid. It prevents the filling freezing onto the ring, protects tortes when stored in the freezer, and is extremely useful when making fillings of various depths, and when smoothing them at the very top.

Freezing: simple, imaginative, economical

A raspberry cream torte demonstrates how to make the most of deep-freezing techniques

Deep-freezing techniques have opened up a whole new perspective in the preparation of tortes and other types of confectionery. Now, combinations of bases and cream fillings that previously were impossible to prepare at home are no longer a problem. Deep-freezing is the greatest boon in the preparation of light whipped cream fillings and mousses, since less binding agent (usually gelatin) is required. When less gelatin is used, the stability of the mold and the consistency of the cream filling are more delicate, and need more careful handling. Therefore, it is important to serve tortes with very light cream fillings, like those in the following recipes, at just the right moment after they have thawed.

RASPBERRY CREAM TORTE
Makes one 9½-inch torte
1 chocolate spongecake ⅝ inch high (see page 74)
For the raspberry cream filling:
7 oz raspberries
½ cup sugar
2 teaspoons gelatin
1½ cups cream
For the white cream filling:
¼ cup sugar, 4 egg yolks
¼ cup milk, pinch of salt
2½ teaspoons gelatin
3 tablespoons white raspberry brandy
1¾ cups cream
For the icing:
1 cup ganache icing (see page 80)
To decorate:
1 tablespoon pistachio croquant (see page 230)
3½ fl oz cream, 2 teaspoons sugar
16 raspberries
You will also need:
8-inch torte ring 1 inch deep
8-inch torte ring 2 inches deep
acetate sheet and strips, baking sheet, parchment paper

A filling as a torte:

Line a torte ring base with parchment paper, place a shallow torte ring on top, and insert a strip of acetate around the sides. Spoon in the raspberry cream and smooth the top.

Cover and refrigerate. When set, allow the torte to stand for a few minutes at room temperature so that the ring can be easily removed.

Remove the strip of acetate by grasping the overlapping end and peeling away in a single movement. Finally, remove the parchment paper.

To make the raspberry cream, cook the raspberries with the sugar until they break down. Strain and allow the purée to cool. When it is almost cold, dissolve the gelatin and stir it in. Whip the cream until stiff and fold into the raspberry mixture just as it is beginning to set. Line the shallow torte ring with a strip of acetate and place on a baking sheet lined with parchment paper. Spoon in the raspberry cream and smooth the top as shown. Cover with a piece of acetate and freeze.

To make the white cream filling, beat the sugar with the egg yolks until frothy. Bring the milk to a boil with the salt and dissolve the gelatin in it. Stir into the egg mixture. Heat to just below boiling point until the custard is thick enough to coat the back of a spoon. Cool until lukewarm, then add the raspberry brandy. Whip the cream until stiff and stir into the custard. Line the deep torte ring with a strip of acetate and assemble the torte as shown.

A cream torte can be made to look very neat. A strip of acetate and the deep-freezing technique produce perfectly smooth sides and a silky gloss on the surface.

Freeze, then stand the torte at room temperature for several minutes. The ring will then be easy to remove, and the sides of the torte will still be protected by the acetate.

To assemble the torte:

Place a spongecake base ½ inch smaller in diameter than the torte ring exactly in the middle of the ring, making sure the acetate strip is flat against the sides of the ring.

Pour the ganache icing over the top. Use a large ladle and complete the step in a single, rapid movement, so that the cream does not set.

Coat the base thinly with the light-colored cream filling, and place the frozen raspberry cream filling exactly in the center, so that the gap around the edge of the ring is uniform.

Use a palette knife to spread the ganache icing from the center to the edge, turning the torte so that the icing is evenly distributed.

Using a pastry bag, fill in the gap with the light-colored cream filling and put the remainder on top of the raspberry filling.

The acetate strip protects the torte from any icing that runs down the sides. Sprinkle the surface with finely broken pistachio croquant.

Using a palette knife, smooth from the center outwards. The acetate strip is the guide and ensures a uniform height.

Remove the acetate strip. The immaculate sides of cream filling are now revealed, and the beautifully glazed surface has a razor-sharp edge.

With a full coffee flavor

Chocolate flavored with coffee is a standard combination in the patisserie and confectionery repertoire

IRISH COFFEE TORTE

It is usually bitter chocolate that is flavored with coffee, although milk chocolate is sometimes used, and even white chocolate is not excluded, as the following recipe shows.

Makes one 9½-inch torte

1 light-colored spongecake base (see page 74)
For the mousse:
1½ cups cream, 1 egg
9 oz white couverture, 3 tablespoons instant coffee powder
3 tablespoons whiskey
For the ganache icing:
4½ oz white couverture, 1 tablespoon instant coffee powder
¼ cup unsweetened condensed milk
For the croquant:
¼ cup sugar, ½ cup roasted blanched hazelnuts
For the croquant base:
6 eggs, separated, ½ cup + 2 tablespoons sugar
½ cup ground walnuts
scraped contents of ½ vanilla bean
½ teaspoon cinnamon, pinch of salt
5 teaspoons water
¾ cup + 2 teaspoons flour
1 recipe croquant (above), 1 tablespoon oil
To moisten:
3 tablespoons sugar syrup, 1 teaspoon instant coffee powder, 3 tablespoons whiskey

To decorate:
16 "coffee beans" made of chocolate
You will also need:
9½-inch torte ring, acetate strip

Prepare the mousse and the ganache icing a day in advance. To make the mousse, heat the cream with the egg for 10 minutes at 158°F. Add the couverture and the instant coffee powder, and dissolve. Blend until smooth. Cool rapidly. Refrigerate for 24 hours. Add the whiskey before use (see below).

To make the ganache icing, melt the white couverture over hot water, stirring constantly and keeping the temperature below 104°F. Dissolve the coffee powder in the condensed milk and gradually stir into the couverture. Stir carefully to blend thoroughly while ensuring that as little air as possible is incorporated, as it will produce bubbles in the icing. Set aside for 24 hours.

To make the croquant, melt the sugar in a saucepan, stirring until it becomes a light caramel. Mix the chopped hazelnuts in well. Roll out on an oiled work surface using a rolling pin. Let cool. Break the cold croquant into pieces and grate.

Preheat the oven to 340°F. To make the croquant base, whisk the egg yolks, 2 tablespoons of sugar, walnuts, vanilla, cinnamon, and salt with the water until frothy. Beat the egg whites with the remaining sugar until stiff. Combine both these mixtures. Blend in the flour and grated croquant together,

Espresso cream torte. The contrasting flavors are the special feature of this fine coffee torte: a somewhat bitter, strong espresso-chocolate flavor between croquant bases topped with a delicate vanilla cream

ESPRESSO CREAM TORTE

Makes one 9½-inch torte

1 croquant base (see Irish Coffee Torte)
For the espresso cream:
7 fl oz cream, 2 tablespoons brown sugar
1 tablespoon instant espresso coffee powder
7 oz couverture, finely chopped
¼ cup soft butter, 4 teaspoons coffee liqueur
To moisten:
4 teaspoons sugar syrup, 2 teaspoons coffee liqueur
For the whipped cream topping:
1 cup cream, 2 tablespoons sugar
scraped contents of ½ vanilla bean
You will also need:
cocoa powder for dusting
24 thin tiles of milk chocolate couverture (2 x 1½ inches)

To make the espresso cream, bring the cream and sugar to a boil. Add the espresso powder and finely chopped couverture, and stir until melted and combined. Transfer to a bowl and allow to cool. Whisk, and add the butter in flakes. Stir in the liqueur. Slice the croquant base in half horizontally. Place one half in a torte ring, spread it with the filling, and cover with the other half. Mix the sugar syrup and coffee liqueur together and use to moisten the top of the torte. Whip the cream with the sugar and vanilla. (If the torte is not to be served the same day, stiffen the cream with 1 teaspoon of dissolved gelatin.) Spread the cream thickly and evenly over the top. Remove the torte ring and coat the sides thinly. Sift cocoa powder on the top. Decorate the sides with tiles of milk couverture.

followed by the oil. Spoon the mixture into a torte ring lined with parchment paper and smooth the top. Bake for 35 minutes. Turn out onto parchment paper sprinkled with sugar. Allow to cool.

Line the torte ring with acetate strip. Cut a ⅝-inch thick layer from the baked croquant base (freeze the remainder to use later as required) and place in the torte ring. Mix the sugar syrup, instant coffee, and whiskey together. Use one third of this

syrup to moisten the croquant base. Stir the whiskey into the mousse and whip. Spread half the mousse on top of the croquant base. Place the spongecake on top and moisten with the remaining syrup. Spread with the remaining mousse. Freeze. To finish the torte, remove the ring, but not the acetate strip. Heat the ganache icing to 82–86°F over hot water, stirring as little as possible, then use to coat the surface of the torte thinly. Remove the acetate strip. Decorate with the chocolate coffee beans.

To make an absolutely flat surface cut a strip of acetate to the correct depth, place it around the torte, and secure it with adhesive tape. Spoon in the whipped cream and smooth the top from center to edge.

Biedermeiertorte and Gentlemen's torte

Two tortes, filled with a light chocolate mousse and flavored with kirsch and raspberry brandy

BIEDERMEIERTORTE

This delicate torte was created to celebrate the Biedermeier Jubilee in Vienna. The filling can be made by the freezer method used for the Raspberry Cream Torte on pages 92–3. It can either form a small-sized torte, to sit inside the larger finished torte, or be spread directly onto the Sachertorte base, with the mousse on top. If you do not want the base of the finished torte to be visible at the sides, trim the diameter ½ inch.

Makes one 9½-inch torte
1 Sachertorte base (see page 88) ⅝ inch deep
For the hazelnut cream filling:
2 egg yolks, 4 teaspoons sugar
scraped contents of ½ vanilla bean
pinch of salt, 1 teaspoon gelatin
2 tablespoons hazelnuts, ground, 5 fl oz cream
⅛ recipe caramelized hazelnuts (see page 102), chopped
For the chocolate mousse:
1½ cups cream, 6 oz couverture, 3 egg yolks
To moisten:
3 tablespoons cherry brandy
For the icing:
1 cup ganache icing (see page 80)
You will also need:
½ cup cream, 1 teaspoon sugar
6-inch torte ring 1 inch deep
9½-inch torte ring 2 inches deep

To make the hazelnut cream, beat the egg yolks with the sugar, vanilla, and salt until frothy. Dissolve the gelatin and mix it thoroughly into the egg yolk mixture. Fold in the hazelnuts rapidly. Whip the cream and mix with the egg yolk mixture and the caramelized hazelnuts. Place the small torte ring onto a smooth base covered with parchment paper or acetate. Spoon in the hazelnut cream and smooth the top. Cover with acetate and freeze.

To make the mousse, bring 3½ fl oz of the cream to a boil. Add the couverture and stir as it melts. Cool to 95°F. Whisk the egg yolks until frothy and fold in rapidly. Whip the remaining cream until stiff and fold in the couverture mixture.

To assemble the torte, line the large torte ring with an acetate strip. Put the Sachertorte base into the ring and moisten with the liqueur. Spread some of the mousse on the base. Let the frozen hazelnut cream stand at room temperature for 5 minutes, then invert it on top of the mousse and remove its ring and parchment paper or acetate. Using a pastry bag and flat tip, fill the gap between the small torte and the sides of the large torte ring with the rest of the mousse. Smooth the top.

Remove the large torte ring, but not the acetate strip. Place a second acetate strip, ¼ inch deeper, around the torte and secure with tape. Cover the top thinly with the lightly sweetened whipped cream. Place in the freezer briefly to firm up. Cover with the icing and remove the acetate strip.

GENTLEMEN'S TORTE

Gentlemen's Torte was originally so called as a discreet way of saying that the filling contained a generous amount of alcohol. In this recipe, the dark Sachertorte base is soaked with raspberry brandy, and the light chocolate cream is also mildly flavored with it.

Makes one 9½-inch torte
1 Sachertorte base (see page 88) 1 inch deep
For the chocolate cream:
1¾ cups cream, 3 egg yolks
6 oz milk chocolate couverture, chopped
2 oz dark couverture, chopped
3 tablespoons raspberry brandy
To moisten:
¼ cup raspberry brandy, 3 tablespoons sugar syrup
You will also need:
9½-inch torte ring
acetate strip, curls of white and dark couverture

Prepare the chocolate cream a day in advance. Heat the cream and egg yolks to 158°F for 10 minutes. Add the chopped couverture, stirring as it melts. Allow to cool and refrigerate for 24 hours.

Place the Sachertorte base on a smooth surface and place the acetate strip and torte ring around it. Mix the raspberry liqueur with the sugar syrup and brush evenly over the base to soak it. Remove the chocolate cream from the refrigerator, stir in the raspberry brandy, and beat with a hand mixer until creamy. Spread over the Sachertorte base. Cover the torte with acetate and freeze.

To finish the torte, remove the ring and acetate strip. Allow the torte to thaw briefly at room temperature, so that the chocolate curls will adhere. Smooth a little of the chocolate cream over the edge of the base and sprinkle the top with chocolate curls.

Loose flakes of white and milk chocolate couverture are mixed and spread with a light touch over the top and sides of the torte.

Sour cherry torte

This delicious and versatile torte tastes as good as it looks

SOUR CHERRY TORTE

The combination of a spongecake tasting richly of chocolate, a cherry cream filling, and the generous use of kirsch is a strong reminder of Black Forest Cherry Cake. But the two could not be more different in taste and texture. The cherry cream filling does not, of course, have to be used exactly as described. It can be spread onto the liqueur-moistened base and then covered with the kirsch cream filling to make a second layer.

Makes one 10-inch torte
1 light spongecake (see page 74)
1 dark spongecake (see page 74)
For the sour cherry cream:
4 oz sour cherries, stoned, 6 tablespoons sugar
1 teaspoon gelatin, 1 cup cream, whipped
For the kirsch cream filling:
4 egg yolks, ¼ cup sugar
¼ cup kirsch
scraped contents of ½ vanilla bean
pinch of salt, 1¾ cups cream
2 teaspoons gelatin
To moisten:
5 tablespoons kirsch
5 tablespoons sugar syrup
To decorate:
7 fl oz cream, a little sugar
milk chocolate couverture curls
16 stewed cherries with stalks, drained
You will also need:
6-inch torte ring 1 inch deep
10-inch torte ring 2 inches deep
acetate strip

To make the cherry cream filling, add the sugar to the cherries and cook through for 2–3 minutes while stirring. Small solid pieces of cherry flesh should remain. Dissolve the gelatin in the hot fruit pulp. Allow to cool. When the cherry mixture begins to

RICE AND CHOCOLATE TORTE

You can substitute raspberry, apricot, or mango purée, and the appropriate sauce, for the strawberry purée used here.

Makes one 9-inch torte
1 chocolate spongecake ⅝-inch deep(see page 74)
14 oz stewed pears with a little juice
For the rice filling:
⅓ cup short grain rice, 1½ cups milk
scraped contents of ½ vanilla bean
pinch of salt
2 oz milk chocolate couverture, ¾ oz couverture
2½ teaspoons gelatin
2 egg yolks, 2 tablespoons sugar
4 teaspoons Jamaica rum, 1 cup cream
For the strawberry meringue:
2 egg whites, 6 tablespoons sugar
2 tablespoons strawberry purée
2 teaspoons lemon juice

You will also need:
9-inch torte ring 2 inches deep
acetate strip, strawberry sauce

Drain the pears and reserve the juice. To make the rice batter, blanch the rice briefly in boiling water and drain. Bring the milk to a boil with the vanilla and salt. Add the rice, bring to a boil, and cook until soft. Chop the couverture into small pieces. Dissolve the gelatin and mix thoroughly into the rice with the couverture. Beat the egg yolks with the sugar and rum until frothy and fold into the rice mixture just as the gelatin begins to set. Whip the cream and fold into the rice mixture.

Line the torte ring with acetate strip. Place the chocolate cake in the ring and moisten with a little pear juice. Spread in some of the rice filling. Arrange the pears on top of the rice in a circle and spoon the remaining rice filling on top. Refrigerate only, as rice is not suitable for freezing.

To make the strawberry meringue, gently heat the egg whites, the sugar, strawberry purée, and lemon juice over hot water to 95°F, and whip until stiff. Spread a layer ½ inch deep over the torte and down the sides. Use a propane torch to brown lightly. Serve the torte with the strawberry sauce.

An icing turntable is a great help when applying the meringue coating. Use a knife to spread the meringue mixture roughly over the torte and then smooth with a dough scraper as you rotate the torte.

set, blend into the whipped cream. Place the smaller torte ring on a smooth base covered with parchment paper or acetate. Spoon in the cream and smooth the top. Cover with acetate and freeze.

To make the kirsch cream filling, beat the egg yolks with the sugar, kirsch, vanilla, and salt until frothy. Whip the cream. Dissolve the gelatin and mix thoroughly into the frothy mixture. Blend the mixture into the whipped cream.

Line the larger torte ring with acetate strip. Slice a ½-inch deep layer from the chocolate spongecake and place in the ring. Mix the kirsch and sugar syrup together and use 3 tablespoons of it to moisten the cake. Spread some of the kirsch cream filling around the base. Let the frozen cherry cream

filling stand at room temperature for 5 minutes, then invert it on top of the cake and remove the ring and acetate. Spread with the remainder of the kirsch cream filling. Slice a thin layer from the light-colored spongecake, place on top, cover with acetate and freeze.

To finish the torte, remove the ring but not the acetate strip. Place a second acetate strip, ¼ inch deeper, around the torte and secure with tape. Moisten the spongecake with the remainder of the kirsch. Whip the cream with the sugar, and spoon onto the torte up to the level of the deeper acetate strip. Smooth the top. Sprinkle milk chocolate couverture curls over the center of the torte and decorate with the well-drained cherries. Remove the acetate strips.

Coconut torte

A perfect combination of two flavors: bitter chocolate and coconut

This is an outstanding example of how useful freezing can be in making high-quality patisserie. In fact, tortes such as this, which are visually stunning and contain a delicate mousse filling, can be constructed only by freezing. If you do not want the base of the torte to be seen, trim it to a slightly smaller diameter. When you place it in the torte ring, you can fill the gap with mousse.

Makes one 10-inch torte

1 Sachertorte base (see page 88), ¾ inch deep
For the coconut cream:
1 cup shredded coconut, 1¼ cups milk
2 teaspoons cornstarch
¼ cup sugar
½ teaspoon gelatin
¾ cup cream, 3 tablespoons coconut liqueur (Malibu)
For the chocolate mousse:
6 egg yolks, ¼ cup sugar
2½ oz dark couverture
2½ oz milk chocolate couverture
5 tablespoons coconut liqueur (Malibu)
1 tablespoon gelatin
1 egg white, 1½ cups cream
For the ganache icing:
2 tablespoons milk, 4 teaspoons cream
2 teaspoons sugar, 1 tablespoon glucose syrup
6 oz milk chocolate couverture
To moisten the spongecake:
¼ cup coconut liqueur (Malibu)
To decorate:
milk chocolate couverture, grated coconut

You will also need:

10-inch torte ring 2 inches deep
6-inch torte ring 1 inch deep
acetate strip

To make the coconut cream, bring the milk and coconut to a boil. Drain through a fine-mesh sieve, squeezing the coconut well and reserving the milk. If necessary, make the reserved milk up to 1¼ cups

with ordinary milk. Mix the cornstarch with a little coconut milk. Bring the remaining coconut milk to a boil with the sugar and add the cornstarch mixture in a trickle, stirring constantly. Cook well. Dissolve the gelatin in the milk, stirring constantly. Cover the cream filling and allow to cool briefly. Whip the cream. Pass the cream filling through a fine-mesh sieve and add the liqueur before the gelatin begins to set. Mix immediately into the whipped cream. Place the smaller torte ring on a smooth base lined with parchment paper. Spoon in the cream filling. Smooth the top. Cover with acetate and freeze.

To make the chocolate mousse, beat the egg yolks with a quarter of the sugar until frothy. Melt both types of couverture in separate double boilers over hot water and stir in the liqueur. Keep this mixture at 95°F. Dissolve the gelatin and then stir

thoroughly into the couverture. Mix loosely with the frothy egg yolks. Whip the egg white and the remaining sugar into soft peaks. Whip the cream. Blend the chocolate mixture with the meringue and whipped cream.

To make the icing, place all the ingredients except the couverture in a saucepan and bring to a boil. Add the chopped couverture. Place a hand blender in the mixture, switch on, and blend thoroughly, using a circular motion and not bringing the blender to the surface. Refrigerate until required, then warm in a microwave oven or over hot water with a minimum of stirring, and use at a temperature of 86°F.

Line the larger torte ring with a strip of acetate, set the Sachertorte base inside, and moisten with the coconut liqueur. Let the frozen cream filling stand at room temperature for 5 minutes, then invert onto the center of the cake and remove the ring and parchment paper. Using a pastry bag with a flat tip, fill the gap between the cream filling and torte ring with mousse. Spread the remaining mousse on top, smooth, cover and freeze. To ice, remove the torte ring but not the acetate strip. Coat with the ganache icing, as shown above right. Remove the acetate strip. Place the torte briefly in the refrigerator for the icing to firm up. To decorate, temper the milk chocolate couverture and finish as shown below.

Acetate strip is very useful when icing with ganache, as the icing can be left to run down the sides. When the acetate strip is removed, the sides are unmarked.

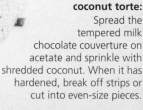

To decorate the coconut torte: Spread the tempered milk chocolate couverture on acetate and sprinkle with shredded coconut. When it has hardened, break off strips or cut into even-size pieces.

Use a knife to mark out the torte into 16 pieces and distribute the coconut-covered couverture strips accordingly.

To blanch hazelnuts, roast them on a baking sheet in the oven at 425°F until the skins show small cracks, but the nuts are still light-colored. Allow to cool. Then the skins will open further and can be removed by rubbing in a cloth.

Hazelnut and chocolate torte

Caramelized hazelnuts and a flourless spongecake tasting richly of chocolate are the basis of this delicate torte

Makes one 9½-inch torte

For the base:

7 eggs, separated

½ cup + 2 tablespoons sugar

scraped contents of ½ vanilla bean

pinch of salt

3 oz couverture

1¼ cups unblanched ground almonds

For the caramelized hazelnuts:

1 cup hazelnuts, blanched and chopped

6 tablespoons sugar, 1 teaspoon water

For the hazelnut cream filling:

½ cup blanched roasted hazelnuts, 1¾ cups cream

2 egg yolks, 1 egg

¼ cup sugar

scraped contents of ½ vanilla bean

pinch of salt, 2 teaspoons gelatin

⅓ recipe caramelized hazelnuts (above)

You will also need:

9½-inch torte ring 2 inches deep

acetate strip

½ cup lightly sweetened whipped cream for spreading

caramelized hazelnuts

couverture and cocoa powder (optional)

Preheat the oven to 325°F. To make the base, beat the egg yolks with 2 tablespoons of the sugar, vanilla, and salt until frothy. Melt the couverture over hot water, cool to 104°F, and mix quickly into the egg yolk mixture. Whip the egg whites with the remaining sugar until stiff. Combine both mixtures and blend in the almonds. Line the torte ring with parchment paper (see page 72) and place on a

Caramelized hazelnuts:

Chop the hazelnuts. Strain to remove very fine particles.

Place the nuts in a hot frying pan and mix with the sugar and water until the pieces of nut are coated all over.

Continue to cook, stirring constantly with a wooden spatula, until the sugar begins to melt and the nuts are coated with a layer of caramel.

Spread out loosely on an oiled work surface, and allow to cool. Crush into small pieces with a rolling pin.

completely flat baking sheet. Spoon in the mixture, smooth the top and bake for 50 minutes. Remove from the oven, turn onto parchment paper sprinkled with granulated sugar and allow to cool.

Prepare the caramelized hazelnuts as shown in the picture sequence on page 102. Only part of the quantity will be used for the hazelnut cream filling and for decoration. The rest will keep in an airtight container.

To make the cream filling, grate or grind the hazelnuts. Whip the cream. Beat the egg yolks and the whole egg with the sugar, vanilla, and salt until frothy. Dissolve the gelatin and add. Stir in the hazelnuts gently and combine with the caramelized hazelnuts and the whipped cream.

Slice a layer ¾ inch deep from the baked chocolate spongecake, as shown on page 75, and freeze the rest. Line the torte ring with an acetate strip. Place the spongecake base in the torte ring. Spoon in the cream filling, smooth the top, cover and freeze.

Let the torte stand at room temperature for 5 minutes, then remove the ring, but not the acetate strip. Place a second acetate strip, ¼ inch deeper, around the first and secure with tape. Cover the top of the torte with lightly sweetened whipped cream. Place in the freezer briefly, so that the acetate strips will come away easily and cleanly. Sprinkle caramelized hazelnuts on top.

The same torte as shown below but with a clear accent on the taste of chocolate. Either dust the top with sifted cocoa powder or sprinkle with finely grated couverture and then cover generously with sifted cocoa powder.

A special chestnut ricer is used to produce the vermicelli-like strands over the torte. A potato ricer can also be used.

Chestnuts and chocolate

A first-class combination as a cream torte or individual squares

SWEET CHESTNUT CREAM TORTE

Sweet chestnut paste is available commercially. If, however, you want to make your own, see page 231. The chocolate batter in this recipe makes two bases, but only one is used here.

Makes one 9-inch torte

For the chocolate mousse:

7 fl oz cream, 5 oz milk chocolate couverture, chopped

2 teaspoons kirsch, 2 egg yolks

For the chocolate spongecake bases (makes 2):

3 eggs, scant ½ cup sugar

scraped contents of ½ vanilla bean

pinch of salt, ½ cup flour

1 tablespoon cocoa powder, 2 tablespoons milk, 2 tablespoons oil

For the sweet chestnut cream filling:

¾ cup chestnut paste, ¼ cup confectioners' sugar, 4 teaspoons rum

1½ cups cream, 2 teaspoons gelatin

To moisten:

4 teaspoons cherry brandy

To decorate:

1 cup chestnut paste, a little vanilla-flavored sugar and rum

16 fresh black cherries or stewed cherries

You will also need:

6-inch torte ring 1 inch deep

9-inch torte ring 2 inches deep

acetate strip, parchment paper, baking sheets

Make the mousse a day in advance. Bring ¼ cup of the cream to a boil and add the couverture, stirring as it melts. Add the kirsch and temper at 89°F. Beat the egg yolks until frothy and fold in quickly. Whip the remainder of the cream and mix in. Place the smaller torte ring on a baking sheet covered with parchment paper or acetate. Spoon in

SWEET CHESTNUT SQUARES

Makes 30 squares

6 tablespoons softened butter, 3 oz couverture, melted

¼ cup confectioners' sugar, 4 eggs, separated

½ cup sugar, ¾ cup flour, sifted

To moisten the cake and for spreading:

¼ cup cherry brandy, ⅓ cup Morello cherry jam, heated and strained

For the chocolate cream:

3½ fl oz milk, 4 teaspoons sugar

scraped contents of ½ vanilla bean, 1 egg yolk

2 heaping teaspoons cornstarch, 6½ teaspoons confectioners' sugar

3½ oz couverture, melted, 2¼ cups cream

For the white cream layer:

2¼ cups cream, 1 tablespoon confectioners' sugar

For the sweet chestnut layer:

1½ cups sweet chestnut paste, mixed with rum and 2 teaspoons vanilla sugar

You will also need:

12 x 10 x 2-inch rectangular mold, 30 cherries

The chestnut squares are 2 x 2 inches. Each piece is decorated with a cherry.

Preheat the oven to 350°F. Cream the butter, warm couverture and confectioners' sugar. Add the egg yolks one at a time. Whip the egg whites with the sugar until stiff. Stir in loosely. Fold in the flour. Place the mold on a baking sheet lined with parchment paper. Spoon in the batter and smooth the top. Bake for 30 minutes. Cool. Cut out the cake, invert it and place in the cleaned mold. Moisten with brandy and spread with jam.

To make the chocolate cream, bring the milk to a boil with the sugar and vanilla. Mix the egg yolk with the cornstarch and 1–2 tablespoons of the hot milk, and add to the milk, stirring over medium heat to thicken it. Add the confectioners' sugar and couverture and temper at 95°F. Whip the cream and stir gradually into the couverture mixture. Spread immediately onto the cake and freeze.

When the chocolate cream is semi-frozen, whip the ingredients for the white cream layer and spread to a uniform depth. Decorate with sweet chestnut paste as shown on page 104.

the mousse and smooth the top. Cover with acetate and freeze overnight.

Preheat the oven to 400°F. To make the chocolate cake, beat the eggs with the sugar, vanilla, and salt. Sift the flour with the cocoa powder onto a piece of parchment paper and trickle it into the batter, stirring constantly. Mix the milk and oil, heat to 125°F, and blend in. Divide the batter into two portions. Line baking sheets with parchment paper, draw two 9-inch circles, and spread the batter on them evenly. Bake for 12–15 minutes, or until a toothpick inserted in the center comes out clean. Turn the cakes onto parchment paper dusted with sugar, remove the parchment paper on which they baked, and allow to cool. If the base of the finished torte is not to be seen, trim one base to 8½ inches diameter, using either a knife or a torte ring as a cutter. Wrap the second base in acetate and freeze.

To make the cream filling, combine the chestnut paste with the confectioners' sugar and rum. Whip the cream. Dissolve the gelatin and carefully stir into the chestnut paste until no streaks are visible. Blend this mixture into the cream.

To assemble the torte, line the larger torte ring with acetate strip. Place the cake base in the ring and moisten with the cherry brandy. Using a pastry bag with a round tip, fill the gap between the cake base and the torte ring with chestnut cream filling. Spread some of the filling over the base and invert the frozen mousse on top. Let stand at room temperature for 5 minutes, then remove the parchment paper or acetate strip from the mousse. Spread the remaining cream filling on the top and sides. Smooth the top. Cover with acetate and freeze.

To decorate the torte, flavor the chestnut paste with vanilla-flavored sugar and rum. Remove the ring but not the acetate strip from the frozen torte. Pass the chestnut paste through a ricer to make strands on top of the torte, as shown on page 104. Trim off overhanging ends. Remove the acetate strip and space the cherries around the edge.

Simple but effective: white couverture curls shaved from the block with a knife.

DARK CHOCOLATE MOUSSE TORTE

Makes two 9-inch tortes 1¼ inches deep

For the bases:
4 egg whites, ¼ cup sugar
3 egg yolks
4½ oz couverture, ½ cup butter
For the mousse:
10 oz couverture, 2½ cups cream, 4 egg yolks
For the icing:
1¾ cups ganache icing (see page 80)
You will also need:
two 9-inch torte rings ½ inch deep
two 9-inch torte rings 1¼ inches deep
acetate strip

Preheat the oven to 350°F. To make the bases, beat the egg whites with the sugar until stiff. Beat the egg yolks until smooth and then stir gently into the meringue. Melt the couverture and butter separately, then mix together — the mixture should be about 95°F — and blend into the meringue. Place the torte rings onto a completely flat baking sheet covered with parchment paper and spoon in the mixture. Bake for 20 minutes. Remove from the oven and allow to cool.

To make the mousse, chop the couverture into small pieces. Place ⅔ cup of the cream in a saucepan and bring to a boil. Add the couverture and melt, stirring constantly. Cool to 95°F. Beat the egg yolks until frothy. In a separate bowl, whip the remaining cream. Mix the egg yolks quickly and lightly into the couverture. Blend the mixture into the whipped cream and continue as shown in the picture. Coat the frozen torte with the ganache icing quickly. Do not allow the torte to thaw, or it will be impossible to ice the delicate mousse.

To prepare the mousse: Melt the couverture and add the egg yolks, which have been whisked until frothy.

Use a whisk to combine the egg yolks and couverture, and to blend in the whipped cream.

Line the deep torte rings with acetate strip. Place the spongecake bases in the rings and spoon in the mousse.

Spread evenly over the bases and smooth with a palette knife. Cover and freeze.

Delicate mousse under a chocolate icing

A melt-in-the mouth ganache icing is the perfect finishing touch

There are many recipes for making chocolate mousse. Each will turn out darker or lighter depending on the chocolate used. The mousse can be made with any number of different flavorings, and with or without whipped cream and meringue. In recipes with light textures or where there is a higher liquid content, for example with additional alcohol, it may be necessary to stabilize the mixture with gelatin. The torte shown here is a combination of delicate mousse with an equally delicate icing and a chocolate base that is made without an ounce of flour.

BLENDED CHOCOLATE MOUSSE TORTE

The white and dark mousses are prepared separately and blended together just before they are put onto the spongecake base.

Makes two 9-inch tortes 1¼ inches deep
2 chocolate bases (see Dark Chocolate Mousse Torte above)
For the white mousse:
6 oz white couverture
2 egg yolks, 13 fl oz cream
6 tablespoons soft butter, 3 tablespoons cognac
For the dark mousse:
6 oz couverture, 3 egg yolks
1½ cups cream, 2 tablespoons soft butter
4 teaspoons cognac

For the icing:

1³⁄₄ cups ganache icing (see page 80)

To decorate:

white chocolate curls

You will also need:

two 9-inch torte rings ¹⁄₂ inch deep

two 9-inch torte rings 1¹⁄₄ inches deep

acetate strip

To make the white mousse, melt the couverture over hot water and cool to 104°F. Beat the egg yolks until frothy and whip the cream. Stir the butter and the cognac into the couverture. The mixture should now be at 95°F. Mix the egg yolk mixture quickly and lightly into the couverture and blend in the whipped cream.

To make the dark mousse, melt the couverture over hot water and cool to 104°F. Beat the egg yolks until frothy and whip 1¹⁄₄ cups of the cream. Stir the butter, the rest of the unwhipped cream, and the cognac into the couverture, which should now be 95°F. Mix the couverture mixture quickly and lightly with the broken egg yolks and blend in the whipped cream.

Line the deeper torte rings with acetate strips and place them on a completely flat base covered with parchment paper. Place the chocolate bases in the torte rings and spoon in the white and dark mousses alternately. Drag a palette knife through the mousses to create a marbled effect. Smooth the tops. Cover the tortes with acetate and freeze. Remove the frozen tortes from the rings and immediately (do not allow them to thaw) ice with the ganache icing. Decorate with white chocolate curls.

Dice and slice

A traditional recipe from Hungary with a new interpretation.
Arrack is a strong alcoholic beverage, which can be made from coconut,
rice or molasses. For this recipe, be sure to get the coconut-flavored one.

STRAWBERRY AND CHOCOLATE SLICES

Makes 25 slices

For the bases:

6 eggs, ½ cup sugar, pinch of salt

scraped contents of ½ vanilla bean

1 cup flour, sifted, 3 tablespoons butter

¼ cup cocoa powder

For the cream filling:

2 teaspoons gelatin

2¼ cups cream, ¼ cup sugar, ¼ cup strawberry purée

4 teaspoons coconut arrack, 1½ oz couverture at 95°F

To moisten:

2 tablespoons sugar syrup, 4 teaspoons coconut arrack

You will also need:

15 x 16½-inch cake pan, parchment paper, foil strips or
a rectangular mold

1 cup ganache icing (see page 80) or 25 striped
chocolate tiles (see pages 58–9)

Preheat the oven to 400°F. To make the base, beat the eggs, sugar, salt, and vanilla together with a hand mixer until frothy. Continue beating, using a circular motion until the batter becomes uniformly creamy and firm. Trickle the flour into the mixture, stirring constantly with a wooden spatula. Line the cake pan with parchment paper and place a strip of foil across the middle widthwise. Spoon half of the batter into one half of the pan. Blend the cocoa powder into the other half of the batter and spoon into the other half of the cake pan. Smooth the tops of both. Bake for 12–15 minutes, watching for doneness. Cut the two cakes to exactly 14 x 8 inches and place a 2-inch deep band of foil around the chocolate cake.

To make the filling, whip the cream with the sugar and mix half of it with the strawberry purée. Dissolve half the gelatin and stir into the strawberry cream mixture. Spread the strawberry cream over the chocolate spongecake. Cover with the light-colored spongecake. Mix the arrack and sugar syrup together, and pour onto the light spongecake.

Dissolve the remaining gelatin. Mix it with the arrack, warm couverture, and the remaining cream. Spread smoothly over the cake. Place the cake in the freezer to firm up the cream fillings. Coat with the ganache icing or cut and decorate with the striped chocolate tiles.

These slices are based on a classic Hungarian recipe, which consists of layers of strawberry, vanilla, and chocolate. In this recipe the vanilla is replaced by arrack to give a different taste.

A nineteenth-century gypsy violinist called Rigo Jansky gave his name to these chocolate dice, which are very popular in Hungary. They are filled with a lot of cream and even more chocolate. This modern version by Karl Schuhmacher, however, is kinder to the waistline.

RIGO JANSKY

Makes 30 squares

For the spongecake:

¾ cup + 2 teaspoons flour

1 tablespoon cocoa powder

3 tablespoons milk, 3 tablespoons oil

4 eggs, ½ cup + 2 tablespoons sugar

scraped contents of ½ vanilla bean, pinch of salt

For the mousse:

¾ cup cream, 11 oz couverture, chopped

6 egg yolks, 2 cups cream, whipped

For the icing:

1 cup ganache icing (see page 80)

For the cream topping:

1¾ cups cream, 1 tablespoon confectioners' sugar

You will also need:

parchment paper, 20 x 12-inch baking sheet

⅓ cup red currant jam

12 x 10-inch mold

In a commercial bakery the individual cakes may be small, but they are made in large quantities. Nevertheless, there is no compromise in precision or quality.

Preheat the oven to 400°F. To make the spongecake, sift the flour and cocoa onto paper. Heat the milk with the oil to 122°F. Beat the eggs with the sugar, vanilla and salt. Blend the flour and cocoa into the batter, followed by the milk-oil mixture. Spread the batter onto a baking sheet covered with parchment paper. Bake for 8 minutes, watching for doneness. Turn the cake onto a paper dusted with sugar, remove the parchment paper, and cut in half lengthwise. Spread one half with the jam and place in the mold.

To make the mousse, bring the cream to a boil and add the couverture, stirring as it melts. Cool to 95°F. Beat the egg yolks until frothy and stir in lightly. Blend into the whipped cream. Take the second half of the cake, which will be used later for the top, and spread thinly with just enough mousse to create a smooth surface. Refrigerate to firm up. Spread the remaining mousse in the mold and refrigerate or freeze.

Coat the top half with the ganache icing and refrigerate again to firm up.

Whip the cream with the confectioners' sugar and spread over the mousse in the mold. Remove the mold, put the cake top in place, and trim. Cut into 2-inch squares with a knife dipped in hot water.

The fillings for the potatoes can be varied. Raspberry or pineapple jam go well with the filling because they both harmonize with the rum. A light ganache cream (see page 156) could be used instead of the butter cream. The colored paper cases look attractive and also help to keep the fingers clean.

Moors' Heads and Potatoes

These traditional little cakes are made with half rounds of spongecake, with chocolate playing an important part as usual

ALMOND PASTE POTATOES

These sweet balls are filled with a light chocolate cream and jam, coated with almond paste, and dipped in cocoa powder.

Makes 24
For the cake:
3 egg yolks
¼ cup sugar
4 egg whites
½ cup cornstarch, 2 tablespoons flour
For the filling:
9 tablespoons butter
3 oz couverture, melted
4 teaspoons rum
3 egg whites, ½ cup sugar
1 cup red currant jelly
For the coating:
½ cup red currant jelly
1 lb almond paste
1¾ cups confectioners' sugar
You will also need:
baking sheets, parchment paper
confectioners' sugar
cocoa powder for dipping
paper cases

Preheat the oven to 375°F. To make the cake, beat the egg yolks with 1 tablespoon of the sugar until frothy. Whip the egg whites until stiff, trickle in the remaining sugar and continue to whip until stiff and dry. First fold the cornstarch into the meringue mixture, followed by the beaten egg yolks, and finally the flour. Spoon the mixture into a pastry bag with a large round tip and pipe 1½-inch mounds spaced well apart onto a baking sheet lined

Pipe 1½-inch mounds spaced apart on a baking sheet.

Preheat the oven to 375°F and bake for 6–8 minutes until light brown.

MOORS' HEADS

Here is a variation on a popular traditional recipe, using an almond soufflé as a base instead of spongecake, ganache icing instead of fondant icing, and a filling of whipped cream and jam.

Makes 30

1 recipe almond soufflé (see page 137)
1 recipe ganache icing (see page 80)
For the filling:
3 cups cream
2 tablespoons confectioners' sugar
⅓ cup raspberry or strawberry jam
You will also need:
baking sheets, parchment paper

Preheat the oven to 325°F. Spoon the almond soufflé mixture into a pastry bag with a large

The original Moor's Head, with chocolate icing and jam, requires only whipped cream as a filling.

round tip and pipe 60 mounds 1½–2 inches in diameter onto a baking sheet lined with parchment paper. Bake for 20 minutes, or until golden brown. Remove and allow to cool.

Using a dipping fork, dip half of the batch into the ganache icing and place on a wire rack to dry.

Place the remainder of the batch in paper cases. Whip the cream with the confectioners' sugar until stiff. Spoon into a pastry bag with a star tip and pipe rosettes onto the bottom halves, leaving a space in the center. Fill with a dab of jam. Top with the icing-coated halves.

The light almond meringue marries well with the delicate, melting ganache icing and the very lightly sweetened whipped cream. Other flavors of jam can, of course, be used for the filling.

with parchment paper, as shown. Bake for 6–10 minutes, until lightly browned. Leave the oven door slightly ajar to allow the steam to escape.

To make the chocolate filling, beat the butter

Roll out the almond paste and cut into 3-inch squares. Place the spongecake balls in the center and bring the corners together.

Pinch the corners together and trim off the excess almond paste. Roll the balls in your hands to make them spherical.

until fluffy, pour in the lukewarm couverture, and stir in the rum. Whip the egg whites until very stiff, adding the sugar gradually while continuing to whip. Fold into the frothy butter mixture.

Use a sharp knife to make a small hollow in the base of the cake bases and place on the work surface. Spoon the cream filling into a pastry bag with a round tip and fill half of the cases. Fill the other half with jam. Sandwich together to form balls.

To make the coating, bring the red currant jam to a boil and spread it over the balls with a brush. Allow to dry briefly. Knead the almond paste with the confectioners' sugar until smooth. Dust the work surface with confectioners' sugar and roll out the paste to ⅛ inch thick, cut into squares, and use to cover the potatoes, as shown in the pictures. Make a few indentations to represent "eyes." Roll the balls in cocoa powder. Shake off the surplus powder. Place in paper cases.

Petit fours

Chocolate cream filling in tiny pastry tartlets, coated with dark or light couverture

These chocolate petit fours are ideal for serving with coffee or tea. The containers are pastry tartlets baked in a variety of shapes. They are filled with various chocolate creams based on two ganaches — a dark one made with bitter couverture and a light one made with milk chocolate couverture — which are beaten until foamy and then flavored.

The petit four molds are lined with a light or dark chocolate pastry. These can be baked and stored in the freezer. Before use, reheat to freshen and make them crisp, to contrast with the soft ganache cream filling. Petit fours will keep for several days, but are best when freshly made.

Chocolate petit fours to keep in stock. The shortcrust pastry cases can be frozen after baking. If they are crisped up in the oven prior to use, they taste absolutely fresh. The ganache cream filling can also be kept in the refrigerator if its container is tightly sealed with plastic wrap. Small quantities can then be prepared relatively quickly when required.

The following basic recipes for cream fillings will make enough for 60–80 items, depending on the amount you put in each tartlet.

For the pastry:
1¼ cups butter, 1¼ cups confectioners' sugar
pinch of salt
scraped contents of ½ vanilla bean
3½ cups flour
6½ teaspoons very dark cocoa powder for the dark pastry
For the dark ganache cream filling:
7 fl oz cream, 10 oz couverture
For the light ganache cream filling:
⅓ cup cream, 10 oz milk chocolate couverture

Preheat the oven to 350°F. To make the pastry, place the butter on a work surface and use a spoon to rub in the confectioners' sugar, salt, and vanilla until soft and creamy. Sift the flour on top and knead in as quickly as possible. When the flour is half worked in, divide the dough into halves. Continue to knead one half briefly until smooth. Sift the cocoa powder over the other half and knead in rapidly. Form the dough into balls, wrap in plastic wrap, and refrigerate for 1–2 hours. Roll out to ⅛ inch thick, line the molds, and bake for 8–10 minutes, watching for doneness.

To make the basic cream fillings, bring the cream to a boil and stir in the finely chopped or melted couverture. Combine thoroughly with a hand blender, as described on page 156. Allow to cool.

These small, sweet confections have something to suit every taste. They are filled with dark or light ganache cream, and are described from left to right in the text below.

⅓ recipe light ganache cream until foamy and pipe onto the tartlets with a star tip. Allow to set. Dip in tempered milk chocolate couverture and sprinkle with pistachio croquant.

Coffee and cognac Whisk ⅓ recipe dark ganache cream with 1 teaspoon instant coffee powder and 4 teaspoons cognac until foamy. Pipe with a star tip into light-colored round tartlets. Spread milk chocolate couverture on parchment paper and pipe a dark couverture lattice on top. Stamp out round shapes and place on top of the cream filling.

Nougat and amaretto Melt 2 oz almond nougat and pipe dabs into light-colored round tartlets. Whisk ⅓ recipe light ganache cream with 4 teaspoons amaretto until foamy. Using a round tip, pipe into the tartlets in rounded mounds. Allow to set. Dip halfway into tempered couverture. Decorate with sugared almonds.

Black Forest style Spread cherry jam into oval chocolate tartlets. Whisk ⅓ recipe light ganache cream with 4 teaspoons kirsch until foamy. Pipe in a spiral using a round tip. Sprinkle with chopped croquant.

Rum Spread hot orange marmalade in light-colored square tartlets and allow to cool. Beat ⅓ recipe dark ganache cream until foamy, then stir in 4 teaspoons dark rum and 2 tablespoons soft butter. Using a star tip, pipe rosettes into the tartlets. Allow to set. Dip in tempered couverture and decorate with a roasted almond flake.

Raspberry brandy Place a dab of raspberry jam in light-colored round tartlets. Stir ⅓ recipe dark ganache cream filling with 4 teaspoons raspberry brandy until creamy but not frothy, and pipe into the tartlets using a round tip. Decorate with white couverture rolls.

Orange almond paste Work 2 tablespoons Cointreau and 1 tablespoon finely chopped candied orange peel into 2 oz almond paste. Fill light-colored rectangular tartlets with the almond paste and smooth the tops. Whisk ⅓ recipe dark ganache cream until foamy and spread around the edges. Allow to set. Dip in tempered couverture and decorate with almond slivers.

Crystallized ginger Fill round chocolate tartlets with finely chopped crystallized ginger. Whisk

Marble cakes

Three recipes for one of the most popular chocolate cakes

Marble cake may not have a very exciting image, but it still remains a firm favorite. Its success began with the discovery of baking powder. However, as the next recipe illustrates, baking powder is not essential for making a very light pound cake. Surprisingly, the cake has no traditional shape, and appears in anything from rings and rectangles to the fluted gugelhupf.

MARBLE POUND CAKE BAKED IN A TUBE PAN

Makes one 8-inch cake

3 eggs, 2 egg yolks, ¾ cup sugar

scraped contents of 1 vanilla bean

grated zest of ¼ lemon

pinch of salt

1¼ cups cornstarch, 6½ teaspoons flour

7 fl oz hot melted butter, 1 teaspoon cocoa powder

You will also need:

8-inch tube pan, butter for the pan

finely sieved bread crumbs

confectioners' sugar

Preheat the oven to 400°F. To make the cake, beat the eggs with the egg yolks, sugar, vanilla, lemon zest, and salt until frothy. Sift the flour and cornstarch together and trickle into the egg mixture while stirring. Add the hot butter and stir the mixture together lightly. Mix one third of the batter with the cocoa powder. Grease the pan and dust with bread crumbs. Spoon the light-colored batter into the pan. Spoon the dark batter into a pastry bag with a flat tip. Insert the tip into the light batter and pipe swirls. Alternatively, use a knife to swirl large spoonfuls of the dark batter into the light batter. Bake for 40 minutes. Remove, stand on a wire rack or turn onto a baking sheet lined with parchment paper. Allow to cool. Dust with confectioners' sugar.

MARBLE CAKE WITH GANACHE ICING

Makes one 8-inch cake

1 recipe marble cake (see above)

For the ganache icing:

6 tablespoons milk, 4 tablespoons cream, 7 teaspoons sugar, 3 tablespoons water

4½ teaspoons glucose syrup, 9 oz couverture, grated

You will also need:

finely chopped peeled pistachios

Make the cake as described in the recipe above. Place on a wire rack or turn onto a baking sheet lined with parchment paper. Place in the refrigerator to cool.

To make the ganache icing, place the milk, cream, sugar, water, and glucose syrup in a saucepan. Bring to a boil, stirring constantly. Remove the pan from the heat. Add the couverture, stirring constantly until completely melted. Place a hand blender in the icing, then switch on and blend thoroughly, using a circular motion. Do not allow the hand blender to come to the surface, or it will trap air bubbles. Temper the ganache icing at 86°F and coat the cake. Sprinkle lightly with the pistachios. Refrigerate until the icing is firm.

With or without icing? If it is merely dusted with confectioners' sugar, a marble cake will dry out much more quickly than if it is enclosed in a layer of chocolate icing. The cake can also be coated with apricot jam and then covered with a chocolate fondant icing. If the cake is to be stored for some time, it can be frozen (see page 119).

MARBLE CAKE

Makes 3 cakes

For the light batter:

6 eggs, separated

1½ cups confectioners' sugar

scraped contents of 1 vanilla bean, pinch of salt

grated zest of ½ lemon, ½ cup sugar

1¼ cups cornstarch, 2½ teaspoons baking powder

1⅜ cups flour, 1¼ cups butter

For the dark batter:

2 teaspoons cocoa powder, 4 teaspoons oil,

2 tablespoons water

You will also need:

three 7 x 3½ x 2½-inch bread pans, butter for greasing

cake or bread crumbs

confectioners' sugar (optional)

Preheat the oven to 475°F. To make the light batter, beat the egg yolks, confectioners' sugar, vanilla, salt and lemon zest until frothy. Whip the egg whites and sugar until stiff. Sift the flour, cornstarch, and baking powder together and trickle into the batter while stirring. Melt the butter and blend in while hot. Fold in the whipped egg whites.

To make the chocolate batter, mix the cocoa powder, oil, and water. Mix evenly with slightly less than half of the light-colored batter.

Grease and dust the bread pans with crumbs. Spoon each batter into a pastry bag with a large round tip. Divide slightly less than half of the light batter between the pans. Pipe the dark batter on top, and add the remaining light batter. Place the pans in the oven and immediately reduce the heat to 400°F. As soon as a light brown crust forms, after about 15 minutes, use a buttered knife to make a slit about ½ inch deep in the tops of the cakes for about three-fifths of their length. Bake for a further 10 minutes at the same temperature, then reduce it to 300°F until fully baked. The total baking time will be 55–60 minutes. Remove from the oven, and allow to cool in the pans for 15 minutes.

Fruit and spice fillings

Chocolate shows its versatility in combination with oranges or ginger

CHOCOLATE CAKE WITH GINGER

A cake made with almond paste and chocolate paste tastes just as good without a filling, but ginger — use stem ginger preserved in syrup — makes it a little more exotic. It is best to let the cake rest overnight, so that the full flavor can develop.

Makes one 12-inch long cake
For the cake:
7 oz almond paste
6 tablespoons soft butter
pinch of salt
scraped contents of ½ vanilla bean
7 eggs, separated
⅓ cup preserved ginger
½ cup + 2 tablespoons sugar
¾ cup flour
½ cup cocoa powder
For the filling:
2 tablespoons ginger syrup
3½ oz almond paste
⅓ cup preserved ginger, minced
4 teaspoons arrack
To decorate:
7 teaspoons apricot jam
2 oz couverture, grated
cocoa powder, preserved ginger (optional)
You will also need:
12-inch ridged bread pan
butter for the pan, bread crumbs

Preheat the oven to 350°F. To make the dough, knead the almond paste with the butter, salt, and vanilla. Add the egg yolks one at a time and stir to a frothy mass. Drain the ginger well, mince, and stir into the almond paste and egg yolk mixture. Whip the egg whites with the sugar into soft peaks. Fold one half into the batter, then the other half. Sift the flour with the cocoa powder. Trickle into the batter and fold in carefully. Grease the cake pan with butter, sprinkle with the crumbs, spoon in the batter, and smooth the top. Bake for 50 minutes. Check for doneness with a wooden toothpick. Turn out the cake and let it rest overnight.

To make the filling, stir the syrup into the almond paste until smooth. Stir in the ginger and arrack. Cut the cake in half lengthwise and spread the filling onto the bottom half. Place the other half on top. Heat and strain the jam, and spread on top of the cake. Sprinkle with couverture and dust with sifted cocoa powder. Decorate with pieces of ginger, if liked.

Called *Rehrücken* in its native Germany, this cake is studded with slivered almonds and then coated with couverture. The spongecake is identical to that in the Orange and Chocolate Ring recipe, and is baked in a 10½-inch ribbed loaf pan.

ORANGE AND CHOCOLATE RING

Makes one 9-inch tube cake

For the cake:

4 oz couverture, 1¼ cups flour

scraped contents of ½ vanilla bean

7 eggs, separated, ¾ cup sugar

1¼ cups ground almonds, 1⅛ cups cake crumbs

For the filling:

3½ oz almond paste, 3 tablespoons orange juice

4 teaspoons Cointreau, ½ cup finely chopped candied orange peel

To decorate:

7 teaspoons apricot jam

dark chocolate curls, white chocolate rolls

You will also need:

9-inch tube pan

butter for the pan, bread crumbs

Preheat the oven to 350°F. Melt the couverture over hot water and cool to 86°F. Beat the couverture with the butter, vanilla and egg yolks until frothy. Whip the egg whites and sugar until stiff. Fold into the chocolate mixture. Mix the almonds and cake crumbs and blend in. Grease the pan with butter, sprinkle bread crumbs on the base, spoon in the batter, and smooth the top. Bake for 50–60 minutes. Check for doneness with a wooden toothpick. Cool and let the cake rest overnight.

To make the filling, knead all the ingredients together. Slice the baked cake into 3 layers and sandwich together with the marzipan mixture. Heat and strain the jam, and use to coat the surface of the cake. Allow to cool. Sprinkle dark chocolate curls over the ring and decorate with white chocolate rolls.

Gugelhupf times two
Once with chocolate chips and once with melted chocolate

Gugelhupf, also called kugelhopf, is the traditional
European cake for celebrating a person's name day.
The original recipe called for a soft yeast dough, but
a fine spongecake is now the norm.

ALMOND GUGELHUPF WITH CHOCOLATE

Small chocolate drops are ideal for this cake,
although chopped couverture can be used instead.
Very fine pieces of chocolate must be strained out,
or they will darken the batter.

Makes one 7-inch cake
¾ cup butter, heaping ½ cup sugar
scraped contents of ½ vanilla bean, pinch of salt
grated zest of ¼ lemon
6 oz almond paste, 4 egg yolks, 4 teaspoons Cointreau
6 egg whites, 2¼ teaspoons cornstarch
1¼ cups flour, sifted
4 oz couverture, chopped, or couverture drops
1 cup walnuts, coarsely chopped
You will also need:
7-inch gugelhupf pan or fluted tube pan
butter for the pan, flaked almonds

Preheat the oven to 350°F. Cream the butter,
2 tablespoons of the sugar, the vanilla, salt, and
lemon zest. Work 1 egg yolk into the almond paste,
then stir to a foamy mass with the remaining egg
yolks and liqueur. Whip the egg whites with the
remaining sugar and cornstarch until stiff. Combine
the butter mixture with the almond paste mixture,
and then fold in the egg whites. Combine the flour
with the couverture and walnuts, and mix into the
batter. Grease the pan and sprinkle with flaked
almonds. Spoon in the batter and bake for 1 hour.

SACHER GUGELHUPF

Makes one 7-inch cake
For the Sacher cake:
7 tablespoons butter, softened, 7½ teaspoons confectioners' sugar
3½ oz couverture, melted
5 eggs, separated, ½ cup + 2 tablespoons sugar
¾ cup + 2 teaspoons flour
2 pieces preserved ginger and 1 cup pecan nuts, coarsely chopped

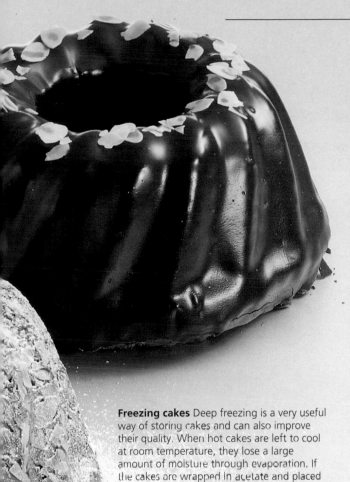

Freezing cakes Deep freezing is a very useful way of storing cakes and can also improve their quality. When hot cakes are left to cool at room temperature, they lose a large amount of moisture through evaporation. If the cakes are wrapped in acetate and placed in the freezer immediately after baking, the crust quickly seals and the cake retains a high degree of moistness. Cakes can be stored in the freezer for a long time. When they are removed and allowed to thaw out slowly at room temperature, they taste fresher than cakes made in the conventional way. The crumb and crust assimilate better, and the structure of the cake becomes more balanced, producing a more pleasing taste and texture. There is the added advantage of having something special on hand in the event of an unexpected visitor.

Masking and Icing:

Pour the strained apricot jam over the gugelhupf, spread it evenly, and remove excess jam.

Pour the chocolate fondant over the gugelhupf and spread it evenly.

Sprinkle the top of the iced gugelhupf evenly with flaked roasted almonds.

For the icing:
1 recipe chocolate fondant icing (see below)
You will also need:
7-inch gugelhupf pan or fluted tube pan
butter for the pan, flour to dust
flaked roasted almonds

Preheat the oven to 350°F. Cream the butter, confectioners' sugar, and couverture. Mix in the egg yolks one at a time. Whip the egg whites and granulated sugar until stiff, and fold into the creamed mixture. Mix the flour with the ginger and nuts, and blend in. Grease the pan and dust with flour. Spoon in the batter and bake for 55 minutes. Turn out onto a wire rack and allow to cool. Coat the cake with apricot jam, and ice as shown in the picture sequence.

Chocolate fondant icing: You have to make more than is needed, to assure a good finish. A lot of excess icing will run off, but it can be saved, and will keep for a fairly long time in a screw-top jar.

To make chocolate fondant icing:

Heat the fondant, without thinning, over a low heat, stirring continuously until it runs smoothly.

Add as much cocoa powder as required to give the desired color and stir until it is mixed in uniformly.

Pour in the warmed couverture. It does not have to be tempered. Stir until it is fully mixed in.

With the addition of the couverture, the fondant becomes visibly thicker. Adjust to the required fluidity by adding sugar syrup a little at a time.

The icing should have a good gloss and flow thickly from the spoon. The temperature of the icing should not exceed 95°F, or the gloss will be lost after it has dried.

Icing ingredients:
1 lb chocolate fondant
cocoa powder as
    required
1½ oz couverture,
    melted
sugar syrup, as required

Three variations on a spongecake From left to right: chocolate and almond cake with almond paste, with candied orange peel, and with chocolate chips.

Chocolate almond cake

With three delicious flavorings

This is a quick and simple recipe provided that each of the flavorings has been prepared in advance.

CHOCOLATE ALMOND CAKE

Makes 3 cakes

3½ oz couverture, 1 oz almond paste

6 eggs, separated, 7 tablespoons butter, softened

scraped contents of 1 vanilla bean

pinch of salt, 6 tablespoons sugar

2 tablespoons cornstarch

1¼ cups ground almonds

You will also need:

three 7 x 3½ x 2¼-inch bread pans

butter and flour or parchment paper for the pans

Preheat the oven to 325°F. Melt the couverture over hot water. Knead the almond paste with 1 egg

For the flavoring:
10 oz almond paste
You will also need:
flour, confectioners' sugar for dusting

To make the flavoring, roll out the almond paste to ⅜-inch thick on a board dusted with confectioners' sugar. Cover with acetate and freeze. Cut the frozen almond paste into small dice, dust with flour, and mix loosely. The almond paste can be stored like this in the freezer. When ready for use, move the desired quantity to the refrigerator for a short time before adding to the batter, so that it is still cold but not frozen and will mix loosely into the batter. Frozen dice will cause the butter to harden and the batter to lose too much volume. Make the cake as described in the recipe for Chocolate Almond Cake.

Allow the cake to cool for 10 minutes in the pan, turn out, and leave until cold. To make a simple decoration, lay a strip of paper down the middle of the cake, then dust with confectioners' sugar.

yolk until smooth, then beat with the remaining egg yolks until frothy. Beat the butter with the vanilla, salt, and melted (but not too warm) couverture. Whip the egg whites with the sugar and cornstarch until stiff. Combine all three mixtures. Mix the almonds with the appropriate flavoring (see recipes below) and blend into the batter. Grease and dust the pans with flour, or line with parchment paper. Spoon the batter into the pans and bake for 40–45 minutes.

CHOCOLATE ALMOND CAKE WITH CANDIED ORANGE PEEL

Makes 1 cake
1 recipe Chocolate Almond Cake batter
For the flavoring:
1½ cups finely diced candied orange peel
Grand Marnier
You will also need:
tempered milk chocolate couverture
strips of candied orange peel to decorate

To make the flavoring, marinate the candied orange peel in Grand Marnier for several days. Make the cake as described above. As soon as it is removed from the oven, brush the underside with Grand Marnier, to give it a better flavor. Allow to cool. Cover with tempered milk chocolate couverture. Decorate with strips of candied orange peel.

CHOCOLATE ALMOND CAKE WITH ALMOND PASTE

Makes 1 cake
1 recipe Chocolate Almond Cake batter

CHOCOLATE ALMOND CAKE WITH CHOCOLATE DROPS AND GINGER

Makes 1 cake
1 recipe Chocolate Almond Cake batter
For the flavoring:
10 oz couverture drops or pieces
⅓ cup preserved ginger, chopped
For the ganache icing:
¼ cup milk
3 tablespoons cream
2 tablespoons sugar, 2 tablespoons water
1 tablespoon glucose syrup, 12 oz couverture, finely chopped or grated
You will also need:
chopped pistachios to decorate

To make the flavoring, pipe chocolate drops as shown on pages 62–3, or cut small pieces from a block of couverture. Mix with the ginger. Make the cake as described in the recipe for Chocolate Almond Cake.

To make the ganache icing, place the milk, cream, sugar, water, and glucose syrup in a saucepan. Bring to a boil, stirring constantly. Remove the pan from the heat. Add the couverture, stirring constantly until completely melted. Place a hand blender in the icing, then switch on and blend thoroughly, using a circular motion (see page 156). Temper the ganache icing at 86°F and coat the cake. Sprinkle with pistachios and refrigerate until the icing is firm.

Chocolate pastry

For large pies or small tartlets, a recommended alternative to light-colored pastry

Chocolate pastry has a bitter taste, which combines best with tangy fillings such as orange cream, red currant meringue, or other fruit. But it also goes well with almonds, walnuts, or — as here — pecan nuts. Work quickly when preparing this pastry, as the cocoa tends to make it crumble more easily than ordinary pastry. If it becomes crumbly, knead with a little egg white until smooth again.

CHOCOLATE PASTRY
2½ cups flour, ¾ cup + 2 tablespoons cold butter
½ cup cocoa powder, 1 cup confectioners' sugar
1 egg yolk, pinch of salt
To bake:
parchment paper, baking beans

To make the pastry, heap the flour onto a board and make a well in the middle. Cut the butter into pieces and place it in the well with the cocoa powder, confectioners' sugar, egg yolk and salt. Mix these ingredients with a fork, working in a little flour at the same time. Using a pastry blender or two large forks, turn in the flour from the outside to the center, until the ingredients resemble fine crumbs. Now knead into a smooth dough. Form into a ball, wrap in plastic wrap, and

Baking blind:

Roll out the pastry evenly and place in the pans. Press the pastry against the sides of the pan with the fingertips.

Trim off excess pastry with a sharp knife. Prick the pastry base several times with a fork.

Place a piece of parchment paper on top of the pastry and fill with baking beans. Preheat the oven to 350°F and bake blind for 20 minutes.

refrigerate for at least 1 hour. Bake the pastry blind, as described in the picture sequence.

CHOCOLATE PECAN PIE

Pecan pie is one of the great American classics. In the following recipe the slightly bitter taste of the chocolate harmonizes well with the pecan nuts. Use a springform pan or a torte pan with a removable base, so that the pastry shell can be removed without damaging it.

Makes one 10-inch pie
1 recipe Chocolate Pastry (above)
For the filling:
1¾ cups pecan nuts, 3 oz couverture
6 tablespoons butter
¾ cup brown sugar, 3 eggs
2 tablespoons cream
¼ cup flour
For the topping:
1 cup pecan halves

You will also need:
10-inch springform pan
parchment paper, baking beans
confectioners' sugar for dusting

Preheat the oven to 350°F. Prepare the pastry and allow to cool, as described on the opposite page. Roll out the pastry evenly and place in the pan. Bake blind for 15 minutes. Remove the beans and parchment paper, and allow to cool.

To make the filling, chop the pecans roughly. Cut or chop the couverture into small pieces. Cream the butter with ¼ cup of the sugar. Add the eggs one at a time and then add the remaining sugar. Stir in the cream and flour. Finally, mix in the chopped nuts and pieces of couverture.

Spoon the filling into the baked pastry case and smooth the top. Top with circles of halved nuts, working from the edge to the center. Bake for 55 minutes. Halfway through the baking, cover with foil to prevent the top burning. Allow the pie to cool slightly before removing from the pan. When cold, dust with confectioners' sugar.

Linzertorte and brownies

Traditional pastries that have become best sellers

CHOCOLATE LINZERTORTE

An old Austrian recipe for delicate almond pastry is combined with a generous amount of couverture.

Makes one 10-inch tart
3 oz couverture, grated
¾ cup ground almonds, unblanched
2¼ cups flour, 1 cup butter
1 cup confectioners' sugar, sifted,
4 egg yolks, pinch of salt, grated zest of ½ lemon
You will also need:
1 cup + 2 tablespoons red currant jelly
parchment paper
10-inch tart pan
1 egg yolk mixed with 1–2 tablespoons milk, to brush the top, confectioners' sugar for dusting

Preheat the oven to 350°F. To make the pastry, heap the grated couverture and almonds onto a work surface. Sift the flour on top and make a well in the middle. Cut the butter into pieces and add it with the sifted confectioners' sugar, egg yolks, salt and lemon zest, and work together quickly to make a dough. Wrap in plastic wrap and refrigerate for 1 hour. Meanwhile, boil up and reduce the red currant jelly by a third. Allow to go completely cold. On a floured surface, roll out half the dough to ½ inch thick, and place in the bottom of a torte pan lined

with parchment paper. To make the sides, roll out about half the remaining dough into a strip 31½ inches long. Place in the pan, and press gently into position. Spread the jelly over the pastry base. Roll out the remaining dough to ¼ inch thick. Cut strips ½ inch wide and make a lattice pattern on top of the jelly. Brush the lattice and edges with the egg yolk mixture. Bake for 40–45 minutes. Remove the tart from the pan and allow to cool. Dust with confectioners' sugar.

CHOCOLATE HAZELNUT SLICES

Makes 15 slices
For the cake:
¼ cup butter, softened
2 oz couverture, melted
2 tablespoons confectioners' sugar
2 eggs, separated
¼ cup sugar, ½ cup flour, sifted
For the meringue:
6 egg whites, 1 cup sugar, 1½ cup ground walnuts
You will also need:
12 x 10-inch cake pan
butter for the pan, fine bread crumbs

Preheat the oven to 325°F. To make the cake, cream the soft butter with the couverture and confectioners' sugar. Add the egg yolks one at a time. Whip the egg whites with the granulated sugar until stiff. Combine the two mixtures and blend in the flour. Grease the base of the cake pan with butter and sprinkle with bread crumbs. Spoon the batter into the pan. Freeze to make it easier to hold the meringue later. The time required to make the meringue is generally long enough for the batter to become firm.

To make the meringue, whip the egg whites with the sugar until stiff. Stir in the walnuts. Spread over the cake batter. Bake for 40 minutes. Slide a small knife around the edge to loosen it from the pan as soon as it comes out of the oven, so that it shrinks a

little as it cools and sinks evenly without breaking the crust. When cold, cut into slices.

BROWNIES

Here is a new recipe for an old favorite.

Makes 15
For the batter:
1¼ cups flour, ½ cup cornstarch
1¼ cups walnuts, coarsely chopped
1½ cups butter, softened
1 cup sugar, 7 oz couverture, melted
scraped contents of 1 vanilla bean
pinch of salt, 5 eggs
For the ganache cream filling:
1 cup cream, 9 oz couverture, coarsely chopped
You will also need:
12 x 10-inch cake pan, foil, baking sheet

Preheat the oven to 325°F. To make the batter, sift the flour and cornstarch together and mix with the walnuts. Cream the soft butter, sugar, couverture, vanilla, and salt. Add the eggs one at a time. Blend in the flour and walnut mixture. Spread the batter in the pan and bake for 50 minutes. Remove from the oven and immediately loosen the sides with a small knife so that the cake will sink evenly as it cools. Leave until cold.

To make the ganache cream, bring the cream to a boil and add the couverture, stirring constantly until it melts. Place a hand blender in the mixture, switch on, and blend thoroughly, using a circular motion. Do not allow the blender to come to the top, or it will trap air bubbles. Cool to 83°F.

Clean the cake pan and place on a baking sheet lined with foil. Turn the foil up around the sides of the pan. Pour in the ganache cream and invert the cake on top of it. Cool. When ready to serve, release from the pan and turn over. Dust with sifted cocoa powder and cut into 15 pieces.

A legendary American recipe: The invention of the celebrated brownie is attributed to a librarian from Maine called "Brownie" Schrumpf. She reputedly forgot to add baking powder when she was making a chocolate cake, and the rest is history.

Crisp and decorative

It is hard to tell whether it is the buttery flavor, the crisp texture, or the decorative appearance that makes these cookies so good

If you want your cookies to look as neat and attractive as the ones shown here, you will have to be quite precise. That means that the dough has to be rolled out absolutely evenly. Thin strips of wood, which can be found in varying sizes in handicraft stores, are a very useful aid. For the designs shown on this page, you will need only two sizes: ½-inch, for rolling out and cutting the squares, and ⅛-inch for rolling out the wrapping for the checkerboard and rolls.

Makes 80
1¼ cups butter
1¼ cups confectioners' sugar
pinch of salt
scraped contents of ½ vanilla bean
3¼ cups flour
2 heaping tablespoons very dark cocoa powder
You will also need:
1 egg yolk mixed with 2 tablespoons milk

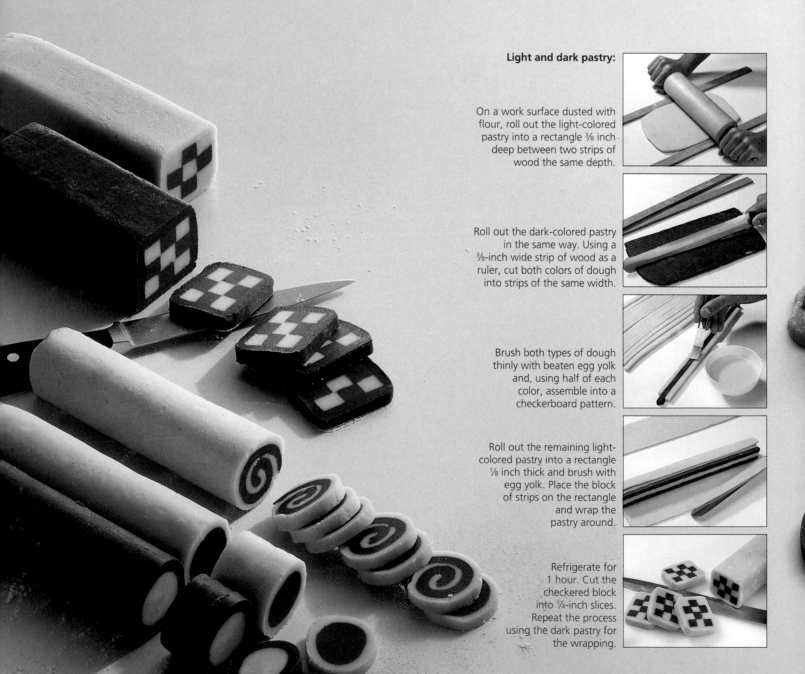

Light and dark pastry:

On a work surface dusted with flour, roll out the light-colored pastry into a rectangle ⅜ inch deep between two strips of wood the same depth.

Roll out the dark-colored pastry in the same way. Using a ⅜-inch wide strip of wood as a ruler, cut both colors of dough into strips of the same width.

Brush both types of dough thinly with beaten egg yolk and, using half of each color, assemble into a checkerboard pattern.

Roll out the remaining light-colored pastry into a rectangle ⅛ inch thick and brush with egg yolk. Place the block of strips on the rectangle and wrap the pastry around.

Refrigerate for 1 hour. Cut the checkered block into ¼-inch slices. Repeat the process using the dark pastry for the wrapping.

The strips of wood help to produce precise squares that look as good at the back as at the front. However, the rolls of pastry have to be shaped by hand. They should have an internal diameter of 1 inch. When they are cold, roll them up in ⅛-inch thick pastry, slice, and bake as for the squares.

Place the butter, confectioners' sugar, salt, and vanilla on a work surface and mix together with a spoon. Sift the flour on top and knead into a dough as quickly as possible. When the flour is half worked in, divide the dough in half. Continue to knead one half briefly until it is smooth. Sift the cocoa powder over the other half and knead in as quickly as possible. Roll each dough into a ball, wrap in plastic wrap, and refrigerate for 1–2 hours.

Preheat the oven to 350°F. Cut both doughs in half and shape one dark and one light portion into rectangles. Reserve the other two halves for the wrapping. Continue as shown in the picture sequence. Place the prepared slices on an ungreased baking sheet spaced well apart. Bake for 12 minutes. Ensure that the pastry does not brown, to maintain a good contrast between the light and dark-colored effects. Remnants of light and dark dough can be rolled up together to produce cookies with an interesting marble pattern.

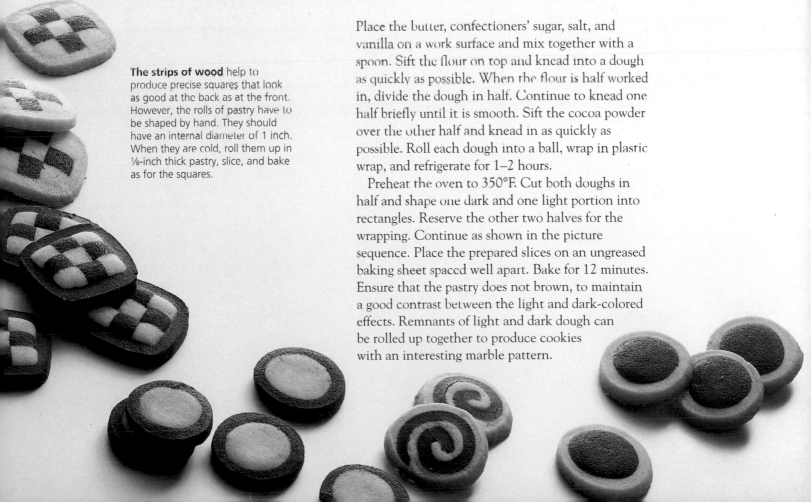

With butter and chocolate

Fancy cookies made from short pastry and couverture — soft for piping, firm for shaping by hand

CHOCOLATE CRESCENTS

Makes about 100

5 oz couverture, 10 tablespoons butter

1¾ cups confectioners' sugar, sifted,

1¾ cups ground almonds

You will also need:

parchment paper, baking sheets

tempered couverture for icing

Preheat the oven to 325°F. To make the dough, melt the couverture over hot water and cool to 89°F. Briefly work in the butter, confectioners' sugar, and almonds. Refrigerate to firm up a little. On a work surface dusted with flour, form 1-inch rolls from the dough. Cut into slices ½ inch thick. Form these slices into rolls 2¼ inches long, shaping the ends into a point. Bend into a crescent shape and space out on a baking sheet lined with parchment paper. Bake until done, watching that they do not brown, or they will taste bitter. Allow to cool. Coat with tempered couverture.

POLOS

Makes about 100

For the cookies:

1 cup + 2 tablespoons butter

1¼ cups confectioners' sugar, 2 teaspoons vanilla sugar

pinch of salt, 2 eggs, 1 egg yolk, 1 cup flour, sifted

For the filling:

2 oz couverture, 9 oz nougat, extra light

about 5 tablespoons unsweetened condensed milk

The crescents call for quite a lot of handling, and shaping requires a fair amount of time, especially for the novice. A quick and easy method is to roll out the dough to ¼ inch thick and then cut out or stamp out shapes. Bake, cool, and cover with couverture.

You will also need:

baking sheets, wax paper (not parchment paper)

tempered couverture to decorate

Preheat the oven to 325°F. To make the cookies, cream the butter with the confectioners' sugar, vanilla sugar, and salt. Add the eggs and egg yolk one at a time. Trickle in the flour while stirring. Line the baking sheets with wax paper (not parchment paper, or the batter will spread). Spoon the batter into a pastry bag with a round tip. Pipe into mounds, spaced well apart. Bake for 12–15 minutes, watching that they do not brown. Allow to cool, then turn half the cookies upside down.

To make the filling, melt the couverture over hot water, mix with the nougat, and temper at 95°F. Also temper the condensed milk at 95°F. Mix just a little of it into the nougat-couverture. This will make it harder. Continue to add small amounts of condensed milk; the mixture will coagulate. As you whisk briskly and add more milk, it will bind again. Spoon it into a pastry bag with a round tip and pipe onto the upturned cookies. Top with the other half. Using a paper pastry bag, pipe lines of tempered couverture over the tops.

NEROS

Makes about 100
For the cookies:
1 cup + 2 tablespoons butter
1¼ cups confectioners' sugar, ¼ cup cocoa powder
2 teaspoons vanilla sugar, pinch of salt, 2 eggs
1¾ cups flour
For the filling:
1¼ cups cream, 10 oz couverture, chopped

To make Neros:

Line a baking sheet with wax paper. Using a round tip, pipe mounds spaced well apart.

Preheat the oven to 325°F and bake for 12–15 minutes until light brown. Check the firmness after about 10 minutes.

You will also need:
wax paper (not parchment paper), baking sheets

Prepare the batter with the cocoa powder, pipe, and bake as for the Polos and as shown in the picture sequence. To make the filling, bring the cream to a boil, and add the couverture, stirring until it melts. Place a hand blender in the mixture, switch on, and blend thoroughly, using a circular motion. Do not allow the blender to come to the top, or it will trap air bubbles. Pour into a flat container to a depth of 1 inch. Cool until it is ready for serving. Do not beat until frothy, or the creaminess will be lost. Finish the Neros as shown in the pictures. Store at 65°F.

Leave the mounds on the paper (do not invert). Using a star tip, pipe ganache cream onto half of the mounds.

Top neatly with the remaining halves, ensuring that no cream oozes out at the sides.

With hazelnuts and almonds

New and old, plain and fancy: cookies with hazelnuts, almond macaroons with chocolate

CHOCOLATE COOKIES

These cookies taste delicious, and are quick and easy to make. Take care with the couverture. It should be chopped as finely as possible. If any pieces are too large, strain them out and chop up small.

Makes about 130
¾ cup soft butter, 1¼ cups brown sugar
¼ teaspoon salt, scraped contents of 1 vanilla bean
2 eggs at room temperature
2½ cups flour, ½ teaspoon baking powder
1¼ cups roasted hazelnuts
6 oz finely chopped couverture
You will also need:
baking sheets, parchment paper

Preheat the oven to 350°F. Cream the butter and sugar. Add the salt and vanilla. Add the eggs one at a time. Mix the flour with the baking powder, nuts, and couverture, and stir into the creamed mixture. Spoon the batter immediately into a pastry bag with a round tip and pipe onto baking sheets lined with parchment paper. The cookies will spread quite a bit, so space them out well. Bake for about 12 minutes until they are light brown. Remove from the baking sheet with a palette knife while still warm.

CHOCOLATE AND RASPBERRY RINGS

Makes about 40
For the cookies:
2¼ cups flour, 10 tablespoons butter, 3 egg yolks
1¾ cups confectioners' sugar, 2 oz couverture, grated
1 cup ground roasted hazelnuts, pinch of salt
grated zest of 1 lemon
For the filling:
⅔ cup raspberry jam

For the icing:
7 oz milk chocolate couverture, tempered
To decorate:
1 cup caramelized hazelnuts (see page 102)
You will also need:
baking sheets, parchment paper

Preheat the oven to 350°F. To make the cookies, knead all the ingredients together. Wrap in plastic wrap and refrigerate for 1–2 hours. Roll the dough out on a floured work surface to ⅛ inch thick. Stamp out rings with an external diameter of 2 inches and an internal diameter of ¾ inch. Place on baking sheets lined with parchment paper and bake for about 12 minutes, until light brown. Allow to cool.

Spoon the raspberry jam into a paper pastry bag and pipe a circle of jam onto half of the cookies. Top with the remaining halves. Dip the tops of the cookies into tempered milk chocolate couverture and sprinkle with caramelized hazelnuts.

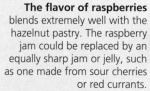

The flavor of raspberries blends extremely well with the hazelnut pastry. The raspberry jam could be replaced by an equally sharp jam or jelly, such as one made from sour cherries or red currants.

Simple almond macaroons (see the recipe for Macaroon Balls on page 132) can also be used just as effectively for this combination of flavors. Other tart jams can be used too.

RED CURRANT MACAROONS

Sweet macaroons with tangy jam and a bitter but gently melting chocolate icing make a popular treat.

Makes about 30

1 recipe Chocolate Macaroons (see below)

½ cup red currant jam, 2 teaspoons glucose syrup

You will also need:

tempered couverture for dipping

Bring the red currant jam to a boil with the glucose syrup and cool to the point where it can be safely spooned into a large paper pastry bag .

Line a baking sheet with parchment paper. Place half of the macaroons upside down and pipe with a large dab of jam. Top with the remaining macaroons halves and press gently together. When cold, dip half of each macaroon into tempered couverture. Scrape off the surplus on the side of the bowl. Place on parchment paper to set.

CHOCOLATE MACAROONS

This macaroon recipe is easy and relatively quick, if you do not count the resting time. To succeed, they must be really dry on the surface, and for this they are best left to rest overnight.

Makes about 60

1 lb almond paste, 1¾ cups sugar

¾ cup ground unblanched almonds

¼ teaspoon cinnamon, 5 egg whites

2 oz chopped couverture, sugar for dusting

You will also need:

baking sheets, parchment paper

Put the almond paste, sugar, almonds, cinnamon, and 1 egg white into a bowl and knead together. Work in the rest of the egg whites one at a time until the mixture is completely smooth and can be piped. Then mix in the chopped couverture. Using a pastry bag with a round tip, pipe 1-inch mounds onto baking sheets lined with parchment paper, spacing them well apart. Dust the macaroons loosely with a little sugar and put aside to dry overnight.

The next day, preheat the oven to 325°F. Bake the macaroons for 12–15 minutes. Leave the oven door slightly ajar to allow the steam to escape. Cool for a few minutes and then remove them from the baking sheet with the parchment paper. Turn over and brush the underside of the parchment with water. After a few minutes the macaroons will lift easily from the paper.

Macaroons and chocolate

A successful variation on a classic cookie

Macaroons and chocolate go together well. The macaroons can either be covered all over with couverture or have one half dipped. A chocolate cream filling is also a splendid addition, as the bitter ganache cream mixed with butter in this recipe shows.

GANACHE HATS
Makes 50–60
For the macaroons:
1 lb almond paste, 1¾ cups sugar
¾ cup ground blanched almonds
5 egg whites
grated zest of ½ lemon
2 oz couverture, finely grated
For the filling:
⅔ cup cream, 9 oz couverture
¼ cup butter, 2 tablespoons dark rum
To decorate:
chopped pistachios
You will also need:
1 lb tempered couverture for dipping
baking sheets, parchment paper

Preheat the oven to 325°F. Prepare the macaroon batter as shown in the picture sequence. It should be firm but capable of being piped. Line the baking sheets with parchment paper. Allow the hats to dry out well before baking. Bake for 12–15 minutes with the door slightly ajar. The macaroons should have a nice crust on the outside but be soft inside. Remove from the baking sheet with the parchment paper, turn over, and brush the underside of the

The cocoa-coated macaroon balls look attractive placed in brightly colored paper cases like the almond paste potatoes on page 110. These prevent the fingers becoming covered with cocoa. The balls can also be dipped in tempered couverture and then rolled in finely crushed almond croquant.

To dip the ganache hats in couverture: Grasp the macaroon with three fingers and, with the cream side down, dip into the couverture as far as the macaroon. Allow to drip, invert, and place on a wire rack. Sprinkle with pistachios. The hats can also be totally covered in couverture by dipping them on a fork.

To make the macaroon batter: Mix the almond paste with the sugar and ground almonds. Stir in the egg whites, one at a time, followed by the grated lemon zest and the grated couverture.

Using a pastry bag with a round tip, pipe into mounds spaced well apart. Dry for 4–5 hours, or overnight.

After baking, apply the cream to the base of the macaroon, shaping it to a point by turning your hand. Set aside to cool.

MACAROON BALLS
WITH BRANDY CHERRIES

Makes about 30

For the macaroons:

1 lb almond paste

1⅞ cups sugar

5–6 egg whites

grated zest of 1 lemon

For the filling:

1 recipe ganache cream filling (see page 132) made with cognac instead of rum

30 Morello cherries preserved in cognac

To decorate:

4 oz couverture, grated, cocoa powder

You will also need:

baking sheets, parchment paper

Make the macaroon batter as shown in the pictures. Line the baking sheets with parchment paper. Spoon the batter into a pastry bag with a round tip and pipe mounds about 1½ inches in diameter, spaced well apart. Allow to dry for 4–5 hours or overnight.

Preheat the oven to 325°F. Bake the macaroons for 12–15 minutes, leaving the door slightly ajar. Remove the macaroons from the baking sheets with the parchment. Turn over and brush the underside of the parchment with water, so that you can remove the macaroons easily. Place half of the macaroons upside down on a baking sheet. Beat the filling until creamy, add the cognac a little at a time, and spoon into a pastry bag with a round tip. Pipe a ring of filling onto the macaroons. Place a well-drained brandy cherry in the center. Top with the remaining macaroon halves to form a ball. Refrigerate until firm. Coat the balls thinly with the rest of the cream filling. Dip immediately into the grated couverture and dust with cocoa powder.

parchment with water so that you can remove the macaroons easily.

To make the filling, bring the cream to a boil and add the chopped couverture, stirring constantly until it melts. Do not let the cream return to a boil. Cool, stirring from time to time to prevent a skin forming. When it is almost cold, pour the cream into a bowl and whip until the volume has at least doubled. Beat the butter, until it has the same consistency as the cream, and stir in. Add the rum a little at a time.

Stars and honey cakes

Classic Christmas cookies, with two examples of how the taste of honey cakes can be enhanced with fruit

CHOCOLATE AND CINNAMON STARS

Makes about 80

1½ cups confectioners' sugar

1 cup ground almonds, 1 cup ground hazelnuts

4 oz almond paste, 3 oz couverture, melted

⅓ cup honey, 2 egg whites, 2 tablespoons cocoa powder

scraped contents of 1 vanilla bean

¾ teaspoon ground cinnamon

For the meringue icing:

2 egg whites, confectioners' sugar as required

You will also need:

metal or wooden strips, ⅜ inch deep

baking sheets, parchment paper

1¼ cups ground almonds for rolling out

Preheat the oven to 325°F. To make the dough, mix all the ingredients together. Roll out between metal or wooden strips (see page 126) on a board sprinkled with ground almonds.

To make the icing, use a wooden spoon to stir the egg whites, adding confectioners' sugar until the consistency is thick, but still soft enough to be slightly runny. Coat the rolled-out dough with the icing and stamp out star shapes, using a cookie cutter dipped in hot water. Place on a baking sheet lined with parchment paper and bake for 10 minutes. The icing should turn a light yellowish brown. Gather up any surplus dough, mix with a little of the ground almonds, and roll out again.

HONEY CAKE

Makes 2

1¾ cups flour, 2 cups rye flour

2 tablespoons water, scant ½ cup sugar, 2 teaspoons vanilla sugar

¾ cup honey, 2 egg yolks, 2 teaspoons cinnamon

pinch each of cloves and ground cardamom

pinch of nutmeg

grated zest of ½ lemon

1 teaspoon ammonium bicarbonate, ½ teaspoon potassium carbonate (available from drugstores or specialist suppliers, see page 234)

4 teaspoons milk, ¼ cup butter

You will also need:

two 10 x 12-inch baking sheets, parchment paper

Prepare the dough a day in advance. Sift the two types of flour. Bring the water to a boil with the sugar and vanilla sugar. Add the honey, and stir until dissolved. Use an electric mixer to work the flour into the hot liquid until it becomes a smooth dough (by hand, this can take up to 30 minutes). Allow to cool.

Combine the egg yolks with the spices and lemon zest, and mix into the dough. Sift the ammonium bicarbonate and the potassium carbonate separately,

and dissolve each in 2 teaspoons milk. Work them into the dough separately (not simultaneously as acid and alkali will neutralize each other). Finally work in the butter.

The next day, preheat the oven to 325°F. On a floured work surface, roll out the dough to ⅛ inch thick. Place on baking sheets lined with parchment paper. Prick with a fork. Bake for 14 minutes. Allow to cool and turn out. Finish one cake with plum jam and the other with raspberry jam, as described in the following recipes.

SLIVOVITZ HONEY BARS

Makes about 90
½ recipe Honey Cake
To moisten and spread:
5 teaspoons Slivovitz (plum brandy)
5 teaspoons sugar syrup, ⅓ cup plum jam
For the almond paste coating:
4 oz almond paste
2 tablespoons Slivovitz (plum brandy)
You will also need:
prunes to decorate
tempered couverture for icing

Make the honey cake as described in the recipe above. Mix the sugar syrup and plum brandy. Bring the plum jam to a boil. Moisten the cake with the brandy mixture and spread with the jam. Allow to

dry a little. Meanwhile, work the Slivovitz into the almond paste, then spread on top of the jam and refrigerate overnight. Using a knife dipped in hot water, cut the cake into bars ¾ x 1½ inches. Place a small piece of prune on each and coat with tempered couverture.

RASPBERRY HONEY BARS

Makes about 90
½ recipe Honey Cake
To moisten and spread:
5 teaspoons white raspberry brandy mixed with 5 teaspoons sugar syrup
⅓ cup raspberry jam, heated and strained
For the almond paste coating:
4 oz almond paste, 2 tablespoons white raspberry brandy
You will also need:
tempered milk chocolate couverture, halved pistachios

Make the honey cake as described above. Mix the raspberry brandy and sugar syrup, and spread on the cake. Spread the hot jam on top. Allow to dry a little. Meanwhile, work the raspberry brandy into the almond paste, then spread on top of the jam and refrigerate overnight. Using a knife dipped in hot water, cut the cake into bars ¾ x 1½ inches. Cover with tempered milk chocolate couverture and decorate with pistachio halves.

Light kisses

Chocolate provides a welcome counterpoint to the sweetness of the meringue

Ideally, leave meringues in the oven overnight so the small foamy bubbles can dry out thoroughly.

MERINGUE PASTE

5 egg whites
1¾ cups confectioners' sugar
pinch of salt
You will also need:
baking sheets, parchment paper

Preheat the oven to 125°F. In a completely grease-free bowl, mix the egg whites, the confectioners' sugar and salt. Take a saucepan large enough to hold the bowl and fill with water to a level that will not overflow when the bowl is placed in it. Heat the water. Whip the egg whites over the hot water until stiff. As soon as the mixture starts to feel warm — around 104–122°F — remove from the heat and whip slowly until cold. If using a hand mixer, use medium speed.

Line the baking sheets with parchment paper. Pipe the meringue onto the sheets using a round or star tip. Bake for at least 8 hours, leaving the door slightly ajar for the steam to escape.

NOUGAT KISSES

Makes about 30
1 recipe Meringue Paste
10 oz dark hazelnut or almond nougat
1 lb tempered couverture
chopped pistachios

Make meringues as described above, using a star tip to drop the paste onto the parchment paper. Melt the dark hazelnut or almond nougat over hot water, cool to 86°F, and spoon into a paper pastry bag. Pipe nougat onto half of the meringue drops and cover with the other half. Dip the tops in tempered couverture; you will use about half the couverture, but the full amount is needed to make dipping easy. Place on parchment paper and sprinkle with chopped pistachios.

RUM AND GANACHE TONGUES

Makes about 50
1 recipe Meringue Paste
For the rum and ganache cream filling:
7 oz milk chocolate couverture
3½ fl oz cream
2 teaspoons glucose syrup
3 tablespoons dark rum
You will also need:
tempered couverture for coating

Make the meringues as described above, using a round tip to pipe the paste into tongue shapes in rows. Mix together all of the ingredients to make a ganache cream filling as shown on page 156 and mix with the rum. Spoon into a pastry bag with a round tip and pipe a strip of cream onto half of the tongues. Top with the other tongues and allow the filling to harden. Dip the ends at an angle into the tempered couverture and place on parchment paper to dry.

ALMOND SOUFFLÉ

Eat these almond meringue confections without delay, at their peak of perfection. The ganache is best stored at 60–64°F. If kept in the refrigerator, bring up to room temperature before serving.

Makes 50

6 egg whites, scant ½ cup sugar
2 heaped tablespoons cornstarch
1¾ cups blanched ground almonds
1½ cups confectioners' sugar
For the ganache cream filling:
1 cup cream, 9 oz couverture, chopped
You will also need:
baking sheets, parchment paper
flaked almonds

Preheat the oven to 325°F. Whip the egg whites with the sugar and cornstarch until stiff. Mix the almonds with the confectioners' sugar and blend into the meringue. Continue as shown in the pictures below. Pipe into mounds and bake for about 15 minutes, leaving the door slightly ajar.

To make the cream filling, bring the cream to a

These small, light cookies can also be made with other chocolate fillings. They could be filled with a bitter chocolate butter cream or the ganache cream could be flavored with rum, Cointreau or kirsch. They also taste good when they are half-dipped in tempered couverture.

Spoon the almond soufflé mixture into a pastry bag with a large round tip and pipe into mounds about 1½ inches high on a baking sheet lined with parchment paper. Sprinkle generously with flaked almonds.

boil, add the couverture, stirring constantly until it melts. Place a hand blender in the cream, switch on, and mix thoroughly, using a circular motion. Pour into a flat-bottomed pan or baking dish so that it cools uniformly. Leave at room temperature to set until it can be piped. Do not stir the cream, as this would destroy the fine texture. Spoon into a pastry bag with a star tip and pipe rosettes onto one half of the almond meringues. Top with the other half and allow to set.

MOCHA BEANS

All meringues, minus the cream fillings, can be stored in an airtight container for 2–3 weeks.

Makes about 50
1 recipe Meringue Paste (see page 136)
2 teaspoons instant coffee powder, 2 teaspoons cognac
For the mocha cream:
½ cup cream, 1 tablespoon glucose syrup
2 tablespoons instant coffee powder
6 oz couverture, chopped, 4 teaspoons cognac
tempered milk chocolate couverture

Prepare the meringue paste according to the basic recipe. At the end, stir in the instant coffee powder

dissolved in the cognac. Using a pastry bag with a round tip, pipe kidney bean shapes onto parchment paper and dry overnight.

To make the cream filling, bring the cream and glucose syrup to a boil and stir in the coffee powder. Add the couverture, stirring until it melts. Place a hand blender in the cream, switch on, and mix thoroughly, using a circular motion. Allow to cool. Beat in the cognac. Using a pastry bag and a round tip, pipe the filling onto the beans. Assemble the beans and dip one end in the tempered couverture.

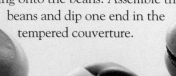

Next to the ordinary bar of chocolate, individual chocolate candies are the true province of chocolate. Experts have applied themselves so single-mindedly and assiduously to this branch of chocolate production that it is reasonable to ask whether it makes sense to produce handmade chocolate candies in small batches, and whether the enthusiastic amateur should even attempt to do so.

The answer is a resounding "No" if such candies are compared with commercial products for their storage quality. However, small-scale production of chocolate candies, be it by a professional running a small business or by an amateur making them as gifts for family and friends, has the advantage over mass production of being absolutely fresh, with no worries about the "sell by" date. The use of choice fresh ingredients ensures high quality; preservatives are not required, and fillings do not have to be sealed with couverture to preserve their shelf-life.

Producing such tiny delicacies can give great creative satisfaction, particularly when people admire the appearance and comment on the exquisite taste of a delicate ganache cream filling or a truffle made with fresh butter.

The history of chocolate candy

In countries and eras in which the sensuous pleasures of life were and are a focus, sweetmeats formed a highlight of the day or meal. In others, where self-denial was a moral duty, people would reward themselves with something sweet, which took on the character of a minor sin. During periods of war or want, sweetmeats used to represent the dream of a return to normal life, of the freedom to eat and drink when and what one chose. For us, sweet goods can be a temptation between the twin goals of staying slim and the prestige afforded by the consumption of luxury items. Unlimited freedom comes at a price.

A little sugar with milk and cocoa, a piece of chocolate — these simple ingredients contain more power and magic than you might think. At moments of the deepest concentration, the senses can focus on the sweetness of chocolate melting on the tongue, providing a moment's breathing space from the intellectual exertions, a pleasure that elevates and enriches the circulation with substances that are essential to our brain cells.

Praline: the first coated candy

The chemistry of the filled chocolate was not yet available to the inspired chef who helped the praline to find a niche at the highest level and at an important moment in world history. At the end of the seventeenth century, the "Eternal Imperial Diet" in Regensburg attempted to control the fate of the 350 or so individual states that comprised Germany after the Thirty Years' War. The government tried to alleviate the tedious business of government and administration with pleasurable distractions. One of these was offered by the German chef serving the French field marshal César de Choiseul, Comte du Plessis-Praslin, who had been sent to Regensburg as an observer by Louis XIV of France. He created an "Imperial Diet Confection," which consisted chiefly of almonds or hazelnuts with a sugary coating, and which he named "praline" in honor of his commander.

Today, of course, chocolate has replaced the plain sugar coating, and there are far more varieties of center than there once were. Many

chocolate candies can be shaped, molded, filled, or coated by industrial processes, but individuality, imagination, and skill can still combine to produce something unique and special.

In the nineteenth century confectioners' shops were a popular meeting place for the whole of society, as this French etching from 1810 shows. Even at this early date, the small sweet delights were displayed on decorative plates and trays.

Chocolate candies are classified and named according to how they are made. Chocolate-coated candies are the originals. Today, as formerly in Regensburg, the centers are produced first. Made of hazelnuts or almonds, croquant or nougat, cream filling or almond paste, they pass on a conveyor belt to an enrobing machine and through a curtain of liquid chocolate. The confection instantly becomes recognizable as a chocolate candy. Depending on the assortment, a scroll of a different colored chocolate may be deposited on top, the machine may cover them with a decorative pattern, beads of sugar may be sprinkled over them, or an almond may be placed on top. All that remains is for them to pass through a cooling tunnel to harden, and then it's straight into the box!

In Regensburg there was no cooling tunnel, but today's home chocolate-maker at least has a refrigerator, a modern convenience far beyond the dreams of the imperial chef.

Filled chocolate candy

Another method of making chocolate candy is to prepare a hollow chocolate mold and fill it with a liquid or cream fillings. First, liquid chocolate is poured into the small compartments of metal or plastic molds. The molds are so cold that the chocolate hardens instantly around the sides. After a specified period of time, the molds are inverted, the surplus chocolate runs out into a special receptacle, and the remainder hardens. Then the filling is put into the shell, and the candies pass on a conveyor belt under a dispenser that puts a dab of liquid chocolate on top of the filling to form the back. One of the charms of making these chocolate candies is that there are no hard and fast rules to fetter or limit the imagination; working with chocolate gives total freedom.

The secret of chocolate figures

Chocolate figures such as the Easter bunny and Santa Claus are generally hollow. Originally, chocolate was poured into a closed mold. With the right amount of liquid chocolate and dexterous handling, the chocolate would set evenly and permeate every hollow and coat every curve. Today, these and other figures, as well as Easter eggs, are made in two halves, each half being made like a hollow chocolate. The edges are then heated gently and the two halves are pressed together.

Layered chocolate candies and truffles

Layered chocolate candies are the most intricate confections to make. Different colors of chocolate and nougat mixtures are layered on top of each other.

"View of a modern chocolate shop" is the caption for this picture in a book on the history of chocolate published in 1931. What looked modern then has a rather antiquated appearance now, but the status of chocolate is as high as ever.

When cold, they are cut into cubes or other decorative shapes. The real art lies in combining flavors that harmonize and complement each other. Layered chocolate candies are, in general, not coated, so that the eye can feast on the promises held out by the various colored layers.

For many chocolate lovers, the truffle represents the crowning glory. Officially, it is often referred to as a "chocolate-type preparation of a particularly high quality," just as the fungus for which it is named is sometimes referred to as a mushroom of particularly high quality. Truffles reveal the true art of getting the mixture right — if the ingredients are not of "a particularly high quality," they do not melt in the mouth and leave a craving for another bite; instead, they leave a film on the teeth, which obstinately refuses to go away.

Sweet anticipation

The best chocolate candies were and still are the products of a highly developed craft. Anyone can enjoy them as they are: sweet morsels, which tempt and tickle our taste buds from the first contact of our lips with the cool, smooth surface, where even this light touch is enough to give a hint of the flavor; through the first bite into the hard brown shell, which has to be breached like the wall around the promised land to release the filling; to the greatest pleasure, when all these tastes melt and mingle in our mouth. For some people, the pleasure is increased by the anticipation, and they are happy to deliberate over which candy to select from the choice presented to them while others wait their turn more or less patiently.

How well chocolate candies go with a cup of strong coffee! How wonderful they look heaped up in profusion in elegant dishes to decorate the table. How well they round off a dinner — a feast for the eyes as well as the palate. And so they have become a ritual in good restaurants: With the coffee comes a silver, crystal, or porcelain stand, filled with miniature chocolates, often astonishing creations of almonds, hazelnuts and chocolate, fruits and spongecake, nougat and croquant. Welcome and wonderful in their own right, they may also arouse images of, and a nostalgia for, a time long past, while their consumption might leave us feeling that it is the present we should treasure.

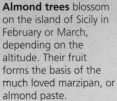

Almond trees blossom on the island of Sicily in February or March, depending on the altitude. Their fruit forms the basis of the much loved marzipan, or almond paste.

Hazelnuts and almonds

Indispensable ingredients to go with chocolate

The seeds of dry-skinned fruits are commonly called "nuts," although botanically this is not correct. Most of them are actually "indehiscent fruits," which means that the shell has to rot or be removed before the seed is released. The only true nut is the hazelnut, in which the three seed skins aggregate to become a hard, woody shell. Whether they are fruits or seeds, we recognize them as nuts, and value them in baking and confectionery for their flavor and texture. **Almonds** (*Prunus amygdalus*) are the most popular, not only on account of the many forms in which they are sold, but also because they are used to make almond paste, or marzipan. The heart-shaped **hazelnut** (*Corylus avellana*) keeps well. Its fat content is 50 percent lower than the almond's, and so it does not turn rancid as quickly. The plump round or oval **walnut** (*Juglans regia, J. nigra*) contains up to 60 percent of unsaturated fats as well as lots of vitamins and minerals. The hard white flesh of the **coconut** (*Cocos nucifera*) has a sweetish taste and is used shredded and grated. The light-green **pistachio** (*Pistacia vera*) contains very oily seeds, which have an almond-like flavor and are useful for decorating cakes and candies. The **brazil nut** (*Bertholletia excelsa*) also has a flavor reminiscent of almonds and is often used as an almond substitute. The **pecan nut** (*Carya illinoinensis*) is closely related to the walnut, but has a slightly sweeter taste. The **cashew nut** (*Anacardium occidentale*) is kidney-shaped, and grows on a thick, fleshy stem called a cashew apple. Cashew nuts are skinned and roasted to remove their sharp taste. The **macadamia nut** (*Macadamia integrifolia*) is the tasty seed of a tree cultivated chiefly in Hawaii, Australia, and New Zealand. It has a high fat content. The **peanut** (*Arachis hypogea*), the seed of an annual herbaceous legume, is contained in a pod that grows underground. The **Spanish chestnut** (*Castanea sativa*) tastes rather floury when raw, but becomes sweet when cooked.

Macadamia nuts and peanuts are just two of the nuts that combine well with chocolate. Simply covered in chocolate, they are a very popular nibble.

Whole almonds, blanched. They must be dry before they can be used for croquant or a decoration.

Slivered almonds. Roasted, they are used chiefly for almond clusters.

Almond halves, blanched. They are a simple decoration to top cakes and tortes.

Chopped almonds can be used in batters, doughs, croquant, and decorations.

Flaked almonds are used to make fine croquant, and are roasted for sprinkling on tortes and small cakes.

Ground almonds. Ground with or without their skins, they can be used in batters, doughs, and fillings.

Chopped pistachios. Their green color makes them especially good for decorating chocolate cakes and candies.

Shelled hazelnuts. Their fine taste harmonizes very well with chocolate in cakes and tortes.

Almond clusters

Couverture and almonds — a quick and easy way to make chocolate candies

The basis for this favorite confection is slivered almonds, which are roasted on a spotlessly clean baking sheet in a preheated 400°F oven until they are light brown. Turn the almonds from time to time with a spatula or wooden spoon so that they brown evenly. Remove from the oven and allow to cool.

The skill required to make the clusters consists of nothing more than mixing almonds with tempered couverture. The almonds should be at least room temperature, but no warmer than the couverture — 77°F is ideal. Use a small saucepan, which should also be warm.

The ratio of almonds to couverture should be at least 2:1. It is advisable to mix only small quantities, so that the couverture does not harden as you work. First place a small quantity of almonds in the saucepan and add sufficient couverture to coat them, but not so much that they are swimming in it. Using a teaspoon, drop small mounds onto parchment paper. When this quantity is used up, prepare another.

ALMOND AND ORANGE CLUSTERS

Other candied or preserved fruit can be used too.

Makes ½ lb

1 cup slivered almonds, 1 tablespoon sugar syrup
6½ teaspoons confectioners' sugar, ⅓ cup candied orange peel, minced
4 oz tempered milk chocolate couverture

Preheat the oven to 375°F. Mix the slivered almonds with the sugar syrup. Spread on a baking sheet and sift the confectioners' sugar on top. Roast until brown, turning frequently. Cool the almonds to 77°F and mix with the candied orange peel. Add to the couverture in batches and drop into mounds on parchment paper or into paper cases. The mixture can also be placed in chocolate shells that have been prepared in advance.

Croquant

Nuts mixed with melted sugar is one of the largest groups of products in confectionery

What we refer to as "croquant" is known in some countries as "nougat." In France, for example, it is known more precisely as "brown nougat," in contrast to white nougat, which is called "*montélimar.*"

The most important aspect of making croquant is melting the sugar as thinly as possible to coat the nuts completely but without letting it turn too dark. A useful addition here is lemon juice (¼ cup to 2¼ pounds of sugar) or glucose syrup (maximum of 10 percent). The ratio of whole nuts to sugar is 1:1. If flaked or chopped nuts are used, the ratio can rise to 1:2, depending on the increased surface area.

Croquant chocolates. Oil-coated whole or roughly chopped nuts are cooked into croquant and placed in small mounds on an oiled sheet. After cooling they are dipped in couverture. The picture below shows whole almonds with dark couverture, whole hazelnuts with milk chocolate couverture and coarsely chopped macadamia nuts coated with dark couverture.

To make croquant:

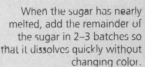

Heat half of the sugar with the lemon juice. If cooking on gas, keep the flame below the level of the sugar, otherwise it will darken at the edges and burn.

When the sugar has nearly melted, add the remainder of the sugar in 2–3 batches so that it dissolves quickly without changing color.

Always ensure that the flame is below the sugar level. Boil until the sugar dissolves but does not darken.

Warm the flaked almonds a little, add to the melted sugar, and stir in immediately until they are completely coated with the sugar.

Turn out onto a work surface oiled with a neutral vegetable oil and spread so that the croquant does not harden into a single mass.

Using a well-oiled rolling pin, roll out into a slab while the croquant is still hot. The depth to which it is rolled will depend on its subsequent use.

Crushed croquant is made by pounding the rolled-out slab with a meat hammer or weight. Place a ring around the croquant so that it does not fly off in all directions. As a semi-finished product, it has a lot of uses in patisserie and confectionery. It is an ingredient in batters and fillings, and is used for decoration.

Pure nougat

Slicing, cutting, coating — the easiest way to make chocolate candy

Nougat is a water-free paste, made from almonds or other nuts, sugar, and couverture, which can be sliced and shaped. After ganache and almond paste, it is the most important basic product in making chocolate candy. In France and many other countries, nougat paste is referred to as "*gianduja*." The basic recipe is very simple:

1 part almonds or other nuts
1 part sugar
1 part couverture

The almonds are roasted to the desired degree of browning. Hazelnuts and other nuts, such as pine nuts, brazil nuts, peanuts, and walnuts, have to be roasted to the point where they can be skinned. The roasted nuts are grated, mixed with sugar, and ground until oily. The mixture is combined with melted couverture and allowed to cool. A second fine grinding imparts the characteristic creamy texture.

The preparation of nougat paste remains the preserve of the professional, since the equipment required would be found only in a well-equipped confectionery. But confectioners, too, often obtain their nougat paste from commercial sources, as these are really the only producers capable of supplying the top-quality, fine-textured products required in making candy.

NOUGAT CHOCOLATES

Nougat is a finished product that can be eaten as is. To make an individual chocolate candy, it can be coated with tempered couverture and decorated. Nougat chocolate candies are very easy to make, and the industry offers a large palette of flavors with which to work. Three examples are shown on this page: squares of dark hazelnut nougat, hearts of dark almond nougat, and rectangles of nougat with cream.

To make individual candies, cut the nougat paste into slices ⅜ inch thick, and then into oblongs, squares, or triangles. It is very economic, as there is practically no waste. If the candies are stamped out with a cutter (for example, hearts, ovals, rings, and so on) the scraps can be used in other fillings for confectionery or patisserie.

Almond paste

Only the best quality is good enough for chocolate candies

There is little point in making your own almond paste, as it is not possible to match the quality of the commercial product in the domestic kitchen.

The basic ingredients of almond paste are almonds and sugar in the ratio of 2:1. Fresh blanched almonds are coarsely ground with the sugar. The almond and sugar mixture is placed in a copper pan set in a *bain-marie* and cooked, while being stirred constantly. When the mixture leaves the sides of the pan and feels dry, it is removed from the heat and cooled as quickly as possible. Sugar syrup is then added and the mixture is ground as finely as possible.

Almond paste has a low sugar content (35 percent maximum), which allows the almond taste to be fully appreciated, and it can be used without additional flavorings. Almond paste also has a soft consistency; if it is to be used for making shapes, it

To dip solid almond paste pieces:

Drop the almond paste pieces into the tempered couverture and immerse fully, using a dipping fork.

Lift out each piece on the dipping fork and shake off the surplus.

Remove the residual couverture by scraping against the side of the bowl or against a piece of wire stretched across the bowl.

The ingredients for these almond paste chocolates are: 1 lb almond paste, 1 cup confectioners' sugar and 4 teaspoons kirsch.

To work the confectioners' sugar into the almond paste:

Heap the confectioners' sugar on a work surface. Add the almond paste in pieces and the kirsch.

Use the hands to knead firmly to a smooth dough. This is easy to do with the small proportion of sugar.

Shape the paste into a rectangle and roll out on parchment paper between two strips of wood to the desired thickness (⅜ inch).

Place on a piece of parchment paper. Hold the fork at an angle and slide the chocolate forwards on its edge onto the paper. Withdraw the fork.

Decorate the surface by drawing the prongs of the fork over the couverture while it is still soft.

PISTACHIO ALMOND PASTE
Makes 40

10 oz almond paste
1 cup ground pistachios, 2 tablespoons maraschino
You will also need:
tempered couverture for dipping
halved pistachios to decorate

Work the ingredients into a paste. Roll out between parchment paper to ½ inch thick, as shown in the pictures. Allow to dry. Dip in couverture, as shown on page 148, and top with half a pistachio.

Dipping pistachio almond paste by hand is demonstrated by Leopold Forsthofer. In candy factories, this time-consuming task has long been taken over by machines.

must be combined with confectioners' sugar — in a ratio of 1:2, for example, for modeling figures.

In candy making, quality has the highest priority, and therefore only a minimum amount of confectioners' sugar or the natural sugar content of the almond paste alone is used, to provide the optimum flavor. The centers are of such a delicate consistency that they have to be coated on their undersides with couverture before they can be properly coated all over (see the picture sequence to the right).

ALMOND PASTE CHOCOLATES

Here, almond paste is mixed with confectioners' sugar and lightly flavored with kirsch. The almond paste is then rolled out on a little confectioners' sugar and cut into ¾ x 1½-inch rectangles. The texture is firm enough not to require a base layer of couverture before dipping (see picture sequence, left). After cutting the almond paste pieces, separate them slightly to allow the sides to dry.

Pistachio almond paste:

Work the finely grated pistachios into the almond paste. Add the liqueur a little at a time.

Place two wooden strips, each ⅜ inch thick, on parchment paper. Press the relatively soft paste flat between the strips.

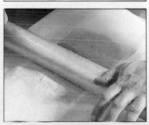

Cover with a piece of parchment paper and roll backward and forward, working from the center.

Remove the upper piece of parchment and coat the surface thinly with couverture. Allow to harden. Remove the wooden strips.

Turn over the slab of almond paste and cut crosswise into 9-inch strips.

Cut lengthwise to make oblongs. Place on parchment paper, separating the pieces to allow them to dry.

Chocolate-covered almond paste

Almond paste with nuts or candied fruit and flavored with liqueur is an outstanding combination

Simple flavored almond paste centers require a thin base layer of couverture, as shown in the pictures accompanying the recipe for pistachio almond paste on page 149. The solid base prevents the dipping fork from sinking into the soft almond paste as the chocolate candies are lifted out of the couverture. This technique is recommended for the recipes on this page; the alternative, which would be to leave the almond paste to dry out until it is firm enough for dipping, would impair the quality.

APRICOT ALMOND PASTE

Use only top-quality dried apricots and nuts for these candies.

Makes about 50 (not illustrated)
⅔ cup dried apricots
14 oz almond paste
½ cup chopped walnuts, 2 tablespoons apricot brandy

WALNUT ALMOND PASTE

Makes about 50
10 oz almond paste, 1 cup ground walnuts
5 teaspoons dark rum
You will also need:
tempered milk chocolate couverture
50 walnut halves

Work the ingredients to a paste. Roll out between strips of wood on parchment paper and spread the underside with milk chocolate couverture(see page 149). Cut out ovals with a cutter. Dip in tempered milk chocolate couverture (see page 148) and place on parchment paper. Decorate with walnut halves.

PINEAPPLE AND MARASCHINO ALMOND PASTE

Makes about 50
½ cup candied pineapple, finely chopped, 3 tablespoons maraschino

You will also need:
tempered milk chocolate couverture

Chop the apricots finely and work into a paste with the other ingredients. Roll out between two strips of wood on parchment paper and spread the underside with milk chocolate couverture. Cut into pieces as shown on page 149. Dip them into milk chocolate couverture, place on parchment paper, and draw a three-pronged dipping fork across the surface, as shown on page 148.

9 oz almond paste
You will also need:
tempered couverture, 3 slices candied pineapple

Soak the pineapple in the maraschino for a day prior to use. Mix with the almond paste and roll out between strips of wood on parchment paper to ⅜ inch thick. Spread the underside with couverture and cut into pieces as shown on page 149. Top each one with a piece of candied pineapple cut to shape. Dip in couverture and place on parchment paper (see page 148).

GINGER AND PECAN ALMOND PASTE
Makes about 50
½ cup crystallized ginger, 6 oz almond paste
¾ cup ground pecans, 2 tablespoons Curaçao
You will also need:
tempered couverture, crystallized ginger

Chop the ginger very finely. Work the almond paste, nuts, and Curaçao to a paste. Roll out between strips of wood on parchment paper. Spread the underside with couverture and cut into pieces as shown on page 149. Dip in tempered couverture and place on parchment paper (see page 148). Decorate each candy with a small piece of crystallized ginger.

COINTREAU ALMOND PASTE
The center of this candy has two components: a gently melting ganache cream filling on an almond paste base flavored with Cointreau.

Makes about 50
For the ganache cream filling:
1 oz dark couverture, 3 oz milk chocolate couverture
3 tablespoons cream

For the almond paste filling:
⅓ cup candied orange peel, very finely chopped
9 oz almond paste, 3 tablespoons Cointreau
You will also need:
tempered milk chocolate couverture
candied orange peel

To make the ganache filling, melt the dark and milk chocolate couvertures together over hot water. Bring the cream to a boil and stir into the couverture. Allow to cool. Place wooden strips on parchment paper as shown on page 149, and spread the ganache filling between them. Refrigerate until set.

To make the almond paste filling, work the candied orange peel into a soft paste with the almond paste and liqueur, and spread over the ganache filling when it has set. Cover with parchment paper, roll until smooth, and cut into large diamond shapes. Dip in tempered milk chocolate couverture and place on parchment paper (see page 148). Decorate with candied orange peel.

Dried fruit candies
With sophisticated fillings or simply coated with couverture

Dried fruits are perfect for transforming into delicate confections with chocolate. As the moisture is extracted from the fruit during the drying process, the sugar content increases to leave a concentrated fruit flavor. When selecting dried fruit, ensure that it has not been stored for a long period, that it smells fresh, has a dry surface, and, as far as possible, is of uniform size.

FRUIT BALLS

Makes about 30

¾ cup dried figs

¾ cup dried apricots

¾ cup dates

¾ cup coarsely chopped walnuts

3½ tablespoons finely chopped candied orange peel

3 tablespoons apricot brandy

You will also need:

tempered milk chocolate couverture for dipping

¼ cup chopped, roasted hazelnuts

Preheat the oven to 250°F. Blanch the figs and apricots briefly and place on a wire rack in the oven for 5 minutes. Mix the figs, apricots, and dates together, and chop not too coarsely. Add the other ingredients and mix into a pliable mass. Cut into three equal pieces. On a work surface dusted with confectioners' sugar, form each piece into a roll 8 inches long. Cut each roll into slices ¾ inch thick. Moisten your hands with a little brandy or apricot brandy and roll the slices into balls. Dip the balls in tempered milk chocolate couverture, place on parchment paper, and sprinkle with hazelnuts.

DATES WITH PISTACHIO ALMOND PASTE CENTERS

Makes 30

30 uniformly sized dates

5 oz almond paste

¼ cup ground pistachios, 1 tablespoon maraschino

You will also need:

tempered milk chocolate couverture

chopped pistachios

Slit the dates lengthwise and remove the stone. Work the almond paste, ground pistachios, and maraschino into a paste. Divide into 30 evenly sized pieces. Fill the dates with this mixture and close the fruit. Dip in tempered couverture, then sprinkle with chopped pistachios.

PRUNES WITH SLIVOVITZ ALMOND PASTE CENTERS

The prunes should be neither too dry nor soft and sticky, as they sometimes are when sold in bags.

Makes 30

5 oz almond paste

2 tablespoons Slivovitz (plum brandy)

30 pitted prunes

You will also need:

tempered couverture

Work the plum brandy into the almond paste a little at a time. Open the lengthwise slit in the prunes and insert a piece of the Slivovitz-flavored almond paste. Close the fruit. Press into the original shape, then dip in tempered couverture.

CHOCOLATE-COVERED DRIED FRUIT

These are neither filled nor made into any special shape. To make them, simply take pieces of dried fruit, trim them if necessary, dip them in tempered couverture, and lift out with a dipping fork. Place them on parchment paper or acetate and make a pattern by drawing the fork across the surface. You can hold fruits such as figs by the stem to dip them. Candied orange peel and preserved ginger are not fruits, of course, but they can be treated in the same way.

Dried pineapple: Dip uniformly sized pieces in tempered couverture, and pipe strands of milk chocolate couverture on top to decorate.

Dried apricots: Dip small choice fruits in milk chocolate couverture.

Dried apple rings: Coat small rings with dark couverture.

Dried mangoes: Cut into pieces, dip in milk chocolate couverture and decorate with circles.

Dried figs: Coat whole fruits with tempered milk chocolate couverture.

Candied orange peel: Not dried fruit, but its peel preserved in sugar. Slice into strips and coat with tempered dark couverture.

Preserved stem ginger: Slice thinly, let dry somewhat, then dip in tempered dark couverture.

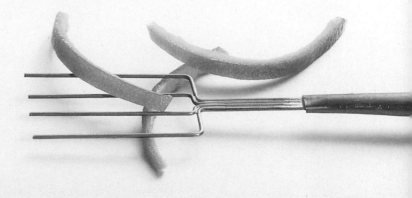

Fresh fruits in chocolate

Easily and quickly prepared, these fruity chocolate candies must be eaten very fresh

The taste of bitter chocolate marries well with that of tangy fruits. Most fresh fruits can be made into candies if they contain sufficient natural sweetness to harmonize with the bitter chocolate. If this is lacking, they need a sugar coating, in the form of fondant, or a base of sweet almond paste before they are dipped.

PHYSALIS

These bittersweet Cape gooseberries are only one example of how quickly a fruity confection can be produced. They can easily be coated in fondant and dipped couverture, and look very attractive if their leaves are left in place.

MANDARIN ORANGES

Divide 3 mandarin oranges into segments, taking care not to damage the membranes. Rest for 2–3 hours. Gently heat 7 oz fondant over hot water to 86°F and flavor with 4 teaspoons Cointreau. Place the mandarin sections on a fork and coat with the fondant. Place on parchment paper and allow to dry. Dip in couverture.

Fresh fruit confectionery tastes best when eaten within two days.

KUMQUATS

Take 30 kumquats and brush under hot water. Dry and halve. On a clean work surface (marble is ideal), knead 7 oz almond paste with 4 teaspoons orange liqueur and ¾ cup confectioners' sugar until smooth. Dust the work surface with confectioners' sugar and roll out the paste to ⅛ inch thick. Cut out rings the same diameter as the kumquats, place half a fruit on each, and press together. Allow to dry for 2 hours, then dip in tempered couverture and place on parchment paper. Sprinkle with grated pistachios.

KIWI FRUIT

Peel 9 oz kiwi fruit (2–3 fruit, depending on size) and cut into slices ¼ inch thick. On a clean work surface, knead 4 oz almond paste with ½ cup confectioners' sugar until smooth. Dust the work surface with confectioners' sugar and roll the paste out to ⅛ inch thick. Spread with couverture. Place the kiwi slices on top and cut out the shape using a knife or cutter. Then coat completely with couverture or dip just the base and sides.

BANANAS

Use small bananas, which tend to be very sweet and taste particularly good with the bitter chocolate coating. Cut the fruit in half lengthwise.If only large bananas are available, cut them in half lengthwise and crosswise. Coat with couverture and sprinkle generously with caramelized hazelnuts (see page 102).

STRAWBERRIES

This fruit requires a sugar coating before dipping in chocolate, as the natural sugar content is too low to develop a good flavor when teamed with the bitter chocolate coating.

Do not wash, but wipe ½ lb strawberries with paper towels. Gently heat 5 oz fondant over hot water to 86°F. Flavor with 4 teaspoons rum. Following the pictures, partially dip the berries in the fondant and set aside to dry. Dip in couverture, place on parchment paper, and allow to set.

STAR FRUIT

Also known as carambola, this fruit has a very attractive shape. Cut the fruit into ¼-inch thick slices and dip in couverture. Sprinkle with granulated sugar.

To dip strawberries:

Grasp the strawberries by the stem and dip in fondant to just short of the top, scrape against the sides of the bowl, and place on parchment paper .

When the fondant has dried (1–2 hours), dip the strawberries in the couverture almost up to the line of fondant.

Ganache

This is the simplest basic cream filling in chocolate-making, but it has the greatest number of variations

Ganache cream is simply magic, and so easy to make. There are only two ingredients, cream and couverture. Mix one part cream to two parts couverture — it can be as simple as that. This ratio gives a filling of medium consistency. It is good for chocolate candies, it can be molded, and it has a balanced flavor. The professional confectioner also adds a little (about 10 percent) glucose syrup to the mixture. This makes the filling easier to work and easier to mold, and it gives it a creamier texture without affecting the taste.

The basic preparation is quite simple. Bring the cream, with or without the glucose syrup, to a boil, add finely chopped couverture, and stir constantly until it melts. The other alternative, as the picture below shows, is to melt the couverture first and stir in the boiled cream. The advantage of this is that the couverture and cream mix together more rapidly and with less effort, but it does not affect the texture or taste.

The consistency of the ganache cream filling depends initially on the ratio of cream to couverture — the higher the proportion of couverture, the firmer the filling — and can be varied according to the use to which it will be put. If it is poured out while still warm and allowed to go cold, it can be cut, like the ganache triangles shown below. The professional calls this a "fatty" ganache. After cooling, and with the addition of other ingredients, such as butter or alcohol, it can be beaten until creamy, and used for spreading or piping.

The hot, boiled cream is stirred into the melted couverture. This is one of two ways of preparing ganache cream. The other method is to melt the chopped couverture in the hot cream.

Cream and ganache triangles:

Place the hand blender in the cream, switch on, and mix using a circular motion.

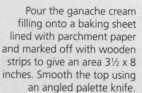

Pour the ganache cream filling onto a baking sheet lined with parchment paper and marked off with wooden strips to give an area 3½ x 8 inches. Smooth the top using an angled palette knife.

Remove from the baking sheet with the parchment. Use a long knife to cut into three strips lengthwise and then diagonally to make 45 triangles.

Using a dipping fork, immerse the triangles in tempered milk chocolate couverture and scrape against the side of the receptacle to remove the surplus. Set on a baking sheet lined with parchment paper.

To decorate, spoon dark couverture into a paper pastry bag and pipe fine strands close together over the triangles.

GANACHE TRIANGLES

In this basic recipe, the ganache is not whipped after cooling.

Makes about 45
10 oz milk chocolate couverture, 3½ fl oz cream
1 teaspoon glucose syrup
You will also need:
parchment paper, 3½ x 8-inch mold or foil strips
tempered milk chocolate couverture for dipping
tempered dark couverture for decoration

Melt the couverture over hot water. Bring the cream to a boil with the glucose syrup and stir into the couverture. Place a hand blender in the hot cream, switch on, and blend thoroughly. Pour into a rectangular mold placed on parchment paper, or onto a flat surface using foil or wooden strips to form the sides, and leave to dry overnight. Cut up and dip in tempered couverture as shown in the picture sequence opposite.

COFFEE CREAM TONGUES

In this recipe, the cold ganache is beaten until creamy.

Makes about 50
⅔ cup cream, 5 teaspoons glucose syrup
1 tablespoon instant coffee powder, 7 oz couverture, finely chopped
You will also need:
parchment paper, baking sheets, tempered couverture
grated white or dark couverture
cocoa powder or confectioners' sugar

Bring the cream to a boil with the glucose syrup. Remove from the heat and stir in the coffee powder. Add the couverture and stir until melted. Place a hand blender in the hot cream, switch on, and blend thoroughly. Allow to cool.

Using a hand mixer, whisk the filling until creamy. Using a pastry bag with a round tip, pipe small tongue-shaped strips onto baking sheets lined with parchment paper and allow to harden. Coat the underside of the tongues thinly with couverture. Dip in tempered couverture. To decorate, sprinkle grated couverture on the coating while it is still soft; use either white couverture dusted with cocoa powder or dark couverture dusted with confectioners' sugar.

Confectioners' sugar or finely grated white couverture — both make a fine contrast with the dark chocolate coating.

Cut with a knife or stamped out with a cutter — both methods are used on the ganache for the chocolate candies shown here. The professional confectioner has special molds for the various shapes that prevent the cream filling from running, but the amateur can use simple rectangular strips of wood covered with foil, as shown on page 156, to produce a uniform depth of filling.

Ganache in all shapes

This versatile cream can be sliced, cut, or piped

AMARETTO GANACHE

Makes about 50
10 oz milk chocolate couverture, 5 tablespoons cream
1 teaspoon glucose syrup, 4½ teaspoons butter, flaked
4 tablespoons amaretto
You will also need:
6 x 12-inch mold
half-moon shaped cutter
tempered couverture
crystallized violets

To make the cream filling, melt the couverture over hot water. Bring the cream to a boil with the glucose syrup and mix into the melted couverture with the butter. Stir in the amaretto. Place a hand blender in the hot cream, switch on, and blend thoroughly. Temper at 83°F and spread in the mold. Allow to harden overnight. The next day, cut out half-moon shapes. Coat with tempered couverture. Draw a fork over each chocolate and decorate with a piece of crystallized violet.

HAZELNUT AND CINNAMON GANACHE

Makes about 50
For the nougat layer:
2 oz milk chocolate couverture
3½ oz extra light hazelnut nougat, chopped
¾ oz unsweetened nougat, chopped
For the cinnamon ganache:
3½ oz milk chocolate couverture, 1½ oz dark couverture
¼ cup cream, ½ teaspoon glucose syrup
¼ teaspoon cinnamon
You will also need:
4 x 12-inch mold
tempered milk chocolate couverture

To make the nougat layer, melt the couverture over hot water and mix with the chopped nougat.

Temper at 83°F and spread in the rectangular mold.

To make the cinnamon ganache, melt the two types of couverture together over hot water. Bring the cream to a boil with the glucose syrup and mix with the couverture. Stir in the cinnamon. Place a hand blender in the hot cream, switch on, and blend thoroughly. Temper at 83°F and spread in the rectangular mold to form a second layer. Allow to harden overnight. Next day cut into 1-inch squares. Dip in tempered milk chocolate couverture. Decorate by drawing a fork across the top.

TEA GANACHE

2½ oz couverture
3½ oz milk chocolate couverture
5 tablespoons milk, 2 tablespoons cream
1 teaspoon glucose syrup
½ cup black tea leaves (Assam or Earl Grey)
1½ teaspoons butter, flaked
You will also need:
6 x 12-inch mold
tempered dark couverture
tempered milk chocolate couverture

Melt both types of couverture over hot water. Bring the milk to a boil with the cream and glucose syrup. Add the tea leaves and allow to infuse for 4 minutes. Strain the liquid through a cheesecloth-lined sieve and squeeze well. Stir into the couverture with the butter. Place a hand blender in the hot cream, switch on, and blend thoroughly. Temper at 83°F. Spread ¼ inch deep in the rectangular mold and allow to harden overnight. The next day, cut into 1-inch squares. Dip in dark couverture. Spoon tempered milk chocolate couverture into a paper pastry bag and pipe diagonal lines on top.

RUM GANACHE

Makes about 50

For the chocolate bases:

milk chocolate couverture

¾-inch diameter round cutter

For the cream filling:

5 oz milk chocolate couverture, 3 oz dark couverture

5 tablespoons cream, 1 teaspoon glucose syrup, ¼ cup dark rum

You will also need:

tempered milk chocolate couverture

tempered white couverture

To make the chocolate bases, temper the milk chocolate couverture, spread thinly onto parchment paper and before it has fully set cut small disks with the cutter. For ease of spreading the ganache filling, do not remove the disks from the paper yet. When they have dried a little, they can be lifted and dipped without difficulty.

To make the ganache cream filling, melt both types of couverture together. Bring the cream to a boil with the glucose syrup and mix into the couverture. Stir in the rum. Place a hand blender in the cream, switch on, and blend thoroughly, using a circular motion. Pour into a receptacle about 1 inch deep and cover with acetate to prevent a skin from forming. Leave until firm but still capable of being piped. Do not stir or process further. Spoon the filling into a pastry bag with a round tip and pipe a mound of cream onto each circle of chocolate. Allow to set overnight. The next day, dip in tempered milk chocolate couverture. Temper the white couverture, spoon into a paper pastry bag and pipe decorative circles on the candies.

Three variations on a theme

The ganache cream, sweetened with fondant and combined with a generous amount of butter, has a particularly delicate creamy texture

COGNAC BALLS
Makes 50
For the ganache cream filling:
⅔ cup cream, 5 teaspoons glucose syrup
7 oz milk chocolate couverture, melted
7 oz dark couverture, melted
¼ cup cognac
For the chocolate bases:
7 oz almond paste
½ cup confectioners' sugar
You will also need:
tempered couverture
6 tablespoons slivered almonds, 2 tablespoons confectioners' sugar

Bring the cream to a boil with the glucose syrup and stir into the melted couverture. Allow to cool.

KIRSCH ROLLS
Makes 50
⅔ cup cream, 1 tablespoon glucose syrup
1 lb milk chocolate couverture, melted
2 oz fondant, ¼ cup kirsch
You will also need:
tempered couverture
tempered milk chocolate couverture

Bring the cream to a boil with the glucose syrup, stir into the couverture, and allow to cool. Melt the fondant over hot water with the kirsch, but do not allow the temperature to go above 89°F. Whisk the cooled cream with a hand mixer and stir in the fondant a little at a time. Continue as shown below. Then dip the candies in tempered couverture and pipe on the milk chocolate couverture decoration.

When the ganache cream is firm but not ice cold, whisk it until creamy, using a whisk or hand mixer. Stir in the cognac a little at a time.

To make the bases, work the confectioners' sugar into the almond paste and continue as shown in the picture sequence at the top of page 161.

Pipe the cream filling onto the bases and coat with tempered couverture as shown in the pictures at the bottom right on page 161. Moisten the slivered almonds with a little water, mix with a little confectioners' sugar and caramelize in a pan, moving them constantly, as shown for the hazelnuts on page 102. Decorate each candy with a slivered almond.

Piping and cutting:

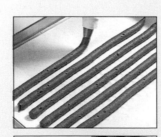

Pipe the beaten ganache cream into rolls, using an pastry bag with a round tip. Line the baking sheet with parchment paper paper.

Refrigerate the cream filling until it has set. Using a warm knife, cut into pieces 1½ inches long.

CROQUANT PEAKS
Makes 50

¾ cup + 2 tablespoons sugar, 2 teaspoons glucose syrup

1 cup flaked almonds, 7 fl oz cream

14 oz couverture, chopped

1 oz fondant, melted, ¼ cup soft butter

You will also need:

tempered couverture

Melt the sugar with the glucose syrup and continue as shown in the picture sequence on page 145. Roll out thinly on a warm work surface and cut out as quickly as possible; despite the warm work surface, croquant hardens very rapidly.

Bring the cream to a boil, add the couverture, stirring constantly until it melts, and allow to cool. Whisk the cream with a hand mixer until frothy. Stir in the melted fondant followed by the soft butter. Spoon into a pastry bag with a star tip and pipe into mounds on the croquant bases, as shown below. Coat with tempered couverture and decorate with small pieces of croquant.

Cognac balls:

Roll out the almond paste to ⅛ inch thick on a work surface dusted with confectioners' sugar and stamp out circles 1 inch in diameter.

Brush the circles thinly with melted couverture and place on the parchment paper, couverture side down.

Whip the ganache mixture until frothy and, using a pastry bag with a round tip, pipe into balls on the almond paste circles.

Croquant peaks:

Place the croquant on a warm surface so that it does not harden too quickly. Use a cutter to stamp out circles 1 inch in diameter.

Attach the croquant circles to the parchment paper with a dab of couverture, so that they do not move as the cream filling is piped on.

Slide the hardened ganache balls into the tempered couverture and immerse them with the aid of a dipping fork. Knock off the surplus.

Stretch a piece of wire over the bowl and tap the balls against the wire several times to knock off the surplus. Set down to dry.

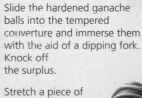

Chocolate truffles

Flavored with amaretto, coffee, or kirsch, these truffles simply melt on the tongue

The name "truffle" reminds us of this candy's resemblance to the exquisite edible fungus, not only in appearance but also in uniqueness of flavor.

The basis of a truffle is usually a ganache cream enriched with butter. The fat permeates the relatively compact filling to produce a delicate and creamy texture. A certain amount of butter — at least 10 percent — is needed to enable the filling to melt on the tongue and to enhance the flavor. The proportion of butter can be increased, of course, if you are not afraid of the calories.

COFFEE TRUFFLES
Makes about 60
For the filling:
½ cup cream
½ cup sugar
2 tablespoons instant coffee powder
5 teaspoons glucose syrup
7 oz dark couverture, chopped into small pieces
6 oz milk chocolate couverture, chopped into small pieces
1 cup butter
You will also need:
tempered dark couverture
1 cup confectioners' sugar

In a separate bowl, whisk the butter until its volume visibly increases.

Make sure that the butter and the chocolate mixture are the same temperature, then gradually stir in the cool chocolate mixture.

Continue beating until the mixture binds to form a homogeneous light brown mass.

Spoon the mixture into a pastry bag with a round tip and pipe bars 2 inches long onto parchment paper. Allow to cool.

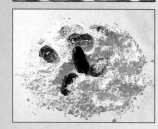

Dip the truffles in couverture, drain well, and roll in confectioners' sugar until completely coated.

To make truffles:

Bring the cream to a boil with the sugar and coffee powder, stirring constantly. Stir in the glucose syrup.

Trickle the chopped couvertures into the hot cream, a little at a time, stirring continuously as they melt.

Amaretto truffle squares are sheer delight, as they melt gently on the tongue.

AMARETTO TRUFFLE SQUARES

⅓ cup cream, scant ½ cup sugar

3 tablespoons amaretto, 10 teaspoons glucose syrup

7 oz dark couverture, chopped

6 oz milk chocolate couverture, chopped, ¾ cup butter

For the almond paste base:

¾ cup confectioners' sugar, sifted

4 teaspoons amaretto, 7 oz almond paste,

You will also need:

7 oz tempered milk chocolate couverture

almond croquant, crushed

Bring the cream, sugar, and amaretto to a boil, and stir in the glucose syrup. Add the couvertures gradually, stirring until melted. Cool. Beat the butter until creamy. When they are the same temperature, stir the chocolate into the butter gradually. Work the confectioners' sugar and amaretto into the almond paste. On a surface dusted with confectioners' sugar, roll out to 7 x 10 inches. Place between 1-inch deep strips of wood on parchment paper and spread the filling on top. Refrigerate until firm. Cut into squares and dip in couverture. Let firm up, then sprinkle with almond croquant.

BLACK FOREST TRUFFLES

Makes about 65

⅓ cup cream, scant ½ cup sugar

3 tablespoons kirsch

10 teaspoons glucose syrup

7 oz dark couverture, 6 oz milk chocolate couverture

1 cup + 2 tablespoons butter

You will also need:

5 oz dark couverture, grated

Bring the cream to a boil with the sugar and kirsch. Stir in the glucose syrup. Chop the couverture into small pieces and add to the hot cream, stirring constantly until melted. Allow to cool. Beat the butter until creamy. When the butter and the chocolate mixture are the same temperature, then add the chocolate mixture gradually, stirring to combine thoroughly. Spoon into a pastry bag with a round tip and pipe small balls onto parchment paper. Refrigerate to set. Dip in couverture.

Truffles made by Godiva in Brussels are well known for their quality. Prepared in such large quantities, coating them with cocoa powder naturally looks somewhat different.

Butter centers

The preparation is simple, the pleasure sublime

BUTTER TRUFFLES

The delicate, melting buttery truffle filling provides an interesting contrast to the thin coating of bitter couverture finished with a layer of cocoa powder. It is not necessary to temper the couverture; just cool it to 86°F.

Makes about 60
For the filling:
⅔ cup cream, ¼ cup sugar
pinch of salt
scraped contents of 1 vanilla bean
7 oz dark couverture, 9 oz milk chocolate couverture
1 cup + 2 tablespoons butter
You will also need:
baking sheet, parchment paper or acetate
dark couverture, thinned with cocoa butter
cocoa powder

Bring the cream to a boil with the sugar, salt, and vanilla. Melt or chop the couverture as finely as possible and stir into the cream. Allow to cool. Cream the butter and stir into the ganache 1 tablespoon at a time. Line a baking sheet with parchment paper or acetate. Spoon the mixture into a pastry bag with a round tip and pipe into balls. Refrigerate to harden. Stand at room temperature for a while before dipping. Dip in the couverture, shake off the surplus, and drop into the cocoa powder. Toss in the powder, and shake off the surplus (see pictures below).

RUM TRUFFLES

Use the recipe for Butter Truffles, above, adding 5 tablespoons of dark rum to the creamed butter. Use a pastry bag with a large round tip to pipe the filling onto parchment paper or acetate in 2-inch strips, as shown on page 160. After cooling, cut into pieces, dip into thin, dark couverture, and then roll in cocoa powder. Roll in the hands to give a more rounded shape.

Piping and dipping:

Using a pastry bag with a round tip, pipe into balls. Start with very little pressure, increase it, and then ease off again, drawing the pastry bag away at the side.

Dip the balls in thin liquid couverture and drain well. Roll in cocoa powder and knock off the surplus.

NUTMEG TRUFFLES

The nutmeg in the butter cream filling and the extra-bitter couverture coating give these truffles an exciting taste. Mix about 10 percent cornstarch into the confectioners' sugar to make a more solid coating, if you like.

Makes about 60
7 fl oz cream, 5 teaspoons glucose syrup
¼ teaspoon freshly grated nutmeg
pinch of salt
7 oz dark couverture, 7 oz milk chocolate couverture
7 tablespoons butter, softened
You will also need:
parchment paper or acetate
tempered dark couverture, confectioners' sugar

Bring the cream to a boil with the glucose syrup. Add the nutmeg and then the salt. Melt or finely chop the couverture and stir into the cream. When the ganache has cooled and begins to set, whisk a little and stir in the butter a little at a time. Spoon into a pastry bag with a round tip and pipe balls onto parchment paper or acetate. Allow to set hard. Dip in tempered couverture and drain well. Roll in confectioners' sugar.

HONEY TRUFFLES

In this truffle filling, all the ingredients can be mixed together. The combination of honey and almond paste gives the truffles an interesting taste.

Makes about 60
¾ cup butter
3½ oz almond paste, in small flakes
¼ cup honey
scraped contents of 1 vanilla bean
7 oz dark couverture, 7 oz milk chocolate couverture
You will also need:
parchment paper
tempered milk chocolate couverture

Beat the butter with the almond paste flakes until frothy. Stir in the honey a little at a time. Mix in the vanilla. Melt both types of couverture to 86°F over hot water and stir into the butter mixture. Spoon into a pastry bag with a large round tip and pipe balls onto parchment paper. Cool and allow to harden. Dip in tempered milk chocolate couverture, drain well, and roll over a wire rack (see picture, right). Place on parchment paper. Small cracks may appear on the surface. If you wish to disguise them, dip the balls a second time.

Use a wire rack to roll the truffles back and forth to achieve the characteristic decorative finish. Then place on parchment paper and allow to set.

Nougat and croquant candies

*Croquant wafers, nougat layers, and other delicate
centers for dipping*

Producing nougat requires a lot of technical effort,
so it is best to buy it. Since nougat contains a
substantial amount of couverture, it has to be
tempered. The optimum working temperature of
83°F is important for trouble-free setting and an
agreeable texture. For the chocolate candies shown
on this page, the mixtures are spread into rectangular
molds. If these are not available, they are quite easy
to make by folding several layers of foil.

NOUGAT BRITTLE

These are shown in the top row in the picture. To
make the almond croquant, combine equal parts of
roasted slivered almonds with sugar, melted until it
caramelizes. Pour onto a flat, oiled baking sheet.
When cool, grate it into fine croquant.

Makes about 40
2 oz milk chocolate couverture, melted
7 oz bitter almond nougat, 2 oz almond croquant
⅔ cup coarsely grated wafer cookies, such as tuiles
You will also need:
4 x 12-inch mold
tempered milk chocolate couverture, slivered almonds

Mix the melted couverture with the nougat, and
temper at 83°F. Mix with the croquant and wafer
cookies and spread in the mold. Allow to harden.
Cut into 1-inch diamond shapes. Dip in tempered
milk chocolate couverture and decorate each with a
slivered almond.

NOUGAT LAYERS

Makes 10
For the white layer:
5 oz extra light hazelnut nougat
2 oz white couverture, melted
For the light-colored layer:
5 oz extra light hazelnut nougat
2 oz milk chocolate couverture, melted
For the dark layer:
5 oz bitter almond nougat, 2 oz couverture, melted
You will also need:
5 x 7-inch mold, tempered couverture

Mix each variety of nougat with the appropriate
melted couverture and temper at 83°F. Spread the
white layer in the mold and allow to set. Spread the
light-colored layer on top and allow to set.
Top with the dark layer and allow to set.
Do not let the individual layers get too
cold, or they may separate when they are
cut. Remove from the mold and cut into
10 squares. The cut sides will later
form the top, so that the
individual colored layers are
visible (see the picture
above). Dip each piece in
couverture, coating only
the base and sides.

CROQUANT WAFERS

The consistency of croquant wafers depends heavily on the mixing. If it is mixed for too short a time, the mixture will not be firm enough to be cut. If it is mixed for too long, it will break when it is cut. The mixture should not be too homogeneous. There needs to be a good balance between the brittleness of the caramel and the softness of the nougat.

Makes about 50 pieces

7 oz extra light hazelnut nougat,

3½ oz unsweetened nougat

5 teaspoons glucose syrup, ¾ cup sugar

You will also need:

baking tray, 4 x 12-inch mold, parchment paper

light and dark tempered couverture

Place both types of nougat on a baking tray and heat in the oven at 125°F until soft enough to work with. Melt the glucose syrup with the sugar until the mixture becomes a light caramel, then pour over the nougat. Using two spatulas, work into the nougat until the mixture binds and is no longer runny. Place a mold on parchment paper and spread the mixture in it. Cover with another sheet of parchment paper and roll out smoothly. Work quickly, as the caramel sets very fast. Cut into 1-inch squares. Dip in milk chocolate couverture and pipe strands of dark couverture on top.

CROQUANT WAFER WITH ALMOND NOUGAT

Makes about 50

10 teaspoons glucose syrup, ¾ cup + 2 tablespoons sugar

3 tablespoons butter

1 cup chopped roasted hazelnuts

For the filling:

5 oz light hazelnut nougat

1½ oz tempered milk chocolate couverture

Bring the glucose syrup to a boil. Trickle in the sugar a little at a time, stirring as it melts, until it caramelizes. When all the sugar crystals have dissolved, work in the butter, and then stir in the hazelnuts. Do not overmix, or the sugar will "die." Pour onto a well-oiled baking sheet and beat with a spatula several times until the mixture no longer spreads. Place in the oven at 300°F until the mixture is soft enough to roll out to ⅛ inch thick — if it is any thicker, it is unpleasant to eat. After rolling out, slide onto parchment paper and warm up again in the oven before cutting into pieces with an oiled knife. When cold, store in a cool, dry place.

For the filling, heat the nougat gently over hot water until soft, and stir until smooth. If it is too soft, it will not hold its shape. Spoon into a pastry bag with a star tip and drop a swirl onto half of the wafers. Place a second wafer diagonally on top and dip one corner into the tempered couverture.

Fill the hollow chocolate molds with the precisely tempered couverture. Hold the mold at an angle so that the excess couverture can run off into a waiting pan or bowl.

Molded candies

Another way to make candies with fabulous fillings

The shells are molded the same way as the hollow chocolates (see pages 66–7). The molds have to be absolutely clean to ensure an even, glossy finish. Fill them with precisely tempered couverture (91°F for dark, 88°F for milk chocolate or white couverture). You may fill them once or twice, depending on the consistency of the chocolate. When the chocolate has set, trim the edges with a spatula.

Note the following points when filling:

1. Some fillings have to be warm so that they are soft enough to be worked. They should not, however, be warmer than 86°F or the chocolate shell will melt.

2. Fill the shells *almost* to the top. Be extremely careful that none of the filling sticks to the lips of the shells, or it will be impossible to seal the candies hermetically.

3. When putting on the "backs," you can spread the chocolate only when the filling is firm; otherwise you have to pipe on the backs.

4. Wait until the candies are cold before turning out of the molds. Transparent molds make it easy to see when the chocolate leaves the sides of the mold.

COGNAC CREAM CHERRIES

Makes 32

32 cherries preserved in cognac, 3 tablespoons cognac, *5 oz fondant*
about 1 lb dark couverture for the shells and backs
For the cream filling:
2 tablespoons cream, ¾ teaspoon glucose syrup
4 oz milk chocolate couverture
1½ tablespoons butter, 3 tablespoons kirsch

The chocolate shells tumble out of the molds immediately if the couverture has been properly tempered and the filling and sealing have been done correctly. They have a perfect, smooth gloss.

Stir the fondant with the cognac over hot water at 86°F until soft. To make the filling, bring the cream to a boil with the glucose syrup. Add the milk chocolate couverture, stirring constantly until it melts. Transfer to a bowl. Place a hand blender in the bowl, switch on, and blend thoroughly. Beat with the butter until creamy, then flavor with the kirsch. Continue as shown in the picture sequence.

To make, fill, and seal hollow shells:

Wipe off the excess couverture with a spatula. Shake and tap the mold to remove any air bubbles.

Grasp the mold from below and invert in one brisk continuous movement. Allow the couverture to run out until it drips only intermittently.

Spread out a piece of parchment paper and prop the mold upside down on two strips of wood. Allow the couverture to harden.

When the couverture has firmed up somewhat, but is still soft, use a metal spatula to scrape off excess couverture around the rims.

When the shells are fully hardened, put a cognac-flavored cherry in each one and pipe fondant on top, so that the shells are at least half-full.

Use a funnel to pour in the ganache cream filling, leaving a tiny gap at the top. Allow the cream filling to set.

Pour couverture over the top of the mold. Smooth and remove the excess with a metal spatula. Refrigerate until set.

When the chocolates have set and are completely cold (the clear plastic mold will show when they are ready), tap the mold and turn them out.

PASSION FRUIT ALMOND PASTE

A simple and delicate filling in a chocolate mold.

Makes 40
For the filling:
flesh of 6 passion fruits (½ cup)
6 tablespoons sugar, 4 oz almond paste
You will also need:
molds
about 1 lb tempered milk chocolate couverture

Bring the passion fruit flesh and sugar to a boil. Reduce by half over a low heat. Pass through a fine strainer. Mix with the almond paste to a consistency that can be piped. Fill the chocolate molds with milk chocolate couverture as shown left. Using a pastry bag with a round tip, fill the shells to just below the rims with the flavored almond paste and spread with tempered milk chocolate couverture to seal (see left).

NOUGAT CREAMS

Shells are particularly easy to make using foil cases.

Makes 30
For the filling:
5 oz light almond nougat, melted, 1 teaspoon honey
6 tablespoons roasted ground almonds
2 oz milk chocolate couverture, melted
You will also need:
30 foil cases, 1 lb tempered milk chocolate couverture
pistachios, finely chopped

Stir all the ingredients for the filling together. Coat the insides of the foil cases with the tempered couverture, drain on a rack, and turn right side up just before the chocolate sets. When the chocolate has hardened, use a pastry bag with a round tip to pipe up to the brim with filling. Make lids by piping tempered milk chocolate couverture onto parchment paper (see page 63). Sprinkle with pistachios.

A small piece of croquant is placed in each shell in a set order. This process, shown here at Godiva in Brussels, calls for the utmost concentration. Each worker is responsible for filling a particular row, so that no shell is missed. It all happens in a flash, as the conveyor belt continues to move, bringing the next tray of empty shells.

RASPBERRY LIQUEUR CREAMS

In this type of candy, the alcohol in the preserved fruit dissolves the fondant to produce a liqueur-like effect. For this recipe, preserve fresh raspberries in a mixture of 2 parts ethyl alcohol and 1 part white raspberry brandy for 4 weeks, or frozen raspberries in the same mixture for 1 week.

Makes 50

25 preserved raspberries, 5 oz fondant
For the filling:
3 tablespoons cream, 1½ teaspoons glucose syrup
5 oz milk chocolate couverture, 3 tablespoons white raspberry brandy
You will also need:
50 round hollow chocolate shells made with milk chocolate couverture, made in advance (see page 168)
tempered milk chocolate couverture for the backs

Drain the preserved raspberries well and reserve the liquid. Place half a raspberry in each shell. Dilute the fondant with a little of the reserved raspberry liquid and heat gently to a maximum of 86°F. Spoon into a pastry bag and half-fill the shells.

To make the ganache, bring the cream to a boil with the glucose syrup, add the milk chocolate couverture, stirring constantly until it melts, and blend thoroughly. Add the white raspberry brandy, cool to 86°F, and use a pastry bag or funnel to fill the shells almost to the brim. Allow to set overnight. Finish off the backs with milk chocolate couverture. When cold, turn out of the mold.

PRUNE AND SLIVOVITZ CENTERS

Soak the prunes in Slivovitz for at least 1 week before use.

Makes 50

7 oz almond paste
4 teaspoons Slivovitz (plum brandy)
5 oz (½ cup) prunes, minced and soaked in Slivovitz
You will also need:
50 round dark chocolate shells, made in advance (see page 168)
tempered dark couverture

Mix the almond paste with the Slivovitz and the prunes until soft. Place in the hollow shells, leaving a tiny gap at the top. Allow to firm up overnight. Finish off the backs with tempered couverture. When completely cold turn out of the mold.

The candies shown here are, from left to right, raspberry cream, honey and caramel, Irish coffee, prune with Slivovitz.

IRISH COFFEE CREAMS
Makes 50

For the coffee cream filling:
5 tablespoons milk, 2 tablespoons instant coffee powder
2 teaspoons glucose syrup, 3½ oz white couverture, melted
⅓ cup soft butter, 2 oz cocoa butter, melted
For the whiskey cream filling:
3 tablespoons cream, 1 tablespoon glucose syrup
9 oz milk chocolate couverture, melted, 2 tablespoons butter, 5 tablespoons whiskey
You will also need:
50 oval milk chocolate couverture shells, made in advance (see page 168)
tempered milk chocolate couverture

To make the coffee cream filling, bring the milk to a boil with the coffee powder and the glucose syrup. Add the melted white couverture, butter, and cocoa butter, and blend thoroughly. Cool to 86°F. Half-fill the hollow shells, using a funnel or pastry bag. Allow to firm up.

To make the whiskey cream filling, bring the cream and glucose syrup to a boil. Add the couverture, butter, and whiskey, and blend thoroughly. Cool to 86°F. Place on top of the coffee cream filling, leaving a tiny gap at the top. Allow to set overnight. Finish off the backs with tempered couverture. When completely cold, turn out of the molds.

HONEY AND CARAMEL CENTERS
Makes 50

½ cup sugar, 3 tablespoons unsweetened condensed milk, 4 teaspoons honey
¼ cup butter, ¼ cup roasted slivered almonds
5 oz cream nougat, ¾ oz couverture, melted
You will also need:
50 rectangular dark couverture shells, made in advance
tempered dark couverture

Melt the sugar and pour in the condensed milk. Add the honey and butter, and blend thoroughly with a hand blender. Cool to 86°F. Spoon into a pastry bag and fill the hollow shells to just under half full. Sprinkle in a few slivered almonds. Melt the cream nougat and couverture over hot water, and temper. Add to the shells to form a second layer, leaving a tiny gap at the top. Allow to set overnight. Finish off the backs with couverture. When completely cold, turn out of the molds.

Fine fillings

Make the shells in advance, and produce your candies twice as fast

One of the advantages of making the chocolate shells in foil cases in advance (see page 168) is that they can be stored easily and taken out in small numbers to make fresh candies.

BLACKBERRY CREAMS

Makes about 60

½ lb fresh blackberries, ½ cup sugar

3 tablespoons dark rum

For the filling:

½ cup cream, 2 tablespoons honey

11 oz couverture, chopped into small pieces

¼ cup dark rum, ¼ cup butter, softened

You will also need:

60 round milk chocolate couverture shells, made in advance

chopped pistachios

Bring the blackberries to a boil with the sugar, then strain. Continue to boil down the liquid to reduce by half. Allow to cool. Add the rum. Spoon the cold blackberry purée into a pastry bag and fill the shells.

To make the filling, bring the cream to a boil with the honey and add the couverture, stirring until it melts and is thoroughly blended. Allow to cool. As soon as the cream filling is firm but not quite cold, whisk until creamy, using a whisk or hand mixer. Add the rum and stir in the soft butter a little at a time. Finish the candies as described below.

To fill blackberry creams:

Use a paper pastry bag to fill the shells a third full with blackberry purée.

Use a star tip to pipe ganache cream rosettes on top. Sprinkle with chopped pistachios.

MOCHA MOONS

Make about 70

For the filling:

½ cup cream

1 tablespoon honey

2 tablespoons instant coffee powder

4 oz dark couverture, chopped into small pieces

9 oz milk chocolate couverture, chopped into small pieces

¼ cup Chartreuse

¼ cup butter, softened

You will also need:

70 crescent-shaped dark couverture shells,
made in advance

tempered dark couverture

Prepare the filling as described in the recipe for Blackberry Creams. Spoon the filling into a pastry bag with a round tip, pipe into the shells, and finish as shown in the picture sequence below.

CHERRY ALMOND PASTE

Makes about 70

4 oz fresh sour cherries

5 tablespoons cognac

1 tablespoon confectioners' sugar

4 oz almond paste

4 teaspoons sugar syrup

3 tablespoons maraschino

For the filling:

½ cup cream, 1 tablespoon glucose syrup

14 oz milk chocolate couverture, chopped finely

¼ cup maraschino

You will also need:

70 square dark couverture shells, made in advance

crystallized violets

Halve the cherries and remove the stones. Mix the cognac with the confectioners' sugar and marinate the cherries in it overnight. The next day, place half a cherry in each of the chocolate shells. Work the sugar syrup into the almond paste until the paste becomes soft, then stir in the maraschino and 4 teaspoons of the cognac used for the marinade. Spoon the almond paste mixture into a pastry bag and pipe over the cherry halves — the shells should be about half full.

To make the filling, bring the cream to a boil with the glucose syrup. Add the couverture and melt. Allow to cool. As soon as the cream is firm but not quite cold, whisk until creamy with a whisk or hand mixer. Stir in the maraschino. Using a pastry bag with a star tip, pipe rosettes on top of the cherry and almond paste filling. Decorate each candy with a piece of crystallized violet.

To fill and seal:

Use a pastry bag with a round tip to fill the crescent shapes with the ganache cream filling, leaving a little gap at the top.

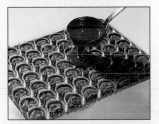

When the ganache has set, pour tempered dark couverture over the shells, distributing it as evenly as possible.

Use a palette knife to spread the couverture smoothly over the whole surface. Hold the mold at an angle over the bowl of couverture and allow the surplus to run off.

Remove the candies from the mold when they have set. You can do this individually or you can invert the entire mold and lift it off.

Just like peas in a pod, these mocha chocolate candies have all turned out identically. Hollow shells prepared in advance take the hard work out of making filled chocolate candies.

Exotic treats

Give your imagination free rein in varying fillings and decorations

At Godiva, in Belgium, all the chocolates are handmade despite the large quantities produced. Even the ganache cream filling is piped by hand in the "Liberty" candies shown here. The white couverture flakes are also applied by hand.

Make the shells in advance and leave them in the molds until filled and decorated.

GRAPPA CREAMS
Makes 50

| ¼ cup cream, 4 teaspoons glucose syrup |
| 3 oz milk chocolate couverture, 1 oz dark couverture |
| 1½ tablespoons butter, 3 tablespoons grappa |
| You will also need: |
| 50 triangular light couverture shells |
| tempered milk and dark couverture |

Bring the cream and glucose syrup to a boil. Add the couvertures, stirring until melted. Transfer to a bowl and blend. Cool to 86°F. Cream the butter and add the grappa. Use a pastry bag with a small round tip to pipe the filling into the shells, leaving a tiny gap at the top. Allow to set overnight.

Spoon the light couverture into a paper pastry bag and pipe tops to seal the shells. While they are still soft, pipe zigzag lines on top in dark couverture. Shake the molds sharply so the couvertures run into each other. When cold, turn out of the molds

NOUGAT CUPS
Makes 50

| 8 oz white couverture |
| 3½ oz dark hazelnut nougat |
| 4 oz light hazelnut nougat |
| You will also need: |
| 50 round dark couverture shells |
| ½ cup chopped roasted almonds, confectioners' sugar |

Melt the white couverture and both types of nougat over hot water, and temper. Spoon into a pastry bag with a small round tip, and pipe into the shells, leaving a tiny gap at the top. Shake the molds to get a smooth surface. When cold, sprinkle with the chopped almonds and dust with sifted confectioners' sugar. Turn out of the molds.

GRAND MARNIER HEARTS
Makes 50

| 7 oz milk chocolate couverture |
| 6 tablespoons butter, softened |
| 4 teaspoons glucose syrup, ¼ cup Grand Marnier |
| You will also need: |
| 50 heart-shaped light couverture shells |
| tempered milk chocolate couverture, cocoa powder |

Melt the milk chocolate couverture and temper at 89°F. Combine the butter and glucose syrup, and mix into the couverture. Stir in the liqueur. Spoon into a pastry bag with a small round tip and pipe into the shells. Tap the mold to release air bubbles. Allow to set overnight. Finish with the couverture, as shown on page 168. When cold, dust with sifted cocoa powder and turn out of the molds.

PASSION FRUIT CREAMS
Makes about 50

For the ganache cream filling:

scant ½ cup cream, 8 oz milk chocolate couverture

¼ cup butter, softened

For the jelly:

6 passion fruits (½ cup fruit flesh)

2 tablespoons butter, scant ½ cup sugar

grated zest and juice of 1 orange

juice of 1 lime, 1 teaspoon gelatin

For the topping:

3½ oz fondant, 4 teaspoons rum

You will also need:

50 oval light chocolate shells

50 dark chocolate drops (see pages 62–3)

Bring the cream to a boil. Add the couverture and melt. Transfer to a bowl. Place a hand blender in the cream, switch on, and then mix, using a circular motion. Do not allow the blender to come to the surface, as this may result in trapped air bubbles. Allow to cool.

Cut the passion fruit in half and use a teaspoon to remove the flesh. Melt the butter and bring to a boil with the fruit flesh and the sugar, cooking until all the sugar has dissolved. Add the orange zest and orange and lime juices, and continue to boil down until the mixture becomes syrupy. Strain. Dissolve the gelatin in the syrup. Allow to go cold. Spoon into a paper pastry bag and pipe into the shells, as shown.

Stir the fondant and rum together over hot water at 86°F until soft. Spoon into a paper pastry bag and pipe on top of the jelly. Leave to stand until the fondant forms a crust. Whip the cream filling until frothy, and stir in the butter a little at a time. The cream should be soft enough to pipe easily. Finish the candies as shown.

To fill chocolate candies:

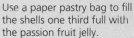

Use a paper pastry bag to fill the shells one third full with the passion fruit jelly.

Use a paper pastry bag to pipe fondant over the top in a spiral, working from the outside to the center. Allow the surface to dry out.

Use a star tip to pipe an oval cream rosette onto each candy. Decorate with chocolate buttons.

Chocolate candies in edible packaging

Boxes made of chocolate are perfect, if rather fragile, gifts and are a testament to the skill of the chocolate-maker

Make cardboard templates for the rectangular box as shown below. To make the boxes, spread a ⅛-inch thick layer of tempered couverture on parchment paper or acetate. Before it has hardened fully, use the templates to cut out the pieces with a knife. Assemble the pieces, using tempered couverture in a pastry bag to glue them together (see page 179). Alternatively, warm the edges on a hot baking sheet and fuse together. Thin some couverture with cocoa butter and brush on to touch up. Striped couverture makes a very attractive lid (for the method, see page 58–9).

To make the oval box, cut the lid and base to the same size from couverture spread on parchment paper. Make the side strip as shown in the small picture on the opposite page. Warm the edge of the strip on a hot baking sheet and set ½ inch in from the edge of the base to fuse. You can use the simplest decorations: broken pieces of couverture lattice or a flower arrangement using piped shapes (see pages 62–3).

WALNUT CARAMELS

A candy or chocolate thermometer is particularly important in this recipe, as it is the only way to determine the correct temperature.

Makes about 100
1 cup sugar, ¾ cup honey, 1 cup cream
7 teaspoons butter, scraped contents of 1 vanilla bean
2 cups chopped walnuts
You will also need:
8 x 10-inch mold or foil strips
tempered dark couverture
tempered milk chocolate couverture

Bring the sugar, honey, cream, butter, and vanilla to a boil, stirring constantly. Continue to boil, checking the temperature continuously until it reaches 252°F. Remove from the heat and stir in the nuts. Place the mold, or strips cut to the right size, on parchment paper and pour in the mixture. Allow to cool until it is firm enough to be cut. Cut into pieces ½ x 1 inch. When cold, coat each piece with tempered couverture and decorate with piped strands of milk chocolate couverture.

The base and lid for the small chocolate box are 3¾ x 5 inches, the long sides are 1 x 4¼ inches, and the short sides are 1 x 3 inches.

All the chocolate candies shown inside the chocolate box can be found in this book. The candies on the tray, which are not in the book, have been made by Dominique Docquier, who runs a one-man business in Belgium, putting a lot of love and only the best ingredients into his work.

MOCHA AND NUT CREAMS
Makes about 80

7 fl oz cream, 2 heaping teaspoons instant coffee powder

¾ lb milk chocolate couverture, melted

For the caramelized nuts:

¾ cup blanched hazelnuts, chopped

1 tablespoon sugar syrup, ¼ cup confectioners' sugar

You will also need:

tempered milk chocolate couverture

Bring the cream to a boil with the coffee powder and stir into the couverture. Use a hand blender to blend thoroughly. Allow to cool. Use a hand mixer to whisk the ganache until light and creamy. Using a pastry bag with a round tip, pipe two strips of the mixture side by side on acetate. Pipe a third strip on top. Moisten the nuts with the sugar syrup and heat on a baking sheet in the oven at 400°F. Sift with the confectioners' sugar and allow to caramelize. Remove from the oven and cool. Sprinkle the nuts on the strips of chocolate and press gently. Cut into pieces and coat with tempered couverture.

The oval band that forms the side of the box is shaped using a strip of acetate (see pages 64–5). The acetate strip coated with couverture is placed inside an oval flan ring used as a mold, and left to set.

Pine cones: Wrap the strips of nougat in the almond paste rectangles. Moisten the edges, seal together, and roll into the shape of pine cones. The surface should have no joins or cracks. Allow to dry overnight, and then nick with a small pair of scissors to make the pattern.

Almond paste in chocolate

At Christmas, almond paste comes into its own

PINE CONES FILLED WITH NOUGAT

Makes 15

scant 1 cup confectioners' sugar

¾ lb almond paste, 5 oz almond nougat

You will also need:

tempered couverture, cocoa butter

confectioners' sugar or cocoa powder

Work the confectioners' sugar into the almond paste. On a work surface dusted with confectioners' sugar, roll out to 9 x 10 inches. Cut into 3 strips lengthwise and 5 strips crosswise. Cut the nougat into 15 pieces, each 2 inches long, and place in the center of the almond paste pieces. Fold, shape, and fashion as shown in the picture sequence to the left. When they have dried out, coat with couverture that has been thinned with a little cocoa butter. Dust with confectioners' sugar or cocoa powder while they are still moist.

CHOCOLATE ALMOND PASTE LOAVES

Makes 20

scant ½ cup confectioners' sugar, 14 oz almond paste

2 tablespoons cream, 3 tablespoons honey

3½ oz couverture, chopped

Work the confectioners' sugar into the almond paste. Bring the cream and honey to a boil, remove from the heat, and add the couverture to melt. Work into the almond paste and let set for 2 hours. Form into a roll, cut into 20 pieces, and shape into loaves. Dry overnight. Coat with thinned tempered couverture.

ALMOND PASTE POTATOES

Makes 35

scant ½ cup confectioners' sugar, 14 oz almond paste

Work the sugar into the almond paste. Form into a roll 1 inch thick. Cut into ½-inch pieces, form into balls and roll in cocoa powder. Make 3 notches.

The Christmas trees are made with almond cluster mixture (see page 144). Using a template, make 5–6 stars of decreasing size with the almond-couverture mixture and place on parchment paper. Assemble them into a tree, using tempered couverture to hold them together.

Country cottage

A lively imagination and a simple design — essentials for an appealing creation

This charming little house is constructed from spread couverture. The technique is described in detail on pages 56–7. Sketch the design first, as in the small picture above, and then make a fair copy on which to base a full-sized cardboard template. This enables you to fix the dimensions accurately before you begin to work with your ingredients.

Cover a work surface with parchment paper and spread the couverture. Using the templates to guide you, cut out the shapes with a small pointed knife. Be careful: The larger the pieces, the greater the tendency of the chocolate to bulge on the parchment. Remove the parchment at the earliest opportunity. You can, however, use this bulging effect to advantage for the roof: Leave the shapes on the parchment until they reach the required curvature. This adds a bit of style to the house.

Warm the edges of the pieces on a hot baking sheet and fuse together immediately. To attach the roof, use the following "contact adhesive" technique (this method is recommended for all pieces that could slip or drop off, such as the arm on a figure). Fill a pastry bag with tempered couverture and pipe along the top edges of the gable end. Place the roof in the desired position and then remove it again immediately. Allow the chocolate to set slightly. Pipe more couverture on top of the previous application. Replace the roof in position and press gently. The chocolate will fuse quickly and cannot be adjusted. Make the ridge tile out of modeling chocolate (see page 182) and fix with couverture.

Decorate the front of the house and gable end with chocolate candies. For a winter version, sift confectioners' sugar very lightly over the model.

Chocolate on show

When using chocolate to make displays, keep the idea simple: It will require less handling and produce better results

The simple technique: Spread tempered couverture on parchment paper or acetate and stamp out shapes with a cutter before it has fully hardened. Remove from the parchment or acetate and allow to dry.

For professional chocolate makers, there is always the question of whether it makes sense to use a valuable commodity, which chocolate undoubtedly is, exclusively for decorative effects and not for the pleasure of eating. They are also concerned, of course, about the quality of their artistic achievement, not least because their works are exposed to the public gaze. In the opinion of Leopold Forsthofer, a master of chocolate sculpture:

Showpieces have their place, whether as small decorations on a torte or as a big display in the window. They are always a good advertisement, provided that one or two ground rules are observed. You should never forget the material with which you are working. The choice of subject should be in good taste. No matter how long you have taken to make them, showpieces should always look clean and crisp. As people often say: "Less is more." The creation should be as stylized as possible, since too many small details spoil the overall effect, and the pieces look contrived. Despite this, there should be a certain wit, which contributes to the charm of the piece. The aim is to produce something that would tempt you to break off a piece of

chocolate to eat. Only then does the idea of creating a showpiece from food become valid. This is the direction in which we strive.

Although they may not have a large public to worry about, amateur chocolate makers will find this very useful advice when creating a display for a birthday party or other family celebration.

The techniques used here have their roots in Catalonia, Spain, where the absence of molds for Easter bunnies and Santa Claus led confectioners to use simple, basic shapes. The work of creative confectioners Antoño Escriba, Francisco Baixas, and Jaime Sabat made these techniques famous.

The simple technique Plain shapes (heart, circle, oval) are cut out of chocolate and assembled to create flat figures, like the rabbit shown below. Spread tempered couverture over a completely flat surface lined with parchment paper, or with acetate if a highly glossy surface is desired. Cut out the shapes before the couverture has fully set. Remove the paper or acetate. Do not leave the shapes on parchment for too long, or the tension will cause them to bulge as they harden.

Hollow mold technique This method, using poured molds such as egg and ball shapes, is described on pages 66–7. You may have to coat large molds two or three times until the chocolate becomes sufficiently rigid. Do not let one layer

You can make the rabbit with basic shapes. The body is half of a heart shape, as are the feet. The head and ears are made with a round cutter. Make a mock-up with cardboard before starting on the real thing.

become too hard or too cold before you apply the next one, otherwise they will separate. Warm the edges of egg or ball halves (press them down gently on a hot baking sheet) to fuse them together. To make half an egg with a solid base (for the clown's feet, for example), place the egg half on freshly spread couverture and leave to set. Remove the parchment and break off the protruding pieces.

Hollow mold sculpture is another relatively easy method of creating models. The picture sequence on pages 66–7 shows how to make the basic molded shapes. The text on page 183 describes how to create the speckled effect on the eggshell.

The fish and the frog can also be made simply, with correspondingly large cutters. For special shapes, such as waves for the fish, make a template from cardboard first.

MODELING CHOCOLATE

The ingredients for modeling chocolate show that you are not meant to eat it.

Makes 1¼ lb
For the dark paste:
1¼ lb tempered couverture
6 tablespoons + 2 teaspoons glucose syrup
5 tablespoons sugar syrup

Combine the couverture with the glucose syrup and stir in the sugar syrup. If the paste is too soft, refrigerate briefly until it can be kneaded. Knead well. The paste can be rolled out like dough and shaped like almond paste. It must remain warm (77–86°F) in order to be shaped. If it is too firm to shape despite being warm, it can be softened with more sugar syrup.

Makes 1⅛ lb
For the white paste:
1 lb tempered white couverture
2 oz cocoa butter, melted
5 tablespoons glucose syrup, 5 tablespoons sugar syrup

Combine the couverture with the cocoa butter and glucose syrup. Stir in the sugar syrup. If the paste is too soft, refrigerate briefly until it is firm enough to knead. Knead well. Wrap in plastic wrap to keep.

As stylized as possible. Before embarking on work with the chocolate, ensure that you know how you want the finished piece to look. A sketch is very useful.

To make tubes, follow the steps shown in the picture sequence. Cut a rectangle of fairly thick-gauge acetate that is longer and wider than the desired length and circumference of the tube. Place the acetate on the work surface. Take a 2-inch wide strip of acetate and place it lengthwise on top of the rectangle so that it defines the length of the finished tube. Spread the tempered couverture an inch or more beyond the edges of the rectangle of acetate. Leave until the couverture has set on the outside and the inner surface is still soft. Remove the acetate strip and the chocolate on it. This will leave a neat edge. Roll up the acetate with the couverture (it will break away neatly from the chocolate beyond the edges) until the two long sides meet and the clear area left where the strip of acetate was removed is uppermost. Lap this clear piece over and secure with rubber bands. Refrigerate until firm, then remove the acetate. To make angled tubes, for arms and legs, cut through the tubes at the required angle with a hot, smooth-bladed knife. Warm the cut edges on a hot baking sheet and fuse together in the opposite direction.

Keep it steady When you construct large figures, you need to make sure they are stable so that they can be transported or stand freely without toppling over. Egg shapes that form the base of a figure (for example, feet) should be fairly thick. Used higher up a figure, these shapes should be thinner, and therefore lighter.

Use chocolate to achieve different decorative effects For example, the clown's bow tie was made with white couverture spread over dark chocolate drops, and then cut out to shape. For the chicken on page 181, drops of dark couverture were dabbed onto the inside of the egg mold with a brush; the mold was then coated with white couverture. Creating decorative effects is described on pages 58–9 and 64–5.

Surface finish If the surface of chocolate figures is subjected to a lot of handling, it will lose its gloss. Joins have to be smoothed over with a knife. To disguise such imperfections, the showpiece can be lacquered with chocolate. Thin couverture with melted cocoa butter to the point where it can be sprayed on with a spray gun. The temperature must not exceed 91°F. Do not spray too thickly, as the chocolate could turn light gray. If necessary, apply a second thin coat. If you do not have a spray gun, you can apply a coat of thinned couverture with a brush. This finishing step is not necessary when the work is carried out cleanly or the chocolate figures are small.

Constructed from tubes. This figure is constructed mainly from tubes, and demonstrates the almost limitless possibilities of how they can be used.

Tube technique:

Spread tempered couverture on a flat sheet of acetate with strips of acetate laid out to define the rectangle. Allow to firm up briefly. Remove the strips.

The couverture should still be pliable on the surface. Lift the rectangle of acetate from the work surface. Proceed with care.

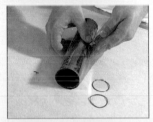

Form a roll, butting the edges of the couverture together smoothly. Lap the free end of acetate around the tube of couverture.

Secure the tube well with rubber bands. The free end of the acetate acts as protection.

When the tube has hardened completely, remove the rubber bands and carefully unroll the acetate.

Use the finished tube just as it is, or cut into pieces diagonally and reassemble the opposite way around to make arms and legs.

CHOCOLATE
DESS

ERTS

This chapter deals with desserts — the crowning touch to a successful meal, in which chocolate plays a significant part.

Most of the cakes, cookies, and candies featured in earlier chapters can be served as desserts, as well as being enjoyed as snacks. However, there are some dishes that belong only to the dessert course. For example, there is the highly popular chocolate flummery, which began its triumphant progress as chocolate pudding; the delicate chocolate mousse, an outstanding example of a chocolate dessert, but also used in light creamy tortes; and the Bavarian creams, parfaits, and all sorts of part-frozen delights made with chocolate.

And, of course, we can never forget chocolate ice cream, made with eggs, sugar, milk, cream and a lot of liquid chocolate. Here is an ice-cold delicacy to rival any commercial product.

In praise of chocolate

"Charlotte Bohémienne" was the name given to this charlotte by Carl Gruber in his *Book of Confectionery* published in 1896. The chocolate cream filling is surrounded by ladyfingers, which are also coated with couverture.

What has a more distinctive aroma than chocolate melting gently in the pan, occasionally releasing a languid, mellow bubble? The impression is that chocolate has always been around, among the almonds and cinnamon, the copper saucepans and porcelain cream pitchers; and that it has always been used to create the most unforgettable climax to a meal.

"Cooking" and "cuisine"

In reality the pleasure gained from this luxury, with its mild yet bittersweet taste, is of relatively recent date. In Auguste Escoffier's famous *Guide Culinaire* (Guide to Cooking), published in France in 1903, there is not a single recipe containing chocolate under the headings "Cold Dishes" and "Cold Desserts." In the chapter entitled "Warm Desserts," which contains almost 220 recipes, there is one recipe for "Chocolate Sauce" and one for "Chocolate Soufflé." There are other desserts flavored with kümmel and kirsch, nuts, oranges, and rum, but no chocolate. On the other hand, in *South German Cooking* by Katherina Prato, which appeared in Vienna a decade earlier, there are forty recipes for chocolate dishes. This may reflect a difference in cultural and economic factors, or the difference between "cuisine" for chefs and "cooking" for the homemaker.

The reason may also have something to do with the information given under the heading "Chocolate" in the *Universal Lexicon of Cooking*, which appeared in 1881. After listing the available types of chocolate — "Vanilla chocolate ... flavored chocolate, to which is added cinnamon, cardamom and a little Peruvian balsam, unspiced health chocolate mixed only with a little sugar, and medicinal chocolate with the addition of Iceland moss, iron, quinine et cetera" — the text warns the reader: "It is not easy to prepare chocolate at home, therefore purchase only the better qualities from high-quality established companies ... ." From what follows it is plain that chocolate was best left alone rather than run the risk of spoiling an important dinner or intimate supper: "... the poorer sorts are always adulterated ... by mixing with flour, wheat,

barley, maize, rice, lentils and peas ... arrowroot, gum arabic, red lead, ochre, cinnabar, powdered brick etc.," not to mention the wonder fat-substitute, which the sharp-eyed housewife of the day recognized as "greased brown paper." However, the reader was comforted by the fact that good-quality chocolate candy was available from reputable commercial producers.

From health to happiness

Even when chocolate was the basis only for drinks, it was valued for more than its taste. At the beginning of the seventeenth century, Francesco Carletti, who had observed the effects of drinking hot chocolate while traveling in Mexico, wrote that it imparted "strength, nourishment, and vigor." A little over two hundred years later Jean-Anthelme Savarin, whose *La Physiologie du goût* was published in France in 1825, asserted that chocolate is wholesome, nourishing, easy to digest, beneficial to people "faced with great mental exertion," and, if drunk regularly, contributes to good health. In 1996, doctors asserted that the phenols in chocolate prevent certain body fats from oxidizing into a more dangerous, artery-clogging form.

Despite this positive health indicator, we now associate chocolate in its many forms more with pleasure. It is not only the rich taste or the variety of textures, but also, of course, the theobromine and other components in the cocoa bean that produce sensations ranging from comfort to exhilaration. These attributes seem to have acted as a great spur to cooks.

In the relatively short time that chocolate has been available as a regular ingredient, an astonishing number of chocolate desserts have been created, some of which have become classics. There are unsurpassable desserts, such as chocolate mousse, served either plain, in the Parisian fashion, or topped with whipped cream. There is also the eternal chocolate flummery, which since the invention of pudding mix has been known, mistakenly, as chocolate pudding. And no list of classic desserts would be complete without that dream-like creation in which melted dark chocolate is poured over swans made of vanilla ice cream with wings of meringue.

Chocolate cherry charlotte

Mini-charlottes such as these obviously make more work than a single large one, but your guests will be delighted

Serves 6
1 recipe Chocolate Spongecake (see page 76)
For the ladyfingers:
5 eggs, separated
¼ cup + 2 teaspoons confectioners' sugar
1¼ teaspoons cocoa powder
1 small egg, 1 teaspoon vanilla sugar, pinch of salt
¾ cup flour sifted with ½ cup cornstarch
For the light chocolate mousse:
1 egg, 1 egg yolk, 1 teaspoon gelatin
2 oz dark and 7 oz milk chocolate couverture, melted
1 tablespoon cognac, 2 teaspoons pear brandy
2¾ cups cream
For the cherries:
14 oz fresh cherries, pitted, 2 tablespoons sugar
2 tablespoons water, 1 teaspoon cornstarch
For the filling and decoration:
7 fl oz cream whipped with 2 teaspoons kirsch
½ cup cream whipped with 4 teaspoons confectioners' sugar
cocoa powder
You will also need:
baking sheets, parchment paper
six 4-inch mousse rings 1¼ inch deep
acetate strip, kirsch

Make the chocolate spongecake. To make the ladyfingers preheat the oven to 300°F. Beat the egg yolks with the confectioners' sugar and cocoa until frothy. Add the whole egg and beat to a thick frothy batter. Add the vanilla sugar. Whip the egg whites with the salt until stiff and fold into the batter.

Finally, fold in the flour mixture. Line the baking sheets with parchment paper. Spoon the mixture into a pastry bag with a round tip and pipe strips ½ x 2 inches onto the baking sheets. Bake for 10 minutes. Cool on a wire rack.

Line the mousse rings with acetate strip. Cut the chocolate spongecake into two layers horizontally, each ¼ inch deep. Cut these into 6 rounds 4 inches in diameter and 6 rounds 3 inches in diameter. Place the larger rounds in the mousse rings.

To make the mousse, beat the whole egg with the egg yolk over hot water until frothy. Dissolve the gelatin in it. Remove from the heat. Stir in the couverture, then the cognac and brandy. Whip the cream until semi-stiff and fold in. Allow to cool.

Preheat the oven to 400°F. Mix the cherries with the sugar and water. Cook in the oven for 15 minutes. Mix the cornstarch to a paste with a little water and use to thicken the cherry juice. Allow to cool.

Spoon 6 tablespoons of the kirsch-flavored cream into a pastry bag with a round tip, and pipe around the edge of each mousse ring. Spoon in the cherries and fill the ring about two-thirds full with the remaining cream. Finish as described in the caption below.

Place the smaller spongecake on top and moisten with kirsch. Spread the chocolate mousse on top and smooth. Refrigerate to firm up. Remove the rings and acetate strips. Before serving, use a round tip to pipe small dabs of whipped cream on the tops of the small tortes, then sift cocoa powder over them. Press the ladyfingers to the sides, arrange on plates, and decorate with the cherries.

Chocolate mousse

This light cream filling can be prepared using all three types of couverture

CHOCOLATE MOUSSE WITH PASSION FRUIT SAUCE

Serves 4

For the mousse:

7 oz couverture, 5 eggs, separated

scant ½ cup sugar, ½ cup cream

2 tablespoons vanilla sugar

3 tablespoons strong coffee

For the passion fruit sauce:

6 passion fruits (½ cup fruit flesh)

2 tablespoons water, 2 tablespoons white wine

¼ cup sugar

½ teaspoon gelatin

To make chocolate baskets, cover any hemispherical shape 3 inches in diameter with foil, and smooth out all the wrinkles. Using a paper pastry bag (see page 62), pipe random strands all over the surface. When hard, remove from the foil.

For the raspberry cream:

3 oz fresh raspberries, ½ cup cream

2 tablespoons sugar

You will also need:

4 little baskets made of couverture

raspberries to decorate

To make the mousse, melt the couverture over hot water. Whip the egg whites with the sugar until stiff. Whip the cream. Beat the egg yolks with the vanilla sugar until frothy and mix in the coffee. Stir in the couverture, blend in the cream using a whisk, and fold in the stiff egg whites immediately. Transfer to a large bowl and refrigerate to set.

Cut the passion fruits in half and remove the flesh with a spoon. Place in a saucepan with the water, white wine, and sugar. Bring to a boil and reduce the liquid by a third. Strain. Dissolve the gelatin in the liquid, stirring briskly. Allow to cool.

Purée the raspberries and strain them. Whip the cream with the sugar, fold in the raspberry purée, and spoon into a pastry bag with a large star tip.

Place two scoops of the mousse on each plate. Place the chocolate baskets beside them and pipe in a portion of raspberry cream. Spoon passion fruit sauce onto the plate and decorate with raspberries.

WHITE AND MILK CHOCOLATE MOUSSE MINI TORTES WITH ORANGE SEGMENTS

Makes 9

For the spongecake:

3 eggs, heaping ¼ cup sugar

scraped contents of ½ vanilla bean, pinch of salt

½ cup flour, ½ cup cornstarch

1 tablespoon milk, 1 tablespoon oil

For the white chocolate mousse:

5 oz white couverture, 5½ tablespoons soft butter

2 tablespoons cognac, 2 egg yolks, 1¼ cups cream

For the milk chocolate mousse:

5 oz milk chocolate couverture

2 tablespoons soft butter

1 tablespoon Grand Marnier, 2 egg yolks,

1 cup cream

For the orange segments:

3 seedless oranges, 3 tablespoons Grand Marnier

¼ cup sugar

You will also need:

baking sheets, parchment paper, plastic wrap

nine 3-inch mousse rings 1¼ inches deep

strips of orange zest, sugar syrup

Preheat the oven to 400°F. To make the spongecake, beat the sugar with the butter, vanilla, and salt. Sift the flour with the cornstarch and trickle into the egg mixture gradually, stirring constantly. Warm the milk and oil to 125°F and blend in. Spread the batter ¼–⅜ inch deep on a baking sheet lined with parchment paper. Bake for 10–12 minutes. Turn out onto a paper dusted with sugar. Allow to cool. Use the mousse ring to cut out 9 bases.

To make each mousse, melt the couverture. Mix with the soft butter and the alcohol, and temper at 95°F. Beat the egg yolks until frothy. Whip the cream. Stir the couverture quickly and lightly into the egg yolks and blend into the whipped cream.

Moisten a baking sheet and cover with plastic wrap. Stroke over the surface with the straight edge of a dough scraper to squeeze out the moisture between the baking sheet and plastic wrap so that the latter adheres without wrinkles. Set the mousse rings on top. Using a pastry bag with a large round tip, pipe milk chocolate mousse into the rings until they are a third full. Spoon the white chocolate mousse into another pastry bag with a large round tip. Press the tip into the milk chocolate mousse until it nearly touches the bottom and fill the ring with white mousse. Place the spongecake bases on top and freeze.

Peel the oranges. Cut the orange segments from the membrane and marinate in Grand Marnier mixed with sugar.

Before serving, allow the mini tortes to thaw at room temperature briefly. Press on the spongecake base and push each one up out of the ring. Cut in half and arrange on a plate as shown above. Decorate with orange segments, marinade, and strips of orange peel cooked briefly in sugar syrup.

A delight to see

Desserts served in glasses

SEMOLINA CREAM FILLING WITH CHOCOLATE SAUCE

The chocolate sauce should be prepared well in advance so that it has time to cool.

Serves 6

For the chocolate sauce:

⅔ cup cream, 1 teaspoon cornstarch

2 oz couverture, chopped

For the cream filling:

1 cup milk, scraped contents of ½ vanilla bean

pinch of salt, scant ¼ cup semolina, 1 teaspoon gelatin

1 egg yolk, 8 teaspoons sugar, 1 cup cream

You will also need:

6 stewed cherries, 6 glasses

To make the chocolate sauce, bring ½ cup of the cream to a boil. Mix the cornstarch with the remaining cream and stir into the boiling cream. Remove from the heat, add the couverture, and stir constantly until melted. Mix with a hand blender. Allow to cool.

To make the cream filling, bring the milk to a boil with the vanilla and salt. Trickle in the semolina, stirring constantly, and allow to boil briefly. Cook until soft. Dissolve the gelatin in the hot semolina. Mix the egg yolk with the sugar and stir into the semolina. Allow to cool. Whip the cream, and just as the semolina is beginning to set, stir in. Spoon the mixture into glasses. Using a funnel, pour chocolate sauce on top and decorate with a cherry.

MILK CHOCOLATE CREAM DESSERT

The easiest-ever dessert.

Serves 5

1¼ cups cream

3 oz milk chocolate couverture, chopped

You will also need:

rectangles of striped couverture (see page 59)

Bring the cream to a boil. Melt the couverture in the cream. Mix with a hand blender for 30 seconds. Cool rapidly and refrigerate for 24 hours. Whip the cream to a soft, semi-liquid consistency. Spoon into glasses and decorate with pieces of striped couverture.

To decorate, add a piece of chocolate lattice (see pages 62–3) and some mint leaves.

WHITE MOUSSE MINI-TORTES WITH PEACHES

Makes 9

For the spongecake:

1 tablespoon milk, 1 tablespoon oil

3 eggs

heaping ¼ cup sugar

scraped contents of ½ vanilla bean

pinch of salt

½ cup flour

½ cup cornstarch

For the white mousse:

9½ oz white couverture

¾ cup butter, softened

¼ cup cognac

3 egg yolks

2⅜ cups cream

For the poached peaches:

1¼ lb peaches

lemon juice, sugar

To decorate:

couverture lattice, mint leaves

You will also need:

baking sheets, parchment paper

plastic wrap

nine 3-inch mousse rings 1¼ inches deep

Preheat the oven to 400°F. To make the spongecake, heat the milk and oil to 125°F. Beat the eggs with the sugar, vanilla, and salt. Sift the flour and cornstarch onto a paper and trickle into the egg mixture, stirring constantly. Blend in the milk-oil mixture. Spread the batter ¼ inch deep on a baking sheet lined with parchment paper. Bake for 10–12 minutes. Remove and turn out onto a paper dusted with sugar. Remove the parchment paper and allow to cool. Using the mousse ring as a cutter, cut out 9 bases.

To make the mousse, melt the couverture over hot water, mix with the soft butter and the cognac and temper at 95°F. Beat the egg yolks until frothy. Whip the cream. Stir the couverture mixture quickly and lightly into the egg yolks and blend into the whipped cream.

Moisten a baking sheet and cover with plastic wrap. Stroke over the surface with the straight edge of a dough scraper to squeeze out the moisture between the baking sheet and plastic wrap so that the latter adheres without wrinkles. Set the mousse rings on top. Spoon the mousse into a pastry bag with a large round tip and pipe into the rings. Smooth the tops, place the spongecake bases on top, and freeze.

Blanch the peaches, plunge into cold water, and remove the skins. Cut the fruit in half, remove the stone, and slice the flesh. Poach gently in a little water with lemon juice and sugar until soft all the way through. Purée a third of the peach slices.

To serve, remove the mousse mini-tortes from the baking sheet and place spongecake side down. After several minutes at room temperature, press out of the rings, preferably directly onto a serving plate. Arrange with the peach purée, peach slices, mint leaves, and chocolate lattice.

Patissière Brigitte Lastin, at Interconti in Vienna, has the professional knack for making designs with couverture.

Bavarian Cream in a chocolate ring

Bavarian cream with raspberries in a white chocolate ring, and with cranberries in a chocolate drop

The basis of a Bavarian cream is always a *crème à l'anglaise*, a custard or vanilla sauce made with milk, eggs, and sugar. Whipped cream is added to give a looser texture. Other flavors, including chocolate, of course, can be used in place of the vanilla. In the two recipes that follow, white couverture is used to enclose the cream filling, and the strong chocolate flavor comes from the sauce.

RASPBERRY CREAM WITH CHOCOLATE SAUCE
Serves 4
For the raspberry cream:
1 cup milk, ½ vanilla bean split lengthwise
3 egg yolks, 6 tablespoons sugar
1½ teaspoons gelatin
5 oz raspberries (fresh or frozen)
3 tablespoons raspberry brandy, 7 fl oz cream
For the chocolate sauce:
5 oz couverture, 5 tablespoons milk
3½ fl oz cream, 2 tablespoons honey
You will also need:
four 3-inch rings of white chocolate (see pages 64–5)
crushed almond croquant (see page 145)
12 raspberries

To make the raspberry cream, bring the milk to a boil with the vanilla bean. Remove the vanilla bean. Beat the egg yolks with the sugar until frothy. Add the hot milk, stirring constantly. Transfer the mixture to a saucepan and, stirring constantly, heat to thicken until you can "blow roses" (see page 230). Dissolve the gelatin in the hot cream. Strain through a fine-mesh sieve into a bowl. Purée the raspberries and strain into the cream. Add the

Chocolate containers:

Chocolate containers can be made easily using the acetate method as described on page 65.

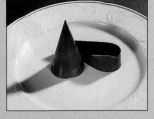

Chocolate in the shape of a teardrop and a cone. These containers are ideal for filling with creams, parfait, or ice cream.

brandy and stir together well. Set aside to cool.

Meanwhile, make the sauce. Melt the couverture over hot water. Bring the milk, cream, and honey to a boil, and stir into the couverture. Place a hand blender in the cream, switch on, and blend, using a circular motion and making sure that the blender remains under the surface. Allow to cool.

Bavarian creams with chocolate sauce. Cranberries are the dominant flavor in one cream, raspberries in the other, and the chocolate sauces provide a welcome contrast.

CRANBERRY CREAM WITH CHOCOLATE AND RUM SAUCE

Serves 4

For the cranberry cream:

1 cup milk, 3 egg yolks, ¼ cup sugar

1½ teaspoons gelatin

7 oz cranberries (fresh or frozen)

6 tablespoons sugar, 7 fl oz cream

For the chocolate and rum sauce:

5 oz couverture, 5 tablespoons milk, 3½ fl oz cream

2 tablespoons honey, 3 tablespoons dark rum

You will also need:

8 white chocolate teardrop rings (see pages 64–5)

whipped cream for the rosettes, pistachio croquant

To make the cranberry cream, bring the milk to a boil. Beat the egg yolks with the sugar until frothy. Add the hot milk slowly, stirring constantly. Transfer to a saucepan, heat slowly, stirring constantly, until you can "blow roses" (see page 230). Dissolve the gelatin in the hot cream and pass through a fine-mesh sieve into a bowl. Allow to cool.

Bring the cranberries and sugar to a boil. Reserve 1 tablespoon of cranberries. Purée the remainder, strain into the cream, stir in, and chill.

To make the sauce, melt the couverture over hot water. Bring the milk, cream, and honey to a boil, and stir into the couverture. Place a hand blender in the cream, switch on, and blend, using a circular motion and making sure that the blender remains under the surface. Allow to cool. Stir the rum into the sauce when it is almost cold.

Place 2 chocolate teardrops on each plate. Whip the cream for the cream filling and blend into the cranberry cream when it is almost cold but still fluid. Pipe into the teardrops and leave to set. Pour the cold chocolate sauce on top. Decorate with a rosette of cream, the reserved cranberries, and croquant.

Arrange the white chocolate rings on plates. Whip the cream for the cream filling, and stir into the raspberry cream when the latter is almost cold but still fluid. Spoon into a pastry bag with a large star tip and pipe thick rosettes into the rings. Allow to set. Pour the cold, but not ice cold, sauce over the dessert. Sprinkle with croquant and decorate with raspberries.

A vanilla or fruit sauce also goes well with the chocolate soufflé. For children, the cognac-flavored plums can be replaced by a non-alcoholic sauce.

CHOCOLATE SOUFFLÉ WITH CHOCOLATE SAUCE AND COGNAC PRUNES

This traditional Austrian dessert is served warm. The cognac-flavored prunes can be prepared in advance, and keep well.

Serves 9–10
For the prunes:
20 prunes, cognac or brandy
For the soufflé:
1 cup milk, 7 tablespoons butter
scraped contents of 1 vanilla bean
pinch of salt
¾ cup flour
2 oz couverture, melted
6 eggs, separated
scant ½ cup sugar
For the chocolate sauce:
1 cup cream
1 teaspoon cornstarch
scraped contents of ½ vanilla bean
3 oz couverture, chopped
To decorate:
½ cup cream, whipped
You will also need:
soufflé dish, butter and bread crumbs
confectioners' sugar

Place the prunes in a screw-top jar, cover with cognac, and put on the lid. Place a folded cloth in the bottom of a saucepan (to prevent direct contact between the jar and the bottom of the pan). Place the jar in the pan and fill the pan with cold water to come halfway up the jar. Cover the pan, bring the water to a boil, and simmer gently for 10–20 minutes, depending on the size of the jar. Allow to cool.

Preheat the oven to 315°F. To make the soufflé, bring the milk to a boil with the butter, vanilla, and salt. Trickle the flour into the mixture, stirring constantly. Allow the paste to dry out briefly so that it leaves the sides of the saucepan. Remove from the heat and stir in the couverture. Stir in the egg yolks one at a time. Whip the egg whites with the sugar until stiff. Combine part of this into the soufflé mixture, and then blend the mixture into the remaining whipped egg whites.

Grease the soufflé dish with butter and sprinkle with bread crumbs. Spoon in the mixture. Stand the dish in a deep pan and fill with boiling water to halfway up the sides of the dish. Bake for 50 minutes.

To make the chocolate sauce, bring ¾ cup of cream to a boil. Stir the remaining cream into the cornstarch with the vanilla and stir this into the boiling cream. Remove from the heat and add the couverture, stirring until it melts. Blend thoroughly with a hand blender.

Divide the soufflé into portions and arrange on plates. Sift confectioners' sugar lightly on top and serve with the hot chocolate sauce, 2 prunes, and a tablespoon of whipped cream.

Baked puddings and soufflés

These baked chocolate desserts are classics in international patisserie

CHOCOLATE SOUFFLÉ

Makes 6 individual soufflés
For the soufflé:
¼ cup butter, softened, ½ cup flour
1 cup milk, 1½ oz couverture
2 heaping tablespoons cocoa powder
5 egg whites, 4 egg yolks
6 tablespoons sugar

You will also need:
six 3-inch soufflé dishes, melted butter, sugar, confectioners' sugar

Preheat the oven to 400°F. Prepare the dishes as shown. Work the flour into the butter, form into a roll, and break into small pieces. Bring the milk, couverture, and cocoa powder to a boil. Stir in the flour–butter paste. Remove the hot, smoothly bound mixture from the heat, and stir in 1 egg white. Transfer the mixture to a bowl and let cool until lukewarm. Stir in the egg yolks one at a time. Whip the remaining egg whites with the sugar until soft. Stir a quarter of the egg whites into the batter, then fold in the rest. Spoon the mixture into molds and stand in a pan of hot water (176°F), with the water 1 inch below the rims. Bake for 40 minutes. Remove from the oven, sift with confectioners' sugar, and serve immediately.

To make a chocolate soufflé:

Grease the dishes with melted, almost cold butter, and dust with sugar. The sides and base must be completely coated. Tip out the surplus sugar.

Pour the milk into a saucepan. Chop the couverture and add. Sift in the cocoa powder and bring to a boil while stirring.

Add the pieces of flour–butter paste one at a time and stir into the boiling milk until the flour binds the liquid into a homogeneous mass.

Whisk the egg yolks into the warm mixture one at a time, and continue to stir until the mixture is smooth and creamy again. Remove from the heat and stir in 1 egg white.

Stir in a quarter of the whipped egg whites with a whisk to lighten the batter. Fold in the remainder of the whipped egg whites with a wooden spoon.

Fill the soufflé dishes to within ½ inch of the top, place in a pan of hot water, and cook in the preheated oven for 40 minutes.

The classic sauce for a chocolate soufflé is *crème à l'anglaise*, a simple vanilla sauce cooked to the point where it coats the back of a spoon. Another fine touch is Crème Chantilly, a semi-stiff whipped cream flavored with vanilla.

Omelets with chocolate

Whether you prefer wafer-thin pancakes or a thick omelet, chocolate is a perfect ingredient for both the batter and the filling

The soufflé filling is spooned into the center of the pancake, which is then folded in half and baked in the oven.

CHOCOLATE PANCAKES WITH SOUFFLÉ FILLING

Serves 8

For the pancakes:

¾ cup butter, 1½ cups milk, 1¼ cups flour

4 eggs, 4 teaspoons vanilla sugar, pinch of salt

grated zest of 1 orange and 1 lemon

For the orange and ginger butter:

¼ cup sugar, juice of 6–8 oranges and ½ lemon

2 tablespoons grated or finely chopped fresh ginger

¼ cup butter, 1 teaspoon vanilla pudding mix

3 tablespoons Cointreau, 4 teaspoons amaretto

zest of 1 orange, blanched

For the filling:

7 fl oz milk, scraped contents of 1 vanilla bean

2 tablespoons butter, softened, ½ cup flour

4 egg yolks, 2 oz couverture, melted,

grated zest of ½ orange

3 egg whites, whipped with ¼ cup sugar until stiff

For the caramelized pear slices:

3–4 pears, washed

1½ tablespoons sugar and 4½ teaspoons butter for each pancake

You will also need:

baking sheet, butter

To make the pancakes, melt the butter until it browns. Stir the other ingredients together until smooth. When the butter has cooled to room temperature, stir into the batter. Cook the pancakes and stack between plastic wrap.

To make the orange and ginger butter, melt the sugar until it colors slightly. Pour in the fruit juices, add the ginger, and reduce by a third. Stir in the butter and thicken with pudding mix mixed with a little water. Remove from the heat, add the alcohol, mix with a hand blender and stir in the orange zest.

Preheat the oven to 400°F. To make the filling, bring the milk and vanilla to a boil. Knead the butter with the flour, break into flakes, and stir into the milk to thicken. On a cold marble slab, work the mixture with a dough scraper until it cools to 131°F. Place in a bowl, add the egg yolks one at a time, and mix to a smooth batter after each one. Mix in the couverture and orange zest. Fold in the stiff egg whites. Place 3 tablespoonsful on each pancake, fold in half, and spread with butter. Place on a buttered baking sheet and bake for 8 minutes.

Cut the pears, unpeeled, into long thin slices. In a large frying pan, melt the sugar, stir in the butter, and caramelize the pear slices on both sides. Place 2 pear slices and 1 pancake on each plate and pour the orange and ginger butter on top.

CARAMELIZED CHOCOLATE OMELET WITH PASSION FRUIT SAUCE

Serves 6–8

For the passion fruit sauce:

12 passion fruits, 6 tablespoons sugar

3 tablespoons mineral water

scraped contents of ½ vanilla bean

For the vanilla sauce:

½ cup milk, ½ cup cream

scraped contents of 1 vanilla bean

¼ cup sugar, 5 egg yolks

For the chocolate omelet:

2 eggs, ½ cup sugar

½ cup butter, 4 oz couverture, melted

To decorate:

pomegranate seeds

segments of 1 large orange, membrane removed

You will also need:

six to eight 3-inch mousse rings 1¼ inches deep

butter and sugar for the rings

six to eight 3-inch round wafer cookies

confectioners' sugar

To make the sauce, halve the passion fruits, remove the flesh, and bring to a boil with the other ingredients. Mix briefly with a hand blender and strain. Mix 1 tablespoon of the seeds back into the sauce.

To make the vanilla sauce, bring the milk, cream, and vanilla to a boil. Beat the sugar and egg yolks until frothy, then add the hot milk, stirring constantly. Cook over hot water until thick enough to coat the back of a spoon. Strain and cool.

To make the omelet, beat the eggs with the sugar over hot water, then remove from the heat and whip to a firm froth. Stir the butter into the warm, melted couverture and fold into the eggs.

Preheat the oven to 375°F. Brush the insides of the mousse rings with butter and dust with sugar. Place the wafers at the bottom, and fill two-thirds with the omelet batter. Dust thickly with confectioners' sugar. Bake for 6 minutes and then place under the broiler for the confectioners' sugar to caramelize fully. Carefully cut around the rings with a knife and set on a plate. Decorate with the two sauces, pomegranate seeds, and orange segments.

Filled with chocolate

Desserts combining chocolate with grenadine and sour cherries

MILLE FEUILLES WITH RUM GANACHE AND GRENADINE SAUCE

Serves 6

7 oz puff pastry, sugar for rolling out

For the filling:

½ cup cream, 3½ oz couverture, chopped

3 tablespoons dark rum

For the grenadine sauce:

4 large pomegranates, 6 tablespoons sugar

2 tablespoons lime juice, ½ cup full-bodied red wine

To decorate:

1 cup cream, 4 teaspoons sugar

You will also need:

baking sheet, sugar for dusting

Preheat the oven to 400°F. Dust the work surface with sugar and roll out the dough to 6 x 9 inches. Dust the surface of the pastry with sugar. Cut into six 3-inch squares. Moisten the baking sheet with water, place the pastry squares on the sheet, and allow to rest for 30 minutes. Bake for 10–15 minutes, until the surface has caramelized. Remove from the baking sheet while still hot and cut each slice in half horizontally.

To make the filling, bring the cream to a boil, remove from the heat, and add the chopped couverture, stirring constantly until melted. Place a hand blender in the cream, switch on, and blend thoroughly, using a circular motion and not allowing the blender to come to the surface. Allow to cool. Whip with a hand mixer until frothy and add the rum. Using a pastry bag with a star tip, pipe a double ring onto the bottom half of each pastry square.

To make the sauce, break open the pomegranates and mix the seeds in a saucepan with the other ingredients. Simmer over a low heat until the mixture has reduced by half. Cool and strain.

To decorate, whip the cream with the sugar to soft peaks and stir in 3–4 tablespoons of the sauce. Place a spoonful of whipped cream on the cream filling, top with the other half of the pastry square, and add the sauce and pomegranate seeds.

and a little water. Working from the center, mix the ingredients together, adding small amounts of water at a time as required, and using your hands to make a pliable dough. Form into a ball and place on a board brushed with oil. Brush with oil and leave to rest for at least 30 minutes.

To make the filling, work the almond paste with a little butter until smooth. Beat with the remainder of the butter, couverture, vanilla, and salt until frothy. Add the egg yolks one at a time. Whip the egg whites with the sugar until stiff. Combine both mixtures and blend in the almonds.

Preheat the oven to 325°F. Spread the towel on a work surface and dust with flour. Place the dough on the towel and roll out with a rolling pin. Then, with lightly clenched fists working under the dough, stretch the dough out wafer-thin to 28 x 40 inches. Spread the filling out lengthwise on the dough to cover about a quarter of the surface. Brush the remaining surface with melted, barely lukewarm butter. Cut off the thick edges of the pastry. Roll up the pastry by lifting the towel at one end and encouraging the dough to roll over on itself, like a jelly roll. Cut in three and place in a buttered cake pan. Brush with butter. Bake for 45 minutes. Brush with butter once or twice while baking.

To make the Royale, mix the egg with the sugar, then stir into the hot milk. After 15 minutes' baking time, pour the Royale over the strudel. Using a fork, prick through the strudel almost to the base so that the Royale will be better absorbed. Divide the strudel into portions and arrange on plates. Sift confectioners' sugar on top and serve with the cherry sauce (see caption) and the honey cream.

Bring the cherries to a boil with the water and sugar. Pour off the juice and heat it with the red wine. Thicken with the cornstarch. Return the fruit to the pan and bring back to a boil.

CHOCOLATE STRUDEL WITH HONEY CREAM AND CHERRIES

Serves 10

For the dough:

2¼ cups flour, pinch of salt

about ½ cup water, 5 teaspoons oil

For the chocolate and almond filling:

2 oz almond paste, ¾ cup butter

5 oz couverture, melted

scraped contents of 1 vanilla bean

pinch of salt, 9 eggs, separated

3½ oz sugar, 1¾ cups ground almonds

For the Royale:

1 egg, 8 teaspoons sugar, 1¾ cups hot milk

For the sour cherry sauce:

7 oz cherries, 5 tablespoons water

¼ cup sugar, ½ cup red wine, 1 teaspoon cornstarch

For the honey cream:

½ cup sour cream, mixed with 2 teaspoons honey

You will also need:

30 x 43-inch dish towel, 9 x 12½-inch cake pan

about ½ cup butter, confectioners' sugar

To make the dough, sift the flour onto a work surface and make a well in the middle. Add the salt

Bûche de Noël

Yule log and ice parfait in a mandarin orange, two exclusive desserts created by Eckart Witzigmann

For the mulled wine sabayon:
2¼ cups mulled wine, 1 cinnamon stick
1 clove, 1 star anise
4 egg yolks, scant ½ cup sugar, ½ teaspoon gelatin
2 tablespoons whipped cream
You will also need:
rectangular cake pan
acetate strips 6¼ x 12½ inches
tempered dark and milk couverture
12½-inch u-shaped mold

Make the spongecake as described on page 74, using a rectangular cake pan. Cut into two 12½-inch long pieces, one to the internal width of the mold, the other to the external width of the mold. To make the mousse, melt the two types of couverture together. Beat the whole egg with the egg yolk over hot water until frothy. The mixture should increase in volume. Dissolve the gelatin in the egg mixture. Remove from the heat. Stir in the couverture followed by the alcohol. Whip the cream until semi-stiff and stir in one third, using a whisk. Mix the remaining cream with the mixed spice and gingerbread, and fold in.

Spread the milk chocolate couverture over the bark-patterned dark couverture (see small photograph) and place the strip, acetate side down, into the mold. Fill one third with mousse, smooth, and place the narrower strip of spongecake on top. Fill up to the edge of the acetate strip with the remaining mousse, smooth, and place the broader strip of spongecake on top. Stand in a cool place.

To make the sabayon, bring the mulled wine to a boil with the cinnamon, clove, and star anise. Reduce by half. Allow to cool. Remove the spices. Whip the egg yolks with the sugar over hot water until creamy. Add the cooled mulled wine and beat until frothy and the volume increases. Dissolve the gelatin in the wine mixture. Place the bowl over iced water and whip the sabayon until cold. Fold in the whipped cream just before serving.

Turn the log out of the mold. After a few minutes, remove the acetate. Slice with a warm knife. Decorate with chocolate leaves (see pages 60–61) and red almond paste berries.

Bark pattern. Spread the dark couverture thinly on acetate strip and make wavy lines by pushing the grain-effect tool forward through the couverture. Allow to set.

CHOCOLATE LOG WITH GINGERBREAD MOUSSE AND A MULLED WINE SABAYON
The traditional French Bûche de Noël is godfather to this fine dessert.

Serves 6

1 recipe light-colored sponge cake (see page 74), substituting ¼ cup ground almonds for 1 tablespoon flour
For the gingerbread mousse:
7 oz milk chocolate couverture
2 oz dark couverture
1 egg, 1 egg yolk, 2 teaspoons gelatin
3 teaspoons cognac, 2 teaspoons pear brandy
2¾ cups cream, 2 tablespoons mixed spice
1 cup finely chopped gingerbread,

CHOCOLATE AND ALMOND PARFAIT WITH STEWED MANDARINS

Serves 15

15 same-size mandarins, washed and dried

For the stewed mandarins:

7 mandarins, 1¼ cups mandarin juice, ¼ cup sugar

grated zest of 1 mandarin

scraped contents of ½ vanilla bean

1 small bay leaf

2 cloves, 1 star anise, 8 coriander seeds

1 teaspoon gelatin

For the chocolate and almond parfait:

3 eggs, ⅝ cup sugar, 5 teaspoons water

2 oz couverture, melted, 4 teaspoons honey

2¼ cups cream

¾ cup roasted flaked almonds

For the orange zest:

1 orange, 3 teaspoons orange juice

3 teaspoons Cointreau, 3 tablespoons grenadine syrup

You will also need:

acetate strip

Begin a day in advance. Cut off the top third of the 15 mandarins and reserve. Remove the flesh completely from the deeper section and squeeze out the juice to use later for stewing the mandarins.

Surround the hollow sections with acetate strip to twice their height and secure with tape.

To make the stewed mandarins, remove the skin and divide the fruit into segments, removing all the fibers. Bring the juice to a boil with the sugar, grated zest, and all the spices. Dissolve the gelatin in it. Allow to cool. Add the mandarin segments and refrigerate overnight. Remove the spices.

To make the parfait, beat the eggs until frothy. Heat the water with the sugar to 244°F. Pour into the eggs in a thin stream, beating continuously until cold. Mix in the couverture and honey. Whip the cream and whisk one third into the parfait. Use a spatula to fold in the remaining cream and the flaked almonds. Spoon the parfait into the hollowed out mandarins so that it stands ½ inch above the rims. Freeze.

To make the zest, peel the orange very thinly, avoiding the white pith. Cut into fine julienne strips and blanch. Drain well. Bring the orange juice, Cointreau, and grenadine syrup to a boil with the julienne strips, reduce by two-thirds, and then cool.

Remove the acetate strips from the fruit and top with the mandarin lids. Arrange on the plate with the stewed mandarins and the orange zest.

Mousse with poppy seeds and chocolate

Whether the mousse is prepared as a single torte or in individual portions, the chocolate sauce makes a particularly fine accompaniment

POPPY SEED AND CHOCOLATE MOUSSE WITH BLACK CURRANT JELLY AND CANDIED CHESTNUTS

Makes 2 small tortes
1 recipe Viennese spongecake (see page 74)
For the black currant jelly:
7 oz black currants, 6 tablespoons sugar
1½ teaspoons gelatin
For the filling:
⅔ cup ground poppy seeds, ½ cup port wine
7 oz white couverture, 1 egg, 1 egg yolk
1¼ teaspoons gelatin
4 teaspoons cognac, scraped contents of ½ vanilla bean
pinch of cinnamon, 2¼ cups cream
For the caramelized chestnuts:
12 chestnuts, 7 fl oz sugar syrup
½ cup orange juice
2 tablespoons Cointreau
1 lb sugar, 1 cup water
10 teaspoons glucose syrup
You will also need:
2 octagonal baking pans 7 inches in diameter, 1¼ inches deep

Make the Viennese spongecake a day in advance. Cut two layers ¼-inch thick from the cake. Cut out a base to fit each cake pan and place in the bottom.

The black currant jelly is also best made a day in advance. Bring the black currants to a rolling boil with the sugar. Strain, pressing the fruit gently. Dissolve the gelatin in some of the hot juice, mix with the remainder of the juice, and set aside to cool.

To make the filling, stir the poppy seeds with the port in a saucepan. Bring to a boil over medium heat and boil down to a dry poppyseed paste. Set aside.

Melt the white couverture over hot water at 104°F. Beat the whole egg and egg yolk over hot water until frothy. Dissolve the gelatin in it. Stir in the melted couverture, then the cognac, vanilla, and cinnamon. Whip the cream to soft peaks. Whisk one third into the couverture, then fold in the remaining cream.

Spoon the filling onto the spongecake base, a third of the way up the pan. Press the surface several times to get a really smooth finish. Freeze until the cream has become firm, then use a teaspoon to spread a thin layer of the firm jelly on top. Freeze until set.

Mix the poppyseed paste into the remaining cream filling and spread on top of the black currant jelly to just below the top of the pan. Freeze.

Fill the pan up to the top with the remaining black currant jelly; the poppyseeds should remain visible. If the jelly has set too hard, warm slightly. Put the pans into a cool place until the mousse is firm.

Peel the chestnuts, as shown in the picture below left. Mix the sugar syrup, orange juice, and Cointreau, and marinate the chestnuts in it overnight. The next day, preheat the oven to 300°F. Wipe the chestnuts dry with paper towels and roast for 5 minutes. In a small saucepan, bring the sugar, water, and glucose syrup to a boil, and boil down to an amber-colored caramel, skimming off the froth from time to time. Place the saucepan briefly in iced water. Put the chestnuts on toothpicks and dip into the caramel, lift out, and allow to drip over the saucepan. As soon as the thread of caramel hardens, shape by hand, leave to set, and trim with scissors. Use for decorating the tortes.

To peel chestnuts: Score the shells crosswise with a sharp knife without cutting into the flesh.

Preheat the oven to 425°F. Place the chestnuts in an ovenproof dish and roast for 10 minutes.

Remove the split shells from the chestnuts while still hot, holding them in a towel.

MILK CHOCOLATE SAUCE

A little extra bitter chocolate gives this light sauce a fine, piquant touch.

Makes ¼ cup

1 cup milk, 1 tablespoon honey

1 vanilla bean, slit lengthwise

2 egg yolks, 1 teaspoon cornstarch

4 teaspoons sugar

2 oz milk chocolate couverture, melted

1 oz extra bitter couverture

Bring the milk to a boil with the honey and vanilla bean. Beat the egg yolks with the cornstarch and sugar until frothy. Stir in 2–3 tablespoons of hot milk. Use this to thicken the boiling milk, then allow to cool. Remove the vanilla bean and mix in the melted couverture. Stir the sauce until smooth and allow to cool.

Hold the caramel-dipped chestnuts over the saucepan so that a long thread forms.

Homemade ice cream

Many people no longer make their own ice cream, but it is worth trying this basic recipe from Eckart Witzigmann

To make ice cream:
Bring the milk to a boil with the cream, half the sugar, the vanilla beans, and salt, stirring occasionally. Beat the egg yolks with the whole eggs and the remaining sugar over hot water. Remove from the heat.

Remove the vanilla beans and whisk the boiling milk mixture into the egg mixture. Place over hot water again.

Using a wooden spoon, stir the mixture until it coats the back of the spoon.

Stir in the glucose syrup, remove from the heat, place over ice water, and stir until cold.

Pass the cream through a fine-mesh sieve to remove any egg white that has run.

Spoon the mixture into an ice cream maker and freeze. Remove the spatula and divide the ice cream into portions.

Chocolate ice cream:
Stir in 4 oz melted couverture with the glucose syrup.

BASIC RECIPE FOR ICE CREAM

This recipe is for vanilla ice cream, but it can be used as the basis for many different flavors, including chocolate, of course. You can use bittersweet chocolate, or ⅔ milk chocolate couverture and ⅓ bittersweet chocolate to give a light-colored bitter chocolate ice cream. Another variation is a mixture of equal parts of hazelnut nougat and couverture.

Makes about 5 cups
2¼ cups milk, 2¼ cups cream
¾ cup + 2 tablespoons sugar
scraped contents of 4 vanilla beans
pinch of salt
8 egg yolks, 4 eggs
4 teaspoons glucose syrup

Cinnamon ice cream: Use only 3 vanilla beans and include 3 cinnamon sticks, 1 star anise, and 1 clove. Remove the spices before adding the boiling milk.

CHOCOLATE FLUMMERY WITH ICE CREAM SAUCE

Serves 4

| 2 oz couverture |
| 2 heaping tablespoons cornstarch |
| 2 egg yolks, scant ½ cup sugar |
| 2¼ cups milk |
| ½ vanilla bean |
| 1 teaspoon gelatin |
| For the ice cream sauce: |
| 2 scoops vanilla ice cream |
| ½ cup strawberry purée or strawberry sauce |
| ½ cup whipped cream |
| To decorate: |
| ¼ lb fresh strawberries, strawberry purée |
| zest of 1 orange |
| lattice made with white couverture (see pages 62–3) |
| You will also need: |
| 4 ribbed or smooth molds |

Melt the couverture over hot water. Mix the cornstarch, egg yolks, and sugar with a little milk. Bring the remaining milk to a boil with the vanilla bean and stir in the melted couverture. Stir in the cornstarch mixture and cook through briefly, stirring constantly. Remove from the heat and stir in the gelatin until it has dissolved completely. Rinse out the molds in cold water and spoon in the mixture. Refrigerate to set.

Stir the vanilla ice cream with the strawberry purée and the whipped cream. Turn out the flummery onto plates and add the ice cream. Decorate with the strawberries, strawberry purée, orange zest, and white chocolate lattice.

CHOCOLATE AND RUM ICE CREAM WITH STRAWBERRY SAUCE

Serve a flavored scoop of chocolate ice cream in a white chocolate ring with strawberry sauce.

Serves 4

| four 3-inch rings made of white chocolate (see page 64) |
| 4 ladyfingers |
| 3 tablespoons dark rum |
| 4 large scoops chocolate ice cream (see page 204) |
| For the strawberry sauce: |
| ½ lb strawberries, ¼ cup sugar |
| ¼ cup water |
| zest of ½ orange, in strips |
| 4 teaspoons dark rum |
| To decorate: |
| a little whipped cream |
| 4 strawberries |

To make the strawberry sauce, wash and hull the strawberries, purée and strain. Bring the water to a boil with the sugar, and add the orange zest and rum. Boil down for 2 minutes. Allow to cool and stir into the strawberry purée. Place a chocolate ring on each plate. Cut a ladyfinger in half and place in the ring, and moisten with rum. Place a scoop of chocolate ice cream on top and pour the sauce over it. Decorate with whipped cream and strawberries.

Decorations made from chocolate are useful to add to the appearance of a dessert, especially if they have been made in advance. This applies to hollow shells and rings (as shown here) as well as to shapes that have been stamped out with a cutter or piped.

A simple combination

*The individual components of this recipe are
extremely simple, but the combination is inspired*

CHOCOLATE WAFFLES WITH PUMPKIN CREAM AND CINNAMON ICE CREAM

Serves 4
For the pumpkin cream:
1 lb pumpkin, 4½ teaspoons butter
1 tablespoon brown sugar
8 teaspoons sugar, pinch ground cloves
¼ teaspoon ground cinnamon, 1 star anise
scraped contents of ½ vanilla bean
½ teaspoon grated fresh ginger
pinch freshly grated nutmeg
2 teaspoons cognac
¼ cup whipped cream

A whole pumpkin is obviously not required for this recipe, but the piece used must be fresh. Using only fresh ingredients is one of the secrets of the culinary art of Eckart Witzigmann.

For the waffles:

1 cup flour, 1 teaspoon cocoa powder

1 cup cream, 2 egg yolks

pinch ground cloves, pinch ground anise

pinch ground cinnamon

scraped contents ½ vanilla bean

grated zest of ½ lemon

2 tablespoons melted butter, room temperature

3 egg whites, pinch of salt, ¼ cup sugar

To decorate:

maple syrup, almond croquant (see page 145)

cinnamon stick

You will also need:

foil for the pumpkin, clarified butter for the waffle iron

confectioners' sugar for dusting

4 scoops cinnamon ice cream (see page 204)

To cook pumpkin:

Preheat the oven to 425°F. Grease a large piece of foil with butter and sprinkle with the brown sugar. Place the pumpkin slices on the foil.

Wrap up in the foil. Cook in the oven for 20–25 minutes. Remove the skin from the flesh.

In a saucepan, bring the pumpkin flesh to a boil with the sugar and spices. Reduce to a thick, dry purée.

To make the pumpkin cream, remove the seeds from the pumpkin and cook the flesh as shown in the picture sequence. Mix the spices, about 1¼ cups pumpkin flesh, and sugar in a saucepan, and bring to a boil. Simmer until it is a thick, dry purée. Strain, stir in the cognac, and stand in a cold place.

To make the waffles, sift the flour with the cocoa powder into a bowl. Add the cream, egg yolks, spices, vanilla, lemon zest, and melted butter. Stir until smooth. Whip the egg whites with the sugar and salt into soft peaks. Whisk one third into the batter, then fold in the remainder. Heat the waffle iron, brush with clarified butter, spoon in the batter, and cook. Cool the waffles on a wire rack. Dust with confectioners' sugar and arrange on plates.

Stir 3 tablespoons of the whipped cream into the pumpkin purée. Stir in the remaining cream so loosely that it creates a marbled effect. Place a scoop of pumpkin cream and a scoop of cinnamon ice cream on the waffles and decorate with maple syrup, almond croquant, and cinnamon stick.

Ice-cold and light

Semi-frozen and served in all sorts of shapes

STRAWBERRY ICE CREAM CHOCOLATE CANDY

Serves 4

For the soufflé batter:

4 egg yolks, ½ cup sugar

¾ teaspoon gelatin

⅝ cup fresh puréed strawberries, 2 egg whites

6 tablespoons cream whipped with 1 tablespoon sugar

For the strawberry sauce:

5 oz strawberries, 1 teaspoon lemon juice

1 tablespoon confectioners' sugar

To decorate:

½ cup cream, 4 teaspoons sugar

You will also need:

24 milk chocolate couverture shell halves 1½ inches in diameter (see pages 66–7)

2 tablespoons tempered couverture

Beat the egg yolks with half of the sugar until creamy. Dissolve the gelatin, and stir in. Heat over hot water, stirring constantly, until the batter is thick enough to coat the back of a spoon. Remove from the heat and stir in the strawberry purée. Transfer the mixture to a large bowl and refrigerate for about 30 minutes until it begins to set. Whip the egg whites with the remaining sugar until stiff. Using a whisk, blend into the cooled strawberry mixture. Fold in the whipped cream carefully with a spoon. Spoon into a pastry bag with a round tip and pipe mounds into the prepared chocolate shell halves. Freeze for 30 minutes. Assemble the shell halves. Spoon the tempered couverture into a paper pastry bag (see page 62) and decorate the tops. Freeze the filled balls for 2–3 hours. To make the strawberry sauce, wash and hull the strawberries, purée and strain. Stir in the lemon juice and confectioners' sugar. To decorate, whip the cream with the sugar until stiff. Spoon into a pastry bag with a round tip. Remove the soufflé balls from the freezer and place 3 on each plate. Decorate with the whipped cream and strawberry sauce.

Soufflé is the name given to this delicate semi-frozen dessert because it looks like a baked soufflé and because it is made with eggs, cream, and sugar. This iced soufflé should be removed from the freezer 1 hour before it is to be served and placed in the warmer part of the refrigerator.

CHOCOLATE AND ORANGE ICED SOUFFLÉ

Serves 12

For the soufflé:

2 oranges

28 sugar cubes

⅔ cup orange juice

8 egg yolks, 1½ teaspoons gelatin

3½ oz couverture, melted

4 teaspoons Cointreau, 4 egg whites

¾ cup + 2 tablespoons sugar, 1½ cups cream

You will also need:

twelve ¼-pint soufflé dishes

parchment paper

cocoa powder

Prepare the dishes. Make sleeves out of a double thickness of parchment paper (for extra rigidity) to extend 1½–2 inches above the tops of the dishes. Wrap around the dishes and secure with tape top and bottom. Place in the refrigerator to cool.

Wash the oranges carefully and dry well. Grate the zest from the oranges and combine with the sugar cubes. Juice the oranges and strain the juice.

Stir the egg yolks and the lemon-sugar together in a pan. Dissolve the gelatin, add to the eggs and sugar, and stir constantly over hot water until the sugar has dissolved and the mixture thickens. Remove from the heat. Stir in the melted couverture, orange juice, and Cointreau. Transfer to a large mixing bowl and refrigerate for 30 minutes.

Whip the egg whites with three-quarters of the sugar until stiff. Blend into the cold orange mixture using a whisk. Whip the cream with the remaining sugar and fold in carefully using a spoon. Spoon into the prepared dishes and freeze. Dust with cocoa powder just before serving.

In the past, people drank "hot chocolate" or "hot cocoa." That is now almost history, or at least outdated, because what we drink today is an "instant drink made with cocoa powder." This practical commodity comes under a variety of brand names, but the one thing that it is not called is "chocolate." To use this name would be misleading, since the amount of cocoa powder contained is low — between 20 and 35 percent; the rest is sugar.

OLATE
RINKS

Chocolate is still available as a drink, although not so widely. Epicures will, of course, always continue to take the trouble to prepare a "real" cup of cocoa, subtly flavored with spices or spirits.

Chocolate is a good drink even when ice-cold. The Aztecs were perhaps the first to recognize this, even if it was in a form that we would not consider very palatable today. Chocolate can be used creatively in all sorts of concoctions, with or without alcohol. It goes well with fresh fruity flavors and with many varieties of ice cream, and naturally makes an appearance in milk shakes.

Drinks

For nearly three hundred years, chocolate in Europe was known solely as a drink. At the court of Louis XIV, the Sun King, its career began with something of a scandal, a washerwomen's rebellion. When these royal laundresses first saw brown stains on the fine white damask table napkins that the King favored, they are said to have refused to touch them. Their revolt did not endure, and they had to bleach out such stains all too frequently, as drinking chocolate was almost a mania among members of the court.

Thick-bodied chocolate

Chocolate was not only drunk from the cup, but also spooned. *The Breakfast*, one of the most charming paintings by François Boucher, shows a young woman who has just spooned chocolate from a cup without a handle. Sitting at the same small table in front of the window, there is a nurse with a child on her lap putting a spoonful of chocolate to its mouth. This is not really surprising, since in the eighteenth and nineteenth centuries chocolate was not a thin liquid drink, but more of a thick cream. In 1708, in one of the first books written about cocoa, there is a description of how the grated cocoa is boiled to a creamy consistency.

According to many recipes, the grated chocolate was whisked with a tablespoon of flour and boiled until it became "velvety and creamy."

From beaker to trembleuse

After the introduction of tea and coffee, the appropriate kind of drinking vessel for them was soon found. But because chocolate, as a new and exotic product, was prepared and spiced in accordance with so many different recipes, to begin with it was served in a variety of vessels.

Prior to the introduction of European porcelain by Johann Friedrich Böttger, who established his works at Meissen, the frothy drink was drunk from beakers. Made of earthenware and, later, porcelain, and frequently imported from China, as were teacups, the beakers were narrow at the bottom and wider at the top. This plain shape was the forerunner of the tall chocolate cups. The first two samples made by Böttger to present to his master and client, the King of Saxony, in 1710 were a glazed and an unglazed beaker. In the typical beaker shape, decorated in green, they were quite simple designs for the fashionable exotic drink of the period.

To prevent the tall beaker from toppling over, a saucer with a relatively deep central hollow was developed to hold it securely. Then, since the chocolate was drunk hot, the beakers were given a handle, sometimes two, like a soup cup. The *trembleuse*, a tall, round cup or beaker with handles and a matching saucer, was introduced in the Rococo period, the era of the greatest refinement in porcelain design. The saucer had a deep central bowl, decoratively pierced and painted, to form a holder. It was designed to prevent the brown liquid spilling onto a featherbed or a silken dress should a lady's small pet dog jump inopportunely onto her lap. The dog, it should be noted, was one essential fashion accessory of the period; another was a servant, whose job it was to serve the chocolate from a specially designed pot with a whisk in the lid, so that he could give it a final stir to create a froth before he poured it out. In addition to these elaborate chocolate cups, a glass of water was always placed on the table. Chocolate was still so thick to drink that it had to be spooned, and a drink of water was useful to clear the mouth.

A step in the right direction

After the French Revolution, in the era of a rising bourgeoisie in Europe, cocoa began to be democratized. It was still not a drink that all classes could enjoy, but it was one that became available to and appreciated by groups of educated people. Indeed, chocolate became the favored morning drink of those individualists who, like cocoa itself, knew no conventions. The great German writer, scientist, and court official Johann Wolfgang von Goethe is a famous example. It is said that Goethe had a sweet tooth from childhood. Although his father was strict and thrifty, his mother arranged "gatherings at the chocolate table." Later, a number of his friends described in their diaries and letters,

somewhat bemused, how, invited to lunch, they had been served only hot chocolate. Goethe was an early riser and always started the day with a cup of chocolate. The globetrotter Alexander von Humboldt told him: "If you drink a cup of chocolate, it keeps you going for the whole day." So Goethe always took a chocolate cup, cocoa, and bars of chocolate with him in his luggage.

Drinking chocolate for all

The drink as it was known then was made by melting a piece of chocolate in a small saucepan on the edge of the newly fashionable solid-fuel stove, where the fire burned enclosed under an iron hot plate. Swirled around with milk or water, the chocolate was enlivened with all sorts of exotic spices, as it had been centuries before, or was flavored with wine, strong coffee, cognac, or rum.

Today the hard cocoa cake is ground into a fine powder, from which some of the cocoa butter has been removed. Lightly fat-reduced cocoa powder must contain at least 20 percent cocoa butter, whereas highly fat-reduced cocoa powder contains between only 8 and 20 percent cocoa butter. Depending on the method of processing and the variety of cocoa bean used, the product can be lighter or darker in color. The lower the fat content of the cocoa powder, the more bitter the taste. Instant drinks containing cocoa represent the final stage of this development. They are made with defatted cocoa powder mixed with finely ground refined sugar, glucose, spices, vitamins, and dried milk. The powder is so finely ground that the minute particles bind together simultaneously and dissolve in cold or hot liquids, a modern solution to the more time-consuming methods of the past.

Chocolate, the "nectar of the Indians," is served. Everybody appears to be enthusiastic about the new luxury commodity of European society in the eighteenth century. Men and women sit together with their drinking chocolate in friendly conversation.

Tejate y champurrado

Ice-cold and very hot — two traditional chocolate drinks from Mexico

Champurrado, the traditional hot chocolate, is prepared here in the area around Mitla, Oaxaca, as it always has been. It is a mixture of *atole* (an old Indian drink made with corn) and chocolate spiced with *piloncillo* (dark sugar) and cinnamon.

Tejate is an ice-cold cocoa drink served, with as much froth as possible, in red bowls. At the market in Octolán, Señora Asunción Martinez Gabriel prepares her own personal recipe.

Tejate, an ice-cold drink from the Mexican state of Oaxaca, is a very popular refreshment at markets and folk festivals. It is prepared in large quantities in giant clay bowls. Each cook prepares it according to her own family recipe, although the main ingredients are usually corn, annatto, shelled cocoa beans, mammee seeds (*Pouteria sapota*), cacao blossoms, sugar, and, optionally, the fatty seeds of the oil palm called *coroso*, or ivory nut. Equal parts of corn and annatto are soaked in water, so that the corn grains swell. Drained and finely ground, this mixture produces a creamy paste called *nicuanextle*. The cocoa beans are roasted over an open fire until the shells burst open and can be removed. The cacao blossoms, nuts, and mammee seeds are also roasted. When they are cold, they are finely ground and mixed with the other roasted ingredients into the paste. Then the mixture is stirred by bare hands and arms in a large vessel and then whipped as cold water is added. When a thick froth has formed, it is pushed to the side and sugar is stirred into the liquid. The *tejate* has to be stirred repeatedly to prevent the annatto from settling on the bottom.

MEXICAN HOT CHOCOLATE

In the annals of history, this is known as "chocolate *caliente*." In place of the traditional tablets of Mexican chocolate, you can use 1 cup cocoa powder mixed with ½ cup of sugar. The chiles go well with the drink, making it more spicy.

Serves 4–6

3¼ cups milk, 1 vanilla bean
9 oz Mexican chocolate tablets, crushed
1 cup water
½ chile, seeds removed
3 tablespoons honey
pinch of salt

Bring the milk to a boil with the vanilla bean and infuse for 10 minutes. Remove the vanilla bean and slit lengthwise. Scrape out the contents and stir into the chocolate and water. Using a whisk, stir into the hot milk and whisk briskly until the chocolate has melted completely. Chop the chile very finely. Stir into the drink with the honey and salt. Serve hot.

Hot chocolate

It can be made with cocoa powder or chocolate, and blends well with a number of flavorings

Orange and chocolate drink is drinking chocolate flavored with reduced orange juice and Grand Marnier. Serve with a spoonful of whipped cream and cocoa powder.

Pure drinking chocolate, prepared only with the finest chocolate and vanilla, and whisked to give a good froth.

IRISH CHOCOLATE

How could it be made any other way? Add a generous amount (at least 5 tablespoons per glass) of Irish whiskey and 2 tablespoons of honey to the Basic Recipe, and top with heavy or whipped cream and grated chocolate.

EGGNOG WITH CHOCOLATE

This sweet punch tastes as good without alcohol as with. For children, simply omit the rum.

Serves 2
4 oz semisweet chocolate
2¼ cups milk
4 egg yolks
½ cup sugar
5 tablespoons dark rum

Grate the chocolate and bring to a boil with the milk. Beat the egg yolks with the sugar until thickened. Stir slowly into the boiling milk, beating continuously. Stir in the rum before serving.

ALMOND COCOA

The almond flavor and taste of chocolate go together very well.

Serves 4
2 tablespoons almonds
1 tablespoon sugar
1 Basic Recipe cocoa
3 tablespoons amaretto

Blanch the almonds and remove the skins. Crush with the sugar in a mortar and cook with 1 cup of the cocoa for 2–3 minutes. Mix with the remainder of the cocoa and the amaretto, and serve with a little whipped cream.

BASIC RECIPE FOR COCOA

Cocoa powder, milk, and sugar are the basic ingredients. The rest is purely a matter of taste; the amount of cocoa powder and sugar can be varied as required.

Serves 4
For medium-strength cocoa:
4½ cups milk
½ cup cocoa powder
¼ cup sugar

Bring the milk to a boil. Mix the dry cocoa powder with the sugar, then mix to a paste with 2–3 tablespoons of cold milk or cold water and whisk into the boiling milk.

DRINKING CHOCOLATE

This has a much more delicate flavor than cocoa, provided that top-quality chocolate is used. It contains more calories because the chocolate has a higher fat content.

Serves 4
1 vanilla bean, 4½ cups milk
4 oz bitter chocolate, 2 tablespoons sugar
You will also need:
1 tablespoon whipped cream, a little grated chocolate

Slit the vanilla bean lengthwise, put in a saucepan with the milk, and bring to a boil. Break the chocolate into a small saucepan and melt in a little hot milk. Remove the vanilla bean and stir the chocolate into the hot milk with the sugar. Top with whipped cream and grated chocolate — a particularly fine finishing touch.

RUSSIAN CHOCOLATE

Add 5 tablespoons of fine cognac to the Basic Recipe above. Top with whipped cream and dust with sifted cocoa powder.

Ice-cold chocolate

Conjure up wonderfully refreshing drinks
with milk and chocolate ice cream

PURE CHOCOLATE

This quick-to-prepare drink has a strong taste of chocolate and a hint of orange. Sharpen the taste by replacing the orange liqueur with dark rum.

Serves 1
3 scoops Chocolate Ice Cream (see page 204)
4 teaspoons crème de cacao, 4 teaspoons orange liqueur
You will also need:
Burgundy glass
1 tablespoon whipped cream, chocolate lattice

In an electric mixer, blend 1 scoop chocolate ice cream thoroughly with the crème de cacao and orange liqueur. Place the remaining ice cream in the wine glass and pour the liquid over it. Decorate with a dab of whipped cream and chocolate lattice.

CHOCOLATE AND ORANGE MILK SHAKE

The glass must be cold, so place it briefly in the freezer shortly before preparation.

Serves 1
2 scoops Chocolate Ice Cream (see page 204)
4 teaspoons Chocolate Syrup (see page 220)
4 teaspoons orange syrup
½ cup milk
You will also need:
cold champagne glass, 1 drinking straw

In an electric mixer, blend the ice cream thoroughly with the two types of syrup, adding the milk a little at a time. Pour into the champagne glass and serve with a straw.

CURAÇAO WITH CHOCOLATE

Always be careful when grating orange and other fruit zest that only the aromatic outer layer is removed, leaving the white pith behind.

Serves 1
2 blood oranges
12 sugar cubes
3 tablespoons Chocolate Syrup (see page 220)
3 tablespoons Curaçao Triple sec
You will also need:
crushed ice (see page 221)
wine glass, 1 tablespoon whipped cream

Wash the oranges well in hot water. Grate the zest and squeeze the juice out of the fruit. Place 7 fl oz of the juice in a saucepan with the sugar cubes, bring to a boil, and reduce by a third. Stand in a cold place. Put crushed ice into the glass, and top up with the reduced juice. Mix the chocolate syrup with the liqueur and pour carefully into the glass. Decorate with whipped cream.

Peppermint, ice, and chocolate — a wonderfully refreshing combination for a sharp long drink. To make a milkshake, replace the crushed ice with 2 scoops of chocolate ice cream, add milk, and blend.

CHOCOLATE AND GRENADINE MILK SHAKE

This is a good drink for children.

Serves 1
2 scoops Chocolate Ice Cream (see page 204)
3 tablespoons grenadine syrup, ½ cup milk
You will also need:
cold wine glass

Place all the ingredients in a cocktail shaker or an electric mixer and blend. Alternatively, place the ice cream in the glass. Pour in the syrup, top up with milk, and mix slowly.

PEPPERMINT CHOCOLATE

Serves 1
3 tablespoons peppermint liqueur
4 teaspoons Chocolate Syrup (see page 220)
2 teaspoons egg liqueur
You will also need:
1 tall drinking glass, crushed ice, mint to garnish

Fill a third of the glass with crushed ice. Pour in the peppermint liqueur. Pour the chocolate syrup and the egg liqueur over the top. Decorate with mint leaves.

Chocolate syrup can be diluted with boiled cream, with alcohol (for additional flavor) or with sweetened condensed milk.

Cool drinks for hot days

Homemade chocolate syrup is the best

CHOCOLATE SYRUP

Keep in the refrigerator in a screwtop jar.

Makes about 2½ cups

2¼ cups cream, ½ cup sugar

2 oz dark cocoa powder, 7 oz couverture, melted

You will also need:

screwtop jar

Bring the cream to a boil with the sugar and sifted cocoa powder. Remove from the heat and stir in the couverture. Strain and cool.

PASSION FRUIT CHOCOLATE

The passion fruit syrup is enough for four cocktails.

Serves 1

For the passion fruit syrup:

6 passion fruits (½ cup fruit flesh), 6 tablespoons sugar, ¼ cup water

For the cocktail:

3 tablespoons passion fruit syrup, 2 teaspoons dark rum

3 tablespoons cream, 3 tablespoons Chocolate Syrup

You will also need:

cocktail glass, white chocolate rolls

To make the syrup, halve the passion fruits and remove the flesh. Bring to a boil with the sugar and water. Reduce by a third, strain, and cool. Mix 3 tablespoons of this syrup, the rum, and cream in a cocktail shaker. Pour into a glass. Carefully pour on the chocolate syrup and top with chocolate rolls.

CHOCOLATE AND COGNAC COCKTAIL
Serves 1

3 tablespoons Chocolate Syrup (see page 220)

3 tablespoons cognac

4 teaspoons crème de cacao, 4 teaspoons cream

You will also need:

cocktail glass

1 tablespoon whipped cream, grated chocolate

Mix all the ingredients in a cocktail shaker and pour the drink into the glass. Decorate with whipped cream and grated chocolate.

LYCHEE DRINK
Serves 1

7 lychees, 2 teaspoons sugar syrup

2 teaspoons lime juice

4 teaspoons dark rum

3 tablespoons Chocolate Syrup (see page 220)

You will also need:

whiskey glass, 3–4 ice cubes, 1 lime

Peel the lychees and remove the stone. Purée the flesh in an electric mixer with the sugar syrup, lime juice, rum, and chocolate syrup. Peel the zest from the lime in a spiral. Place the ice cubes in the glass, pour the drink over them, and decorate with the lime zest.

LONG COCONUT DRINK
To make the crushed ice, place several ice cubes in a dish towel and crush with a rolling pin, or crush in a food processor. Transfer to a bowl.

Serves 1

4 teaspoons rum, 3 tablespoons coconut liqueur

4 tablespoons pineapple juice

You will also need:

tall drinking glass, crushed ice

3 tablespoons Chocolate Syrup (see page 220)

1 tablespoon whipped cream

Mix the rum, coconut liqueur, and pineapple juice in a cocktail shaker. Fill the glass a third with crushed ice and pour the drink over it. Slowly pour in the chocolate syrup. Place a dab of whipped cream on top.

BANANA MARTINIQUE
Serves 1

1 medium banana, peeled, ½ cup milk

4 teaspoons dark rum

3 tablespoons crème de bananes

5 tablespoons Chocolate Syrup (see page 220)

You will also need:

3–4 ice cubes, tall drinking glass, 1 slice lime

Place the banana, milk, rum, crème de bananes, and chocolate syrup in a cocktail shaker and mix well. Place the ice cubes in the glass and pour the drink over them. Decorate with a slice of lime.

SAVORY
CHOC

Despite its great familiarity, cocoa still retains a suggestion of the exotic. A magical fruit, a fruit of love, unfailingly invigorating when mixed with red-hot Tabasco or pepper. Had it not found its way as the drink of the Catholic princesses of Spain into the aristocratic society of a sober-minded Europe, it would surely have been condemned as a witches' brew.

Cocoa had an easy passage into the rounds of Christian festivals, high points of the Church year. Traditional cakes came to be iced and filled with it. It trickled into mixing bowls and dusted cream and milk like a dark-colored snow. But why should melted chocolate serve only to hold together hazelnuts and almonds as the French king's chef dictated? Why not dip a strawberry into the bitter cream? Why not dice firm fruits, such as bananas and pineapples, and dip them into the hot, sweet chocolate?

Whatever happened in the past, diverse chocolate fondues made of bitter or milk chocolate, with or without alcoholic flavorings, have now become smash hits. There are many creations that cannot be categorized in the traditional list of chocolate fare as dessert, patisserie, or candy. They include chocolate noodles, turkey with *mole*, the Mexican sauce, and even hare in glossy dark brown chocolate sauce.

OLATE

Noodles with chocolate

Chocolate-brown noodles, whether boiled or in a soufflé, are a favorite sweet main course

To make the noodles, sift the flour with the cocoa powder onto a work surface and make a well in the middle. Add the confectioners' sugar, vanilla, and the eggs to the well.

CHOCOLATE NOODLES WITH APRICOT AND PASSION FRUIT SAUCE

If you make these noodles for children, omit the apricot brandy.

Makes about ¾ lb
2 cups flour, ½ cup cocoa powder
¼ cup confectioners' sugar
scraped contents of 1 vanilla bean
4 eggs, 1–2 tablespoons water, as required
For the sauce:
12 passion fruits (1 cup fruit flesh)
½ cup sugar, ½ cup white wine, 9 oz fresh apricots
4 teaspoons apricot brandy, ½ cup cream
4 teaspoons sugar
You will also need:
1 tablespoon macadamia nut croquant (see page 145)

Place all the ingredients for the dough as shown left, and start mixing from the center with a fork. Gradually stir in the flour from the edge and then knead with the hands to a smooth dough. If the mixture is hard to work, add a little water. Wrap in plastic wrap and let rest for 30 minutes.

Roll out the dough several times to the desired thickness in a pasta machine, gradually reducing the settings. Cut the noodles ⅛-inch wide and place them on a cloth to dry for 2–3 hours.

Meanwhile, prepare the macadamia croquant as shown for croquant on page 145.

To make the sauce, halve the passion fruits and remove the flesh with a spoon. Bring to the boil with the sugar and white wine, and reduce by a third. Lightly score the skin of the apricots, blanch briefly, plunge into cold water, and remove the skins. Halve the fruits and remove the stones. Purée the fruit with a hand blender. Strain the passion fruit sauce and the apricot purée together. Mix in the apricot brandy. Cool. Whip the cream with the sugar to soft peaks and stir into the cold sauce.

Cook the noodles *al dente* in lightly salted boiling water. Drain. Serve with the sauce and croquant.

BAKED NOODLES WITH CHOCOLATE AND HAZELNUTS

Serves 4

1¾ cups flour
2 eggs, 1 teaspoon oil, 1 pinch of salt
water as required
For the chocolate and hazelnut mixture:
6 tablespoons butter, ¾ cup confectioners' sugar
4 eggs, separated
¾ cup ground roasted hazelnuts
3 oz couverture, grated
½ cup bread crumbs
½ teaspoon ground cinnamon, grated zest of ½ lemon
You will also need:
baking dish, butter, bread crumbs
confectioners' sugar

To make the noodles, sift the flour onto a work surface and make a well in the middle. Add the remainder of the ingredients and mix in, using a fork at first to draw in flour from the edge. Work in all of the flour and knead to a smooth dough. Wrap in plastic wrap and let rest for 30 minutes.

Roll out the dough and, using a knife or pasta machine, cut into ¼-inch strips. Cook until *al dente* in lightly salted boiling water. Drain and rinse under cold running water.

Preheat the oven to 400°F. Prepare the chocolate and hazelnut mixture as shown in the picture sequence. Spoon the mixture into a greased baking dish dusted with bread crumbs. Bake for 25–30 minutes. Dredge with sifted confectioners' sugar.

To make the chocolate and hazelnut mixture, beat the butter with half of the confectioners' sugar and the egg yolks until frothy.

Whip the egg whites with the rest of the confectioners' sugar until stiff and fold into the egg yolk mixture.

Mix the hazelnuts, couverture, bread crumbs, cinnamon, and lemon zest, and stir into the egg mixture.

Rinse the noodles under cold running water, fold into the chocolate and hazelnut mixture, and spoon into the prepared dish.

A hint of chocolate

As a savory flavoring, chocolate is both sweet and bitter

For sauces that are intended to blend with meat or poultry, chocolate can positively enrich the taste. But proceed with care and use it sparingly so that it does not become overpowering. It can be used in a sauce for braised beef, for veal, or, if combined with a little cream, for game. Ultimately, chocolate is a flavoring for the cook who likes to experiment.

WILD HARE IN CHOCOLATE SAUCE

Serves 4
For the ragout:
1 hare, about 3½ lb
6 tablespoons oil
½ cup diced onions
½ cup diced carrots
6 tablespoons diced celeriac
2 red chiles, halved and seeded
2 garlic cloves, peeled
1 sprig fresh rosemary
2 sprigs fresh thyme
2 bay leaves
5 crushed juniper berries
10 peppercorns
3 cloves
¼ cinnamon stick
2¼ cups red wine (Burgundy)
1 cup game stock
2 oz couverture, grated
salt, freshly ground pepper
2 oz shallots
You will also need:
½ lb sweet chestnuts
1 teaspoon thyme leaves

Preheat the oven to 425°F. Remove the meat from the carcass. Remove the skin and sinews. Cut the flesh into 1-inch cubes. Chop the bones and trimmings into small pieces.

Heat 4 tablespoons of the oil in a roasting pan and sear the bones and trimmings. Add the vegetables, herbs, and spices, and brown evenly. Pour in half of the red wine. Cover and braise in the oven for 25 minutes. Add the remaining red wine from time to time during this period. Then add the stock and braise for a further 1½ hours. Strain the contents of the roasting pan into a saucepan and reduce the liquid a little. Melt the couverture in the sauce, stir well, and season to taste.

Meanwhile, score the chestnuts crosswise with a small sharp knife, taking care not to damage the flesh. Place on a baking sheet and bake for 20 minutes. Remove from the oven and take the split shells off the hot chestnuts.

Season the hare flesh with salt and pepper. Heat the remaining oil in a frying pan, add the meat, and brown all over. Peel and quarter the shallots and sauté briefly with the meat. Add to the sauce with the chestnuts and braise for 10–15 minutes. Sprinkle with thyme leaves and serve. Small white bread dumplings are a perfect accompaniment.

Mole comes from Nahuatl, the language of the Aztecs, and means "sauce." The best known are *mole poblano* (from the state of Puebla) and *mole oaxaqueño* (from the state of Oaxaca). Each cook has his or her own "secret" recipe. A large range of ready-made products is also available in the form of powder or paste.

Commercial production:

A small business in Atocpan, Mexico, offering fourteen kinds of *mole* in the form of powder or paste.

Tortillas, an important accompaniment for *mole poblano*, are deep-fried until dark brown.

The ingredients are pulverized by rollers. The facial mask is for hygiene, and also acts as protection against the hot chiles.

Mole in all colors — the pastes are sold as semi-finished products and will keep for a relatively long time.

Mole is traditionally served with chicken and turkey.

Mole

A special spicy mixture from Mexico, with lots of chiles and chocolate

Mole is an extremely tasty sauce, served mainly with chicken or turkey. The uninitiated might look slightly askance at first — the combination of chiles and chocolate sounds very strange indeed. However, it is not the sweetened chocolate, associated with candies and cakes, for which this sauce is prized, but the slightly bitter chocolate that gives it a creamy consistency.

MOLE POBLANO

Makes about 5 cups
For the spicy mixture:
1 white onion, 7 cloves of garlic, 2 tomatoes
5 oz pork lard
½ banana, cut into ¼-inch slices
½ cup each of sesame seeds, almonds and peanuts
½ cup raisins, ¼ cup pitted prunes
¼ teaspoon each of coriander seeds and anise,
½ cinnamon stick
¼ croissant (1 day old), ½ tortilla
1½ cups light poultry stock, salt
For the chile mixture:
7 mulatto chiles, 4 ancho chiles, 1½ pasilla chiles
¼ chipotle chile, ½ white onion, 2 cloves of garlic, salt
2 oz Mexican chocolate (spiced with cinnamon)
2 tablespoons sugar, 2⅔ cups poultry stock

Halve the onions. Cut one half roughly into dice and dry-fry in a heavy frying pan. Cut the other half into slices. Dry-fry the cloves of garlic and remove the skins. Blanch the tomatoes, skin, quarter and fry.
Now wash and soak the chiles.

Meanwhile, melt a little lard in a large saucepan. First fry the garlic and remove it, then fry the diced onion with the tomato quarters. Remove them and fry the banana slices with the seeds, nuts, dried fruit, and spices. Cut up the croissant and tortilla into small pieces and purée with all the sautéed ingredients and the stock in several batches in a food processor. Brown the onion slices in the remainder of the lard, add to the purée, season with salt, and simmer over a low heat for 1 hour, stirring occasionally.

To make the chile mixture, drain the chiles, reserving the water for use later. Slice them lengthwise and remove the seeds. In a food processor, purée the chiles with the onion, garlic, and a little of the water used for soaking the chiles. Strain, and salt to taste. At 10-minute intervals, stir the mixture into the simmering spicy mixture. Finally, add the chocolate and sugar, and stir until melted. As soon as the mixture comes back to a boil, add the stock. Cover the saucepan and simmer the *mole* for 2–3 hours.

Glossary

Ammonium bicarbonate: Raising agent for honey cakes and gingerbread; can be purchased from drugstores, cake decorating stores, and specialist suppliers (see page 234).

Angled palette knife: *See* Palette knife.

Arrack: A strong alcoholic beverage distilled from coconut, and sometimes from rice and molasses.

Bain-marie: A pan of hot water in which a dish containing food can be heated or cooked slowly and gently; a double boiler; a water bath.

Bake blind: To prebake a pastry base before adding a filling or topping. The pastry is pricked with a fork and lined with parchment paper or foil, which is then sprinkled with baking beans or dried beans to weigh it down. It is baked for 8–12 minutes. The lining and beans are removed and the pastry is left to cool.

Bavarian cream: A dessert based on custard, lightened with whipped cream and bound with gelatin.

Beating: Process used in preparing meringue, whipped cream, spongecake batter, sauces, and custards. A whisk, hand mixer, or hand blender is used to work the mixture to a light, airy texture.

Beat warm and cold: Technique used in patisserie. A mixture is beaten over a heating source (over hot water or in a *bain-marie*) to a large volume, and then beaten away from heat. Flour or cornstarch can then be stirred in without lumps forming, and the mixture will be very stable. Note: Ingredients should be beaten together cold first, so that warm beating will be trouble-free.

Blanch: To boil briefly or plunge in boiling water and then rinse in ice-cold water; a method used to prepare or peel vegetables, fruit, and nuts.

Blend in: To draw in carefully and mix ingredients of different consistencies with the aid of a spatula. A light, frothy mixture should not decrease in volume, therefore always fold a lighter mixture into a heavier one.

Blend thoroughly: To mix a cream or icing, such as ganache icing, to a smooth consistency with a hand blender. Place the blender in the mixture before switching on. After switching on, move the blender in circles, keeping the blade below the surface of the mixture so that no air bubbles are created.

"Blowing roses": Technique for checking the consistency of custard or cream. Bring to just under boiling point, stirring constantly, until the custard coats the back of the spoon in a thin layer. If you blow on the surface, it will make wrinkles, reminiscent of a rose.

Brown nougat: Alternative name for croquant.

Caramelize: To dip mainly fruit and nuts in caramel and leave to harden on a lightly oiled tray.

Chartreuse: French liqueur, distilled from ingredients including wine, angelica root, cinchona bark, ginger, orange zest, and lemon balm.

Cocoa butter: Pale yellow fat of the cocoa bean, sold in blocks. Melts at 90–95°F.

Cocoa cake: Conched cocoa mass from which the acid has been removed, molded in blocks, containing at least 50 percent cocoa butter.

Cocoa liquor: Ground cocoa, basic material in the production of chocolate and cocoa powder.

Confectioner's funnel: Utensil for pouring liqueur fillings into chocolates.

Confectioner's harp: Special utensil for cutting chocolates in geometric shapes.

Couverture: The type of chocolate used to make chocolate bars and candies, icings, and cream fillings. It can be eaten without further processing.

Crème à l'anglaise: Vanilla sauce or thick custard, used for a variety of desserts.

Crème Chantilly: Whipped cream flavored with vanilla.

Crème patissière: Confectioners' custard, made from milk, sugar, and egg yolk, and bound with cornstarch.

Croquant: French word meaning "crunchy," applied to a mixture of melted sugar and nuts.

Crystallized ginger: Ginger cut into pieces and preserved in sugar.

Crystallized violets: Candied violet petals used to decorate chocolate candy.

Curaçao: Aromatic liqueur made from bitter oranges.

Dead icing: Icing whose surface has lost its shine, due to crystallization of the sugar.

Decorating comb: A plastic comb with notches of differing sizes, used to create straight or wavy lines and stripes.

Dipping fork: Special fork for dipping, immersing, removing, and decorating candies or small baked goods in tempered couverture or icings. The fork may have 2–6 prongs, and be round, oval, or spiral.

Dry out To leave iced goods or glacéd fruits to stand at an even temperature to dry out, so that they conserve their shine and do not become dull.

Edible starch: Binding agent used in cakes and creams, manufactured from cereals, tubers and roots. Wheat powder and cornstarch are very fine, while potato starch is coarser.

Egg whites, whipped: For meringue, sugar should be added to the egg white a little at a time. For spongecakes, the egg white should be whipped to soft peaks, and the sugar added all at once rather than trickled into the mixture. This creates a dense, frothy substance, which, when mixed with egg yolk, or an egg-yolk-and-butter mixture, has a much firmer and better texture.

Firm up: To leave chocolate, mousses, icings, or toppings to cool and become firm. This procedure is necessary if clearly separate layers are to be created.

Fondant: Soft icing made from the finest sugar crystals and sugar syrup. The basic mixture is white, but color may be added, and it can be flavored with liqueurs.

Ganache: Cream created by mixing boiled cream and couverture.

Gelatin: Tasteless, transparent gelling agent. It should always be sprinkled on a little cold water and left without being stirred for 1–5 minutes, as stated on the package. It can then be dissolved directly in hot liquid. To add to a cold liquid, it has to be melted over hot water until it reliquefies.

Gianduja:: The word for "nougat" used in France, Switzerland, and Italy; consists of equal quantities of almonds, sugar, and couverture.

Ginger: Ginger preserved in syrup may be called preserved ginger, stem ginger, or Canton ginger.

Glucose syrup: A very thick syrup made from dextrose, starch, and water. Increases viscosity and prevents unwanted crystallization, but does not affect taste. Can be purchased from cake decorating stores and mail order suppliers (see page 235).

Grand Marnier: French liqueur made from bitter oranges and brandy.

Hazelnuts, to peel: Spread the nuts on a baking sheet and roast in the oven at 400°F until the skins burst. Leave to cool briefly, wrap in a clean dish towel, and rub off all the skins.

Maraschino: A cordial or liqueur distilled from wild cherries.

Masking: To spread heated and strained jam over the surface of a cake before icing, to ensure a smooth surface, or before sprinkling with decorations so that they stay in place.

Meringue: Frothy mixture of egg white and sugar, dried, rather than baked, in the oven.

Milk ganache: Ganache cream made with milk chocolate couverture.

Millefeuille: Literally "a thousand leaves," the French term for flaky pastry.

Moisten: To pour liquid flavorings such as alcohol or sugar syrup over light bakery products.

Nougat: Paste made from almonds or other nuts, sugar, and couverture.

Palette knife: Thin, flat knife with a rounded end, used for smoothing batter, creams, and icing, and for cooling couverture. Palette knives may be short or long, straight or angled.

Paper pastry bag: Homemade pastry bag made from wax paper or parchment paper, to be used once and thrown away. Has the advantage that the opening can be cut to any size.

Parfait: A mixture of egg white and cream to which different flavorings are added, often semi-frozen.

Pipe: To shape mixtures or cream fillings using a pastry bag with a tip.

Preserved ginger: *See* Ginger.

Reduce: To boil down a liquid in order to concentrate the flavor.

Roll out: To pass a rolling pin over a sheet of pastry to ensure even thickness.

Sabayon: Frothy wine sauce, made from whisked egg yolks, Marsala, sugar, and flavorings.

Seal: To cover, spread, or pipe the top or back of a filled chocolate candy.

Setting point: The moment at which a mixture, jelly, or cream filling becomes thick and firm.

Sugar, to boil: Bring 1 lb sugar and 1 cup water to the desired temperature.
Thin thread: 219°F. To test, moisten index finger and thumb in cold water, then cover with a little syrup. When the fingers are opened and closed quickly, short threads will form.
Thick thread: 226°F. Test as for small thread, but the thread will be longer. This highly concentrated sugar is used in compotes and jam.
Small pearl: 234°F. To test, dip a small wire loop in the syrup and blow through it lightly; small bubbles will form.
Large pearl: 237°F. Test as for small pearl, but large, linked bubbles should form. Used for fondant and Italian meringue.
Soft ball: 240–244°F. To test, dip the thumb and index finger in ice-cold water, take a little syrup from the spoon, and dip immediately in the icy water. You should be able to shape the syrup easily into a small ball. Used for Italian meringue and butter cream.
Soft crack: 284°F. When a little of the sugar is poured into iced water, it will become firm immediately, but will remain somewhat sticky. Further boiling will harden it.
Hard crack: 307–310°F. When a little of the sugar is poured into iced water, it will become as brittle as glass and no longer be sticky. Used for glazing fruit, for spun sugar, and for pouring and piping decorations.

Sugar syrup: Place 1 lb sugar in a saucepan with 2¼ cups water, and stir over low heat until the sugar is completely dissolved. Boil for 1 minute, then remove from the heat. The syrup is used to moisten cakes, and is added to cream fillings and confectionery.

Sweet chestnut paste: To make, boil the chestnuts in their skins in water until soft. Cut open and remove the contents. Press through a fine-mesh sieve. Mix 10 parts of chestnut purée with 3 parts confectioners' sugar. Add a little vanilla and rum if liked. The paste will keep for several days in a refrigerator, and for a lengthy period in a freezer.

Tartlet: Small, blind-baked pastry case for petits fours and other confections.

Temper: Slow warming and cooling of couverture to produce hard, lustrous chocolate with good flavor and storage qualities. Heated couverture, fondant, and other mixtures can be cooled by smoothing and scraping together with a palette knife on a table-top or marble slab.

Truffles: Term used by confectioners for cream ganache blended with butter, usually shaped into balls.

Whipped cream: Always whip fresh heavy or whipping cream rather than using commercially whipped cream. The cream should not be too stiffly beaten, otherwise it loses volume and flavor. Whipped cream used for decoration should always be lightly sweetened in order to bring out its delicate, buttery flavor.

Work in: To knead a solid or semi-solid ingredient with another dry ingredient, such as butter and flour, almond paste and confectioners' sugar.

Zester: Gadget that scrapes rather than cuts fine shreds of rind from citrus fruits.

Equipment and utensils: Precision in patisserie and confectionery is essential. Sometimes this calls for a standard of equipment beyond that found in the ordinary domestic kitchen.

1 Rectangular cake pan

2 Set of pudding basins

3 Mixing bowls

4 Large mixing bowls for eggs

5 Torte rings

6 Acetate strip

7 Ladles

8 Measuring jug/pitcher for large quantities of liquid

9 Measuring glass for small quantities of liquid

10 Whisk attachment for an electric mixer

11 Electric hand mixer with whisk

12 Electric hand blender

13–14 Whisks

15 Dough scraper

16 Curved wooden spatula

17 Straight wooden spatula

18 Spoon

19 Serrated kitchen knife

20 Straight palette knife

21 Angled palette knives

22 Rubber spatula

23 Knives in various sizes

1 Marble slab

2 Rolling pin

3 Foil

4 Parchment paper

5 Wax paper

6 Saucepans

7 Spatula

8 Parchment paper for pastry bags, parchment pastry bags

9 Molds for hollow figures: Santa Claus, Easter rabbit, and Easter egg

10 Strainers

11 Dipping forks, for dipping, lifting and decorating candy

12 Meat hammer to crush croquant

13 Round cutters with fluted edge

14 Square cutters

15 Oval and round cutters with plain edge

16 Flower-shaped cutters

17 Digital thermometer

18 Candy cutters for chocolates in various shapes: square, triangle, heart, flower, crescent

19 Pastry bag with round and star tips in various sizes

20 Decorating comb with different edges

21 Square wire cake rack

22 Round wire cake rack

23 Pomponette molds

24 Torte ring base

25 Baking sheet

26 Pastry brushes

Suppliers

Check the Yellow Pages for local cake-decorating stores, for ingredients and equipment; restaurant supply stores, for equipment; art supply stores, for acetate; and gourmet food stores, for special ingredients.

The following sources can supply their products by mail order. Some of them may also have mail-order catalogs or stores in your area.

EQUIPMENT AND INGREDIENTS

Maid of Scandinavia
3244 Raleigh Avenue
Minneapolis, MN 55416
1-800-328-6722

Parrish
314 West 58th Street
Los Angeles, CA 90037
(1-213) 750-7650

Albert Uster
1-800-231-8154

Williams-Sonoma
PO Box 7456
San Francisco, CA 94120
(1-415) 421-4242

EQUIPMENT ONLY

Beryl's Cake Decorating Equipment
PO Box 1534
North Springfield, VA 22151
(1-703) 256-6951

Bridge Kitchenware
214 East 52nd Street
New York, NY 10022
(1-212) 688-4220

INGREDIENTS ONLY

Assouline and Ting Inc.
314 Brown Street
Philadelphia, PA 19123
1-800-521-4491

Chef's Pantry
P.O. Box 3
Post Mills, VT 05058
1-800-666-9940

Cocolat
2547 Ninth Street
Berkeley, CA 94710
(1-415) 843-1182

Confetti
4 Embarcadero Center
San Francisco, CA 94111
(1-415) 362-1706

Fencliff House
P.O. Box 177
Tremont, OH 45372
(1-513) 390-6420

La Cuisine
323 Cameron Street
Alexandria, VA 22314
1-800-521-1176

Paradigm Chocolate Company
5775 S.W. Jean Road
#1064
Lake Oswego, OR 97035
1-800-234-0250

S.E. Rycoff
761 Terminal Street
Los Angeles, CA 90021
(1-213) 622-4131

Index

A

B

C

Picture Credits

p. 7: Compañía Nestlé S.A. de C.V., Mexico City, Mexico; pp. 6, 18, 20, 21: Imhoff-Stollwerck-Museum, Cologne: pp. 8, 9, 11, 12, 13, 16, 17, 29, 37, 44, 45,. 46: Info-Zentrum Schokolade, Düsseldorf; pp. 10, 40: Cadbury Ltd, Bournville, England; p. 26: Kartographie Huber, Munich; p. 39: Cacaofabriek DeZaan, Koog an de Zaan, Netherlands; WaltraudBerger.

Acknowledgements

The authors and publishers wish to thank all those whose have contributed to this book with their advice, help and expertise, especially:

Lee Oon Teik, Malaysian Embassy, Bonn

Helen Davies, Cadbury Ltd, Bournville, England

Christine Henvinck, Callebaut, Lebbeke,Belgium

LauraB. DeCaraza Campos, Mexico City

Paul Ziegler and Peter Gassmann, Carma-PfisterAG, Dübendorf, Switzerland

Demetrio Carrasco, Mexico City

Enrique Gordillo, Compañía Nestlé S.A. deC. V., Mexico City

Hugo Dinges, Herne

Dominique Docquier, Hannut, Belgium

Eduardo Ferrarini, Firma Slogan immagine e comunicazione, Bologna, Italy

Jean Galler, Galler, Chaudfontaine, Belgium

Patricia Simon, Godiva, Brussels, Belgium

Dr. Gerhard Haas,Constance

Wolfgang Hamester, Hamester Gustav F.W. GmbH, Hamburg

Imhoff-Stollwerck-Museum, UschiBaetz, Cologne

Rüdiger Funke, Info-Zentrum Schokolade, Düsseldorf

René Kramer, Lugano, Switzerland

Dato' Dr. Hashim A. Wahab, Kota Kinabalu, Malaysian Cocoa Board, Sabah, Malaysia

Andrea Schürpf, Max Felchlin AG, Schwyz, Switzerland

Gordon Gillett, Nestec Ltd., Vevey, Switzerland

Alexander Klein, Nestlé Côte d'Ivoire, Abidjan, Ivory Coast

Restaurant Las Cazuelas deAtocpan, San Pedro Atocpan, Mexico

Elsa B. de Sada, Mexico City

Schokoladen-Erzeuger Compañía La Soledad, Oaxaca

Carola Steup, Mexican State Tourist Office, Frankfurt.